lonely planet

W9-BOM-915

BARCELONA

TOP SIGHTS, AUTHENTIC EXPERIENCES

Andy Symington

Contents

Plan Your Trip

Top Experiences 35

Dining Out 129

Treasure Hunt 151

Bar Open 171

Map Scale

N
0 ————————— 2 km
0 ————————— 1 miles

Recinte Modernista ◎
de Sant Pau

Gràcia & Park Güell

Gaudí's fairy-tale woodland park and the intriguing district of Gràcia, full of *barrio* life, await exploration. (Map p254)

La Sagrada
Família ✝

La Ribera

The trendiest part of the old town, with first-rate tapas, medieval architecture and a stunning Modernista concert hall. (Map p250)

🏛 Quadrat d'Or

◎ La Pedrera

Passeig
de Gràcia 🅿
◎
**Casa
Batlló**

Palau de
la Música
Catalana
◎

⊗ La Ribera
Museu Picasso
🏛 ⊗ El Born

Museu Frederic Marès
🏛
La Catedral ✝ 🏛

MACBA 🏛
ercat de la Boqueria ◎
La Rambla ◎

✝ Basílica de Santa
Museu Maria del Mar
d'Història
de Barcelona

**Barceloneta
the Waterfront &
El Poblenou**

Pretty beaches, a waterfront promenade and bountiful seafood make for a memorable day on the Mediterranean.

Palau 🅿
Güell

Barcelona's 🏛
Waterfront

Fundació
Joan Miró
🏛

*Port
Vell*

*Mediterranean
Sea*

◎ **Exploring
Montjuïc**

**La Rambla &
Barri Gòtic**

Stroll Barcelona's famous boulevard, then lose yourself in the Gothic quarter. (Map p250)

Welcome to Barcelona

Barcelona is an enchanting seaside city with boundless culture, fabled architecture and a world-class drinking and dining scene. This combination plus a harder-to-define magic in the air makes it one of the world's greatest cities.

Barcelona's architectural treasures span millennia. Towering temple columns, ancient city walls and subterranean stone corridors provide a window into Roman-era Barcino. Fast forward a thousand years or so to the Middle Ages by taking a stroll through the shadowy lanes of the Gothic quarter, past tranquil plazas and soaring 14th-century cathedrals. In other parts of town bloom the sculptural masterpieces of Modernisme, a mix of ingenious and whimsical creations by Gaudí and his Catalan architectural contemporaries. The Sagrada Família, still under construction, is already one of the planet's most sublime buildings.

Barcelona has long inspired artists too, including Salvador Dalí, Pablo Picasso and Joan Miró, whose works are on bold display in the city's myriad museums.

Art of another sort adorns the groaning bar-tops and stylish plates of Barcelona's tapas bars and avant-garde restaurants. Catalan cooking blends the tradition of using flavourful, market-fresh ingredients, with a hint of French savoir faire and a modern twist of molecular wizardry.

Add this to lazy days on the beach, paddling or cruising the deep blue sea, strolling into classy boutiques and quaffing sessions in sociable vermouth bars, and you have just a fraction of the intoxicating cornucopia that is Barcelona.

Barcelona is an enchanting seaside city with boundless culture, fabled architecture, and a world-class drinking and dining scene.

Plaça d'Espanya

★ BARCELONA ★

Tibidabo
Mountain
(1km)

Park Güell

Camp Nou, Pedralbes & La Zona Alta

A medieval monastery, an intriguing museum and lofty Tibidabo – all capped by football thrill at Camp Nou.

◎ **Museu-Monestir de Pedralbes**

L'Eixample

Modernisme rules in the city's 19th-century 'extension', replete with masterpeices by Gaude and others (Map p254)

◎ **Camp Nou**

Estació Sants

El Raval

A once-seedy area that's now home to cutting-edge museums, and bohemian bars and eateries. (Map p249)

Museu Nacional d'Art de Catalunya (MNAC)

Montjuïc, Peble Sec & Sant Antoni

Home to manicured parks, excellent museums and cinematic city views. (Map p256)

Plan Your Trip
This Year in Barcelona

Barcelona

There's always something happening in Barcelona. Traditional fiestas maintain their riotous blend of popular religion, devil-may-care revelry and time-honoured customs. Meanwhile, concerts, festivals and modern celebrations keep things ticking right through the year.

Clockwise from left: Festes de Santa Eulàlia (p7); Festa Major de Gràcia (p13); Festival del Grec (p12); Festes de la Mercè (p14)

2020

★ Top Festivals & Events

Festes de Santa Eulàlia, February

Primavera Sound, May or June

Festival del Grec, July

Festa Major de Gràcia, August

Festes de la Mercè, September

Plan Your Trip
This Year in Barcelona

January

Barcelonins head to the Pyrenees for action on the ski slopes, while others simply enjoy a bit of post-holiday downtime (school holidays go to around 8 January).

☆ Gran Gala Flamenc   1 Jan
Bringing in the New Year in style, this major flamenco performance at the Palau de la Música Catalana (p106) features the acclaimed guitarist and composer Chicuelo along with other top musicians and performers.

⚜ Reis (Reyes)   5 Jan
On 5 January, the day before Epifanía (Epiphany), children delight in the Cavalcada dels Reis Mags (Parade of the Three Kings; pictured above), a colourful parade of floats and music, spreading bonhomie and boiled sweets in equal measure.

◉ Éluard y Picasso   to 23 Feb
This exhibition at the Museu Picasso (p80) explores the friendship between the painter and French surrealist poet Paul Éluard,

⚜ Festes dels Tres Tombs   17 Jan
In addition to live music and *gegants* (papier mâché giants worn over the shoulders of processionists), the festival dedicated to Sant Antoni features a parade of horse-drawn carts in the neighbourhood of Sant Antoni (near the Mercat de Sant Antoni).

who was a significant source of emotional support during the Spanish Civil War and beyond.

February

Often the coldest (and seemingly longest) month in Barcelona, February sees few visitors. Nonetheless, some of the first big festivals kick off, with abundant Catalan merriment amid the wintry gloom.

☆ Nights at the Opera   Jan-Jun
Aida (13 Jan-2 Feb), Verdi's much-loved bigger-than-Ben-Hur opera will take the Liceu by storm. This production uses the well-loved stage sets of the historic Catalan designer Mestres Cabanes. *The Clemency of Titus* (19-27 Feb & 17-29 Apr), Mozart's penultimate opera, with an Italian libretto, will feature sopranos Carmela Remigio and Myrtò Papatanasiu alternating in the role of Vitellia, conducted by Philippe Auguin.

☉ Countercultural Sculpture   to 1 Mar
The major exhibition, *Object, Totem and Matter: Post-war Sculpture in Catalonia*, runs throughout the winter at the Museu Nacional d'Art de Catalunya (p56),and looks at how avant-garde sculptors subverted norms under the dictatorship.

🎊 Festes de Santa Eulàlia   12 Feb
(http://lameva.barcelona.cat/santa eulalia) This big winter fest celebrates Barcelona's first patron saint with a week of cultural events, including parades of *gegants* (papier-mâche giants), open-air art installations (pictured above), theatre, *correfocs* (fire runs) and *castells* (human castles).

🎊 Carnestoltes (Carnaval) 19-25 Feb
(http://lameva.barcelona.cat/carnaval) Seven weeks before Easter, the carnival involves several days of fancy-dress balls, merrymaking and fireworks, ending on the Tuesday before Ash Wednesday. More than 30 parades happen around town on the weekend. Down in Sitges a wilder version takes place.

☉ Charlotte Posenenske: Work in Progress   to 8 Mar
MACBA (p94) hosts this retrospective of the German sculptor whose reconfigurable works resemble air-conditioning ducts. Posenenske was determined not to impose any message or meaning on the viewer, so it's down to you and your interpretations.

Plan Your Trip
This Year in Barcelona

March

After chillier days of winter, March brings longer sunnier days, though still cool nights (light-jacket weather). There are relatively few tourists and fair hotel prices.

🎊 Festa de Sant Medir 3 Mar
This characterful religious procession in Gràcia includes the throwing of sweets to the masses, who await with buckets and bags to catch the treats (pictured above).

☆ Barcelona Obertura Spring Festival 19-30 Mar
A top-notch line-up of classical musicians and singers makes this festival an exciting prospect. Choral performances, opera, chamber music and orchestral works are scheduled across two venues.

🍺 Barcelona Beer Festival mid-Mar
Craft beer has hit the scene in full force in Barcelona. Come see the latest taste-makers in action at this three-day beer and food fest (www.barcelonabeerfestival.com), with more than 300 craft beers on hand.

03

🏃 Barcelona Marathon 8 Mar
Runners descend on Barcelona every March to participate in the city's spring marathon; it usually starts and finishes at Plaça d'Espanya, passing Camp Nou, La Pedrera, La Sagrada Família, Torre Agbar, El Fòrum, Parc de la Ciutadella, Plaça de Catalunya and La Rambla.

CHRISTIAN BERTRAND/SHUTTERSTOCK ©

April

Spring arrives with a flourish, complete with wildflowers blooming in the countryside, Easter revelry and school holidays, although April showers can dampen spirits. Book well ahead if coming around Easter.

🎎 Setmana Santa (Easter) 5-12 Apr

On Palm Sunday people line up to have their palm branches blessed outside the cathedral, while on Good Friday you can follow the floats and hooded penitents in processions from the Església de Sant Agustí (Plaça de Sant Agustí 2), located in El Raval.

☆ Barcelona Open 18-26 Apr

The city's premier tennis tournament, an important fixture of the international clay-court season, sees some top names slug it out (pictured above).

✕ Alimentaria 20-23 Apr

Though it's a serious trade fair (www. alimentaria-bcn.com) rather than a gastro festival, for foodies this is well worth visiting. A highlight is the show-cooking area, where top chefs demonstrate their skills.

🎎 La Diada de Sant Jordi 23 Apr

Catalonia honours its patron saint, Sant Jordi (St George), on 23 April. Traditionally men and women exchange roses and books – La Rambla and Plaça de Sant Jaume fill with book and flower stalls.

🏃 Passejada Amb Barret 19 Apr

Inspired by New York's Easter Parade, this 'Stroll with a Hat' welcomes the spring with a casual walk along Rambla de Catalunya. Make sure you wear your hat!

🎎 Feria de Abril de Catalunya late Apr

Andalucía comes to the Parc del Fòrum with this weeklong southern festival featuring flamenco, a funfair, and plenty of food and drink stalls. It kicks off in late April.

Plan Your Trip
This Year in Barcelona

NATURSPORTS/SHUTTERSTOCK ©

05

May

With sunny days and clear skies, May can be one of the best times to visit Barcelona. The city slowly gears up for summer with the opening of the chiringuitos (beach bars).

☆ D'A – Festival Internacional de Cinema d'Autor de Barcelona   late Apr–early May
(www.dafilmfestival.com) This well-curated film festival presents a selection of contemporary art-house cinematic works.

♣ Salón del Cómic   early May
(www.ficomic.com) Spain's biggest comics event takes place over three days. It's usually held in early May but has been held as early as late March, so keep an eye out.

♣ Festa de Sant Ponç   11 May
To commemorate the patron saint of beekeepers and herbalists, Carrer de l'Hospital in El Raval is taken over by a long market selling artisan honey, herbs and more.

☆ Primavera Sound   late May or early Jun
(www.primaverasound.com) For one week in late May or early June, the open-air Parc del Fòrum stages an all-star line-up of international bands and DJs. There are also associated concerts around town, including free open-air events at the Parc de la Ciutadella and the Passeig Lluís Companys.

☆ Spanish Grand Prix   mid-May
The Spanish Grand Prix is held at the Circuit de Barcelona-Catalunya, northeast of the city (pictured above).

☆ Ciutat Flamenco   late May
(www.ciutatflamenco.com) One of the best occasions to see great flamenco in Barcelona, this festival is held over two weeks at the Teatre Mercat De Les Flors (p202) and other venues.

CHRISTIAN BERTRAND/SHUTTERSTOCK ©

June

Tourist numbers are soaring as Barcelona plunges into summer. Live music festivals and open-air events give the month a festive air.

✿ Cors Muts   1 Jun

After a weekend of out-of-town revelry over the Pentecost (or 'Second Easter' weekend), these gaudily dressed bands of musicians return to the *barrios* of Raval and Barceloneta in a big parade on the Monday afternoon.

☆ Festival Pedralbes   early Jun–mid-Jul

This summertime fest (www.festival pedralbes.com) takes place in lovely gardens and stages big-name performers – many of them old-timers (Beach Boys, Sting, Blondie) from early June to mid-July.

✿ Corpus Christi   11 Jun

Honouring the Holy Communion, and held on the Thursday after Trinity Sunday, Corpus Christi is celebrated in Barcelona with a big procession of *gegants* and the traditional 'L'Ou Com Balla', where eggs are seen to 'dance' in fountains across the city centre.

☆ Sónar   18-20 Jun

Sónar is Barcelona's massive celebration of electronic music, with DJs, exhibitions, sound labs, record fairs and urban art (pictured above).

✿ La Revetlla de Sant Joan   23 Jun

On 23 June locals hit the streets or hold parties at home to celebrate the Revetlla de Sant Joan (St John's Night), which involves drinking, dancing, bonfires and fireworks. In Spanish, it's called 'Verbenas de Sant Joan'.

✿ Pride Barcelona   late Jun or early Jul

Barcelona's Pride festival (www.pride barcelona.org) is a couple of weeks of celebrations held late June or early July with a crammed program of culture and concerts, along with the traditional Pride march on Saturday.

Plan Your Trip
This Year in Barcelona

CHRISTIAN BERTRAND/SHUTTERSTOCK ©

07

July

Prices are high and it's peak tourist season, but it's a lively time to be in the city, with sun-filled beach days, open-air dining and outdoor concerts.

☆ Cinema Lliure
a la Platja   late Jun–early Aug
(www.cinemalliure.com) This free cinema festival on the beach usually shows a mix of independent films from around the world. Bring a blanket and a picnic, and enjoy movies on the big screen.

☆ Rock Fest Barcelona   early Jul
(www.rockfestbarcelona.com) This three-day festival draws big names in hard rock and metal music.

☆ Crüilla   mid-Jul
(www.cruillabarcelona.com) This popular music festival runs over three days and features an eclectic line-up covering everything from rock to flamenco (pictured above).

☆ Sala Montjuïc   Jul–early Aug
(www.salamontjuic.org) Picnic under the stars while watching a movie at this open-air cinema, which also features concerts.

☆ Festival del Grec   Jul
(http://grec.bcn.cat) The major cultural event of the summer is a month-long fest with dozens of theatre, dance and music performances held around town, including at the Teatre Grec amphitheatre on Montjuïc, from which the festival takes its name.

FELIX LIPOV/SHUTTERSTOCK©

☆ Brunch in the Park   Jul–mid-Sep
(http://barcelona.brunch-in.com) Every Sunday from July to mid-September, you can enjoy a day of electronic music at an outdoor space on Montjuïc. It attracts a mix of young families and party people.

2020

August

The heat index soars; barcelonins leave the city in droves for summer holidays, as huge numbers of tourists arrive. It's a great time to hit the beach.

☆ Música als Parcs Jun-Aug

Music in the Parks is a series of open-air concerts held in different parks and green spaces around the city. More than 40 different concerts feature classical, blues and jazz groups.

♟ Circuit Festival mid-Aug

(www.circuitfestival.net) Running for about two weeks, this is a major gay fiesta with numerous party nights, including an epic final all-day, all-night event in a waterpark (pictured above). There's a parallel lesbian event, GirlieCircuit (www.girliecircuit.net).

🎇 Festes de Sant Roc mid-Aug

For four days in mid-August, Plaça Nova in the Barri Gòtic becomes the scene of parades, *correfoc* (fire runs), a market, traditional music and magic shows for kids.

🎇 Festa Major de Gràcia mid-August

(www.festamajordegracia.org) Locals compete for the most elaborately decorated street in this popular weeklong Gràcia festival held around 15 August. The fest also features free outdoor concerts, street fairs and other events.

🎇 Festa Major de Sants late Aug

(www.festamajorsants.cat) The district of Sants hosts an eight-day fest with concerts, outdoor dance parties, *correfocs* and elaborately decorated streets.

Plan Your Trip
This Year in Barcelona

CONCEALED RESONANCES/SHUTTERSTOCK ©

09

September

After a month off, barcelonins return to work, although several major festivals provide ample amusement. Temperatures stay warm through September, making for fine beach days.

⚜ Diada Nacional
de Catalunya   11 Sep
Catalonia's national day curiously commemorates Barcelona's surrender on 11 September 1714 to the Bourbon monarchy of Spain, at the conclusion of the War of the Spanish Succession (pictured above).

⚜ Festa Major
de la Barceloneta   29 Sep
This big September celebration in Barcelona honours the local patron saint, Sant Miquel, on 29 September. It lasts about a week and involves plenty of dancing and drinking, especially on the beach.

🍷 Mostra de Vins i
Caves de Catalunya   late Sep
At this wine and *cava* event, you can taste your way through some of the top wines of

⚜ Festes de la Mercè   24 Sep
(www.bcn.cat/merce) Held around 24 September, the city's biggest party involves four days of concerts, dancing and street theatre. There are also *castells* (human castles), fireworks displays, a parade of giants, and *correfocs* (fire runs).

FRANCISCO GONCALVES/GETTY IMAGES©

Catalunya. It's usually held at Port Olímpic over four days, coinciding with the Festes de la Mercè at the end of September.

October

While northern Europe shivers, Barcelona enjoys mild October temperatures and sunny days. With the disappearance of the summer crowds, and lower accommodation prices, this is an excellent month to visit.

🏃 Liber 7-9 Oct
(www.libereurope.eu) This major international book fair brings together authors, publishers and keen readers for a few days at the beginning of October.

☆ Symphony for the Ears Oct
L'Auditori is a modern building with amazing acoustics, and seeing a show here is a must for music lovers. Visit www.auditori.cat to see the program and buy tickets.

☆ Festival de Jazz de Barcelona throughout Oct
(pictured above; www.jazz.barcelona) With an excellent program of high-quality concerts throughout the month, this long-standing festival is a musical highlight.

✕ Mercat de Mercats Oct
The 'market of markets' is a celebration of Catalan cooking and those wonderfully locally sourced ingredients that have made Barcelona such a foodie destination. Over one weekend in October, this food fair features great foods, wines and workshops. Held in front of La Catedral.

Plan Your Trip
This Year in Barcelona

GURBIDI08R/SHUTTERSTOCK©

November

Cooler days and nights arrive in Barcelona, along with occasional days of rain and overcast skies. For beating the crowds (and higher summer prices), though, it's an excellent month to visit.

✿ Día de Todos los Santos   1 Nov
All Saint's Day is traditionally when locals visit the tombs of family members, then get together for the Castanyada, when roasted chestnuts and other winter foods are eaten (pictured above).

☆ L'Alternativa   mid-Nov
(www.alternativa.cccb.org) Showcasing feature-length and short films, plus premieres by new directors, the Barcelona Independent Film Festival includes free and ticketed events.

☆ LOOP Barcelona   Nov
(www.loop-barcelona.com) LOOP features video art and avant-garde films shown in museums, theatres and non-traditional spaces (like food markets) around the city. It usually runs for a few days in November.

☆ Camp Nou   Nov
See a football match at Camp Nou, hallowed ground for football fans across the globe. There are likely league, cup or Champions League games to choose from this month. Or take a self-guided tour of the stadium and learn about the sport's most famous players at FC Barcelona's museum.

CHRISTIAN BERTRAND/ SHUTTERSTOCK ©

☆ Festival Mil·lenni   late Nov–May 2021
(www.festival-millenni.com) Running from November to May each year, this festival consists of a series of high-profile concerts in various venues around town.

2020

12

December

As winter returns barcelonins gear up for Christmas, and the city is festooned with colourful decorations. Relatively few visitors arrive, at least until Christmas, when the city fills with holidaying out-of-towners.

Fira de Santa Llúcia
late Nov-Dec

(pictured above; http://en.firadesanta llucia.cat) This holiday market has hundreds of stalls selling all manner of Christmas decorations and gifts – including the infamous Catalan Nativity scene character, the *caganer* (the crapper).

Christmas
24 Dec–6 Jan

Christmas in Spain is a two-week affair, with the major family meals on the nights of Christmas Eve and New Year's Eve, and lunch on 6 January.

Nochevieja (New Year's Eve)
31 Jan

On 31 December, the fountains of Montjuïc (Font Màgica) take centre stage for the biggest celebration in town. Crowds line

Christmas Crappers
Dec

At Christmas some rather unusual Catalan characters appear. The *caganer* (crapper) is a chap with dropped pants who balances over his unsightly offering (a symbol of fertility for the coming year). There's also the *caga tío* (poop log), which is supposed to *cagar* (crap) out gifts on Christmas Day.

up along Avinguda Reina Maria Cristina to watch a theatrical procession and audiovisual performance (plus *castells*), followed by fireworks at midnight.

Plan Your Trip
Hotspots For...

CULTURE VULTURES

◉ **MACBA** The city's top destination for contemporary art, with amazing views to boot. (p94)

◉ **Fundació Joan Miró** A comprehensive collection of this local's works, in a brilliant building. (pictured; p60)

✖ **Enigma** A work of art in itself before you even get to the 40-course tasting extravaganza. (p147)

✖ **Els Quatre Gats** Admire the Modernista decor in this historic restaurant. (p137)

✪ **Gran Teatre del Liceu** Enjoy state-of-the-art acoustics in this atmospheric venue on La Rambla. (p196)

GASTRONAUTS

◉ **Barcelona's Food Markets** Several brilliant produce markets are dotted across the city. (p48)

🅐 **La Ribera** Stroll this intriguing district and browse its gourmet shops. (p108)

✖ **Disfrutar** Have the meal of your trip at this highly inventive molecular gastronomy restaurant. (pictured; p144)

✖ **La Barra de Carles Abellán** A visual treat, this modern celebration of seafood is a Barceloneta highlight. (p142)

✪ **Espai Boisà** Whip up some classic tapas and Catalan dishes in this excellent cooking school. (p210)

ROMANTICS

◉ **Park Güell** Stroll the gardens and admire the views among Gaudí's Modernista fantasies. (p68)

◉ **Barri Gòtic** Amble around the historic centre and explore its hidden corners. (p86)

✕ **La Vinateria del Call** This exquisite little old-town eatery is perfect for cosy dining. (p135)

✕ **Can Recasens** This enchanting warren of candlelit rooms backs up the atmosphere with delicious food. (p141)

✦ **Swing Maniacs** Learn swing dancing at a drop-in class, then hit the dance floor. (p210)

VIEWFINDERS

◉ **Teleférico del Puerto** Old-fashioned cable car with awesome perspectives. (p63)

◉ **Basílica del Sagrat Cor de Jesús** Worth the trip for the mesmerising view. (pictured; p99)

✕ **Barraca** Superb seafood to match the sublime sea outlook. (p142)

✕ **Martínez** Paella and tapas high up on Montjuïc. (p147)

☕ **Mirablau** At the foot of Tibidabo, with magnificent vistas over the city. (p191)

HISTORY BUFFS

◉ **Museu d'Història de Barcelona** Probe the city's intriguing past. (p112)

◉ **Temple d'August** Examine the best of Barcelona's ancient temples. (p67)

◉ **Via Sepulcral Romana** This assemblage of tombs originally stood outside the city limits. (pictured; p47)

✦ **Runner Bean Tours** Take the Gothic Quarter walking tour to explore the city's history. (p211)

✕ **La Granja** Check out the section of old city wall in this cafe. (p134)

Plan Your Trip
Top Days in Barcelona

©PERESANZ/SHUTTERSTOCK©

Barcelona's Must-Sees

On your first day in Barcelona, visit the city's major highlights: stroll La Rambla, explore the atmospheric lanes of the Barri Gòtic and linger over the stunning artistry of La Sagrada Família. History, great architecture and a celebrated food market are all part of this sensory-rich experience.

Day

01

❶ La Rambla (p42)

It heaves with visitors, but there are still treasures worth seeing on this iconic thoroughfare. Don't miss the Miró mosaic, and key buildings facing La Rambla, including the Gran Teatre del Liceu (p196) and the 18th-century Palau de la Virreina (p45).

➲ La Rambla to Mercat de la Boqueria

🚶 Find the market's entrance on La Rambla's west side.

❷ Mercat de la Boqueria (p50)

This staggering food market is packed with culinary riches, but you have to know where to look. Skip the touristy juice bars and head to the back for authentic, delectable food stalls and tapas bars.

➲ Mercat de la Boqueria to Barri Gòtic

🚶 Head back down La Rambla, then turn left into Plaça Reial after passing Carrer de Ferran.

© ANSHARPHOTO/SHUTTERSTOCK ©

❸ Barri Gòtic

Delve into Barcelona's old city. Cross picturesque Plaça Reial (p47) before wandering narrow lanes that date back to at least the Middle Ages. Make your way to the magnificent Catedral (p64), then visit the Temple d'August (p67).

⬣ Barri Gòtic to Cafè de l'Acadèmia

🏃 Cross Cross Plaça de Sant Jaume, walk along Carrer de la Ciutat and take the first left.

❹ Lunch at Cafè de l'Acadèmia (p136)

Arrive early to get a seat at this small atmospheric restaurant serving excellent Catalan cuisine. The multicourse lunch special is fantastic value.

⬣ Cafè de l'Acadèmia to La Sagrada Família

Ⓜ Take Line 4 north from Jaume I; transfer at Passeig de Gràcia for Line 2 to Sagrada Família.

❺ La Sagrada Família (p36)

Roll the drums, turn on the stage lights and get ready for one of Spain's most-visited sights. This one-of-a kind religious monument is as unique as the Pyramids and as beautiful as the Taj Mahal.

⬣ La Sagrada Família to Tapas 24

Ⓜ Take Line 2 back to Passeig de Gràcia. Walk southeast down the street of the same name, then take your second left.

❻ Evening Bites at Tapas 24 (p143)

This great basement spot does innovative takes on traditional tapas. It's a top place for a light bite or a full meal.

From left: La Rambla (p42); Bridge of Sighs, Barri Gòtic

Plan Your Trip
Top Days in Barcelona

© LITTLEAOM/SHUTTERSTOCK ©

Mar i Muntanya (Sea & Mountain)

This itinerary takes you along the promenade that skirts the Mediterranean, then into the old fishing quarter of Barceloneta before whisking you up to the heights of Montjuïc for fine views, fragrant gardens and superb art galleries – including two of the city's top museums.

Day

02

❶ Waterfront (p88)

Start the morning with a waterfront stroll; this scenic but once-derelict area experienced a dramatic makeover for the 1992 Summer Olympics. Look north and you'll see Frank Gehry's shimmering fish sculpture, while to the south rises the spinnaker-shaped tower of the W Hotel.

↪ Barceloneta Beach to Can Ros

🏃 Look for Carrer del Almirall Aixada just north of the rectangular beach sculpture. Can Ros is about 350m back from the beach on this road.

❷ Lunch at Can Ros (p142)

Take your pick of the seaside restaurants if you want the view, but otherwise head back a few streets to this family-run gem, which has been dishing up excellent seafood for generations.

↪ Can Ros to Teleférico del Puerto

🏃 Walk to the southern end of Barceloneta and you'll see the cable car to your right.

KATSIUBA VOLHA/SHUTTERSTOCK ©

❸ Teleférico del Puerto (p63)

After lunch take a scenic ride on this aerial cable car for fantastic views over the port and the dazzling city beyond. At the top, you'll arrive in Montjuïc, a minimountain that's packed with gardens – both sculptural and floral – and also hosts a few first-rate museums.

➲ Teleférico del Puerto to Fundació Joan Miró

🚋 Take the cable car up to Montjuïc, disembark and follow the main road 800m west.

❹ Fundació Joan Miró (p60)

See a full range of works by one of the giants of the art world. Paintings, sculptures and drawings by the prolific Catalan artist are displayed along with photos and other media. Outside is a peaceful sculpture garden with views over Poble Sec.

➲ Fundació Joan Miró to Museu Nacional d'Art de Catalunya

🚶 Follow the path through the sculpture gardens east, take the steps up to the main road and continue east to the museum.

❺ Museu Nacional d'Art de Catalunya (p56)

Not to be missed is the incomparable collection of artwork inside this enormous museum. The highlight is the impressive Romanesque collection – rescued from 900-year-old churches in the Pyrenees. Out front, you can take in the view over Plaça d'Espanya to the distant peak of Tibidabo.

➲ Museu Nacional d'Art de Catalunya to Tickets

🚶 Descend toward Plaça d'Espanya. Turn right before the fountain, left on Carrer de Lleida and right on Avinguda del Paral·lel.

❻ Dinner at Tickets (p147)

You'll need to book weeks in advance, but it's well worth the effort to score a table at Tickets, one of Barcelona's hottest attractions. The celebrated restaurant, run by the Adrià brothers, showcases an ever-changing menu of molecular gastronomy.

From left: Barceloneta Beach (p91);Teleférico del Puerto (p63)

Plan Your Trip
Top Days in Barcelona

DLEIVA/ALAMY STOCK PHOTO ©

La Ribera

Like adjacent Barri Gòtic, La Ribera has narrow cobblestone streets and medieval architecture galore. Yet it's also home to high-end shopping, a brilliant Modernista concert hall and a treasure trove of artwork by Picasso. Great restaurants and a fanciful green space complete the Ribera ramble.

Day
03

❶ Museu Picasso (p80)

Many of Picasso's early masterpieces are held among his 3500 works in this museum. As impressive as the artwork are the galleries themselves – set in a series of merchant houses dating back to the 14th century.

↻ Museu Picasso to El Born

🚶 Stroll southeast along Carrer de Montcada.

❷ Window Shopping in El Born (p161)

The medieval streets of El Born hide an abundance of shopping intrigue, from magic shops to purveyors of fine wines, along with plenty of eye-catching fashion boutiques.

↻ El Born to Cal Pep

🚶 Walk across Plaça de les Olles.

❸ Lunch at Cal Pep (p140)

For lunch, head to this bustling eatery for some of the city's tastiest seafood tapas.

↻ Cal Pep to Basílica de Santa Maria del Mar

🚶 Stroll northwest along Carrer de la Vidriería and turn left on Carrer de Santa Maria.

©STEVE LOVEGROVE/SHUTTERSTOCK©

❹ Basílica de Santa Maria del Mar (p116)

A few blocks away, this captivating church is built in the style of Catalan Gothic. The 14th-century masterpiece soars above the medina-like streets surrounding it.

⭕ Basílica de Santa Maria del Mar to Parc de la Ciutadella

🚶 Walk northeast on Carrer de Santa Maria and pop inside the Born Cultural and Memorial Centre to see the old city ruins, before continuing to the park.

❺ Parc de la Ciutadella (p84)

After the compact streets of La Ribera, catch your breath and stroll through the open green expanse of this manicured park. You'll find sculptures, a small zoo, the Parlament de Catalunya and the centrepiece – a dramatic (if utterly artificial) waterfall dating from the 19th century.

⭕ Parc de la Ciutadella to Palau de la Música Catalana

🚶 Take Carrer de la Princesa back into El Born and turn right after 200m, making your way northwest.

❻ Palau de la Música Catalana (p198)

Designed by Domènech i Montaner in the early 1900s, this intimate concert hall is a Modernista masterpiece, with luminescent stained glass and elaborately sculpted details throughout. Come for a concert, but it's also worth returning for a guided tour.

⭕ Palau de la Música Catalana to El Xampanyet

🚶 Make your way back (southeast) to Carrer de Montcada.

❼ El Xampanyet (p179)

Just up the road, El Xampanyet is a festive spot to end the night. Sample mouth-watering bites and let your cup brim with ever-flowing *cava* (Catalan sparkling wine). It's usually crowded but friendly; just politely elbow your way in.

From left: El Born shops (p161); Basílica de Santa Maria del Mar (p116)

Plan Your Trip
Top Days in Barcelona

LUCAS VALLECILLOS/ALAMY STOCK PHOTO ©

Art & Architecture

This tour takes you up to the enchanting park Gaudí designed overlooking the city, down the elegant architectural showpiece avenue of Passeig de Gràcia and into El Raval. There you'll find the city's top contemporary art museum anchoring Barcelona's most bohemian neighbourhood.

Day
04

❶ Park Güell (p68)

Go early to Park Güell to beat the crowds and see the early morning rays over Barcelona and the Mediterranean beyond. Stroll the expanse of the park, ending your visit at Casa-Museu Gaudí (p70), where you can learn more about the life and work of the great Catalan architect.

➲ Park Güell to Gràcia

Ⓜ Take Line 3 from Vallcarca to Fontana or walk (it's just one stop).

❷ Gràcia

The village-like feel of Gràcia makes for some great exploring. Stroll from plaza to plaza along the narrow shop-lined lanes, stopping perhaps at open-air cafes along the way. Good streets for browsing include Carre de Verdi, Travessera de Gràcia and Carrer de Torrijos.

➲ Gràcia to Botafumeiro

🚶 Walk southwest along Travessera de Gràcia and turn right on Carrer Gran de Gràcia.

❸ Lunch at Botafumeiro (p149)

One of Barcelona's best seafood restaurants. If the tables are full, you can usually get a spot at the bar.

◯ Botafumeiro to Passeig de Gràcia

🏃 Amble southeast along Carrer Gran de Gràcia, which leads into Passeig de Gràcia after 400m.

❹ Passeig de Gràcia

Head to L'Eixample to see high-concept architecture. Passeig de Gràcia is a busy but elegant boulevard lined with exquisite Modernista buildings, including Gaudí's La Pedrera (p76) and Casa Batlló (p52).

◯ Passeig de Gràcia to MACBA

🏃 Continue on Passeig de Gràcia, cross Plaça de Catalunya to La Rambla and turn right on Carrer del Bonsuccés.

❺ MACBA (p94)

A few streets away from Placa d'Espanya you'll reach the city's top contemporary art gallery, MACBA. It houses an excellent range of Catalan and European works from WWII to the present.

◯ MACBA to El Raval

🏃 Walk along Carrer dels Àngels and turn left on Carrer del Carme.

❻ El Raval

Spend the early evening strolling the lively multicultural streets of El Raval. Stop for a breather in the pretty courtyard of the Antic Hospital de la Santa Creu (p46) and check out Gaudí's Palau Güell (p92).

◯ El Raval to Koy Shunka

Ⓜ Take Line 3 from Paral·lel to Catalunya.

❼ Dinner at Koy Shunka (p137)

End your night with a feast at Koy Shunka, where the haute cuisine is a magnificent marriage of Catalan creativity and Japanese tradition. The tasting menus are worth the hefty price tags.

From left: Casa-Museu Gaudí (p70); La Pedrera (p76)

Plan Your Trip
Need to Know

Daily Costs

Budget:
Less than €60

- Dorm bed: €11–30
- Set lunch: from €11
- Bicycle hire per hour: €5

Midrange:
€60–200

- Standard double room: €80–140
- Two-course dinner with wine for two: €50
- Walking and guided tours: €15–25

Top end:
More than €200

- Double room in boutique and luxury hotels: €200 and up
- Three-course meal at top restaurants per person: €80
- Concert tickets to Palau de la Música Catalana: around €45

Advance Planning

Three months before Book accommodation and reserve a table at a top restaurant.

One month before Check out reviews for theatre and live music, and book tickets.

One week before Book tickets for top sights like La Sagrada Família. Browse the latest nightlife listings, art exhibitions and other events to attend while in town. Reserve spa visits and organised tours.

Useful Websites

Barcelona (www.bcn.cat) Town hall's official site with plenty of links.

Barcelona Turisme (www. barcelonaturisme.com) City's official tourism website.

Lonely Planet (www.lonely planet.com/barcelona) Destination information, hotel bookings, traveller forum and more.

BCN Mes (www.bcnmes.com) Website for a trilingual monthly print mag of culture, food, art and more.

Spotted by Locals (www. spotted bylocals.com/ barcelona) Insider tips.

Arriving in Barcelona

El Prat airport Frequent *aerobúses* make the 35-minute run into town (€5.90) from 5.35am to 1am. Taxis cost around €25.

Estació Sants Long-distance trains arrive at this large station near the centre of town, which is linked by metro to other parts of the city.

Estació del Nord Barcelona's long-haul bus station is located in L'Eixample, about 1.5km northeast of Plaça de Catalunya, and is a short walk from the Arc de Triomf metro station.

Girona-Costa Brava airport Sagalés runs direct services between Girona-Costa Brava airport and Estació del Nord bus station in Barcelona (one way/ return €16/25, 75 minutes).

Currency

Euro (€)

Languages

Spanish, Catalan

Visas

Generally not required for stays upto 90 days. Some nationalities need a Schengen visa.

Money

ATMs are widely available (La Rambla has many). Credit cards are accepted in most hotels, shops and restaurants.

Mobile Phones

Local SIM cards can be used in unlocked phones. Data packages are readily available.

Time

Central European Time (GMT/UTC plus one hour)

Tourist Information

Oficina d'Informació de Turisme de Barcelona (p239) provides maps, sights information, tours, concert and events tickets, and last-minute accommodation.

For more, see the **Survival Guide** (p235)

When to Go

Sweltering July and August are peak tourist season and crowds swarm the city and its beaches.

For pleasant weather, but without the sea dips, come in May.

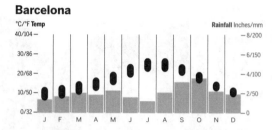

Barcelona

Reus airport Hispano-Igualadina offers a service that runs between Reus airport and Estació d'Autobusos de Sants to meet flights (€11.60/17 one way/return, two hours).

Getting Around

Barcelona has abundant options for getting around town. The excellent metro can get you most places, with buses and trams filling in the gaps. Taxis are the best option late at night.

Metro The most convenient option. Runs 5am to midnight Sunday to Thursday, till 2am on Friday and 24 hours on Saturday. Targeta T-10 (10-ride passes; €10.20) are the best value; otherwise, it's €2.20 per ride.

Bus A hop-on, hop-off Bus Turístic, from Plaça de Catalunya, is handy for those wanting to see the city's highlights in one or two days.

Taxi You can hail taxis on the street (try La Rambla, Via Laietana, Plaça de Catalunya and Passeig de Gràcia) or at taxi stands.

On foot Barcelona is generally best explored on foot.

What to Take

- Money belt
- Earplugs for noisy weekend nights
- Trainers or walking shoes
- Bathing suit
- Swim towel
- Sunglasses
- Sunscreen
- Hat
- Rain jacket or umbrella
- Reading material (try page-turners by Carlos Ruiz Zafón or Manuel Vázquez Montalbán)

What to Wear

In Barcelona just about anything goes and you'll rarely feel uncomfortable because of what you're wearing. That said, Catalans are fairly fashion-conscious and well dressed. Most folk dress smart casual, with something perhaps a bit dressier if going somewhere special in the evening. If you're planning on going to up-market nightclubs, bring something stylish (sandals or sneakers are a no-go).

Meanwhile, La Catedral and La Sagrada Família advertise a policy of no admittance to those in baseball caps, sleeveless tops or shorts. The rule isn't always enforced, but it's best not to take the risk.

Plan Your Trip
What's New

JORDI C/SHUTTERSTOCK ©

Food Trucks

The city's appetite for street food is apparently insatiable and regular pop-up food markets now include Eat Street (http://eatstreet.barcelona), All Those (www.allthose.org) and Van Van (www.vanvanmarket.com).

Barcelona's Notorious Prison

The newest attraction to tour in Barcelona is the city's historic 114-year-old prison, La Model (www.lamodel.barcelona). The prison only closed down in 2017 and in 2018 started offering fascinating tours giving a sneak peek inside its walls.

Luxury & Urban Style

The latest addition to Barcelona's hotel scene is Ian Schrager's **Barcelona Edition** (☏ 93 626 33 30; www.editionhotels.com/barcelona; Avinguda de Francesc Cambo 14; d from €290; Ⓜ Jaume I). Located right next to the colourful Mercat de Santa Caterina, the hotel is an urban hub where guests can hang with local hipsters, join in the vermouth hour at Bar Veraz or head down into the basement for a clandestine performance at Cabaret.

Poblenou Renaissance

This formerly industrial 'hood is on the make, with new galleries, colourful shops and restaurants forming the intersection for the creative tech and design folk who are increasingly moving here.

Cereal Cafes & Brunch Bars

Brunch menus are as popular as ever with weekend queues often out the door, but the latest craze to hit the city is cereal cafes. Order a bowl of your favourite childhood breakfast, complete with multicoloured crunch, mini-marshmallows or lots of chocolate, and pair it with a bottle of flavoured milk.

Above: Food trucks at Castell de Montjuïc (p63)

Plan Your Trip
For Free

MSTEPANPHOTOGRAPHER/SHUTTERSTOCK ©

With planning, Barcelona can be a surprisingly affordable place in which to travel. Many museums offer free days and some of the best ways to experience the city don't cost a cent – hanging out on the beach, exploring fascinating neighbourhoods and parks, and drinking in the views from hilltop heights.

Festivals & Events

Barcelona has loads of free festivals and events, including Festes de la Mercè (p14) and Festes de Santa Eulàlia (p7). From June to August, the city hosts Música als Parcs (Music in the Parks), a series of open-air concerts held in different parks and green spaces around the city. Stop in at the tourist office or go online (www.bcn.cat) for a schedule.

Walking Tours

Numerous companies offer pay-what-you-wish walking tours. These typically take in the Barri Gòtic or the Modernista sites of L'Eixample. Of course, the guides expect a contribution.

Sights

Entry to some sights is free on occasion, most commonly on the first Sunday of the month, while quite a few attractions are free from 3pm to 8pm on Sundays. Others, including the Centre d'Art Santa Mònica (p46), Palau del Lloctinent (p67), Temple d'August (p67) and Antic Hospital de la Santa Creu (p46), are always free, and the Basílica de Santa Maria del Mar (p116) is free in the morning and evening.

Picnics

You can eat very well on a budget if you stick to set menus at lunchtime. For even less, you can put together a picnic of fruit, cheese, smoked meats and other goodies bought at local markets. The obvious choice is Mercat de la Boqueria (p50), but you'll find fewer crowds and an equally good selection at the Mercat de Sant Antoni (p51) on the western edge of El Raval. La Ribera has the handy Mercat de Santa Caterina (p110).

Above: Papier-mâché giants, Festes de la Mercè (p14)

Plan Your Trip
Family Travel

TVERNHOVNETS/GETTY IMAGES ©

Catalan Style

Going out to eat or sipping a beer on a late summer evening at a *terraza* (terrace) needn't mean leaving children with minders. Locals take their kids out all the time and don't worry about keeping them up late. To make the most of your visit, try to adjust your child's sleeping habits to 'Spanish time' early on, or else you'll miss out on much of Barcelona. Also, be prepared to look for things 'outside the box': there's the childlike creativity of Picasso and Miró (give your children paper and crayons and take them around the museums), the Harry-Potter-meets-Tolkien fantasy of Park Güell and La Pedrera, and the wild costumes, human castle-building and street food at festivals.

Eating with Children

Barcelona – and Spain in general – is super friendly when it comes to eating with children. Spanish kids tend to eat the Mediterranean offerings enjoyed by their parents, but some restaurants have children's menus that serve up burgers, pizzas, tomato-sauce pasta and the like. Good local – and child-proof – food commonly found on tapas menus are *tortillas de patatas* (potato omelettes) or *croquetas de jamón* (ham croquettes).

Filferro (☑93 221 98 36; www.facebook.com/elfilferro.barceloneta; Carrer de Sant Carles 29; tapas €2-7, mains €7-9; ☺10am-1am Tue-Sun; 🛜✏; MBarceloneta) is a tapas and snack bar where you can enjoy the Mediterranean breeze, while the children play in the adjacent playground.

Babysitting

Most of the midrange and top-end hotels in Barcelona can organise babysitting services. Otherwise **T5 Serveis** (☑93 412 56 76; www.5serveis.com; Pelai 50, 3r 1a, Barcelona) offers babysitting services.

CHRISTIAN BERTRAND/ALAMY STOCK PHOTO ©

Need to Know

Supplies Nappies (diapers), dummies, creams and formula can be bought at any of the city's many pharmacies. Nappies are cheaper in supermarkets.

Accessibility The narrow streets of the Ciutat Vella, with their unpredictable traffic and cobbled streets, are less buggy-friendly than the rest of Barcelona.

Metro Barcelona's metro is accessible and great for families with buggies. Be mindful of pickpockets.

Change facilities Generallly widely available and clean.

Cots Usually available in hotesl (ask for una cuna); reserve ahead.

High chairs Many restaurants will have at least one.

Best Family-Friendly Meals

La Nena (p148)

Bar del Convent (p139)

Granja M Viader (p137)

Pepa Tomate (p148)

Granja La Pallaresa (p135)

Parks & Gardens

Barcelona has many parks and gardens that make a great break from the city and give children a chance to run around, including Parc de la Ciutadella (p84) and Park Güell (p68).

From left: Parc de la Ciutadella (p84);
Parc d'Atraccions (p99)

TOP EXPERIENCES

The very best to see and do

La Sagrada Família interior

ANA CANDIDA/SHUTTERSTOCK ©

La Sagrada Família

If you have time for only one sight-seeing outing, this is it. The Sagrada Família inspires awe by its sheer verticality, remarkable use of light and Gaudí's offbeat design elements.

Great For...

☑ **Don't Miss**

The apse, the extraordinary pillars and the stained glass.

In the manner of the medieval cathedrals La Sagrada Família emulates, it's still under construction after more than 130 years. Work began in 1882 and is hoped (although by no means expected) to be finished in 2026, a century after architect Antoni Gaudí's death.

A Holy Mission

The Temple Expiatori de la Sagrada Família (Expiatory Temple of the Holy Family) was Antoni Gaudí's all-consuming obsession. Given the commission by a conservative society that wished to build a temple as atonement for the city's sins of modernity, Gaudí saw its completion as his holy mission. As funds dried up, he contributed his own and in the last years of his life he was never shy of pleading with anyone he thought a likely donor.

REBIUS/SHUTTERSTOCK ©

❶ Need to Know

Map p254; ☎93 208 04 14; www.sagrada-familia.org; Carrer de la Marina; adult/child €15/free; guided tours €24 for 50 minutes; audio tour €7; ⊙9am-8pm Apr-Sep, to 7pm Mar & Oct, to 6pm Nov-Feb; Ⓜ Sagrada Família

✕ Take a Break

Cantina Mexicana (☎93 667 66 68; www.cantinalamexicana.es; Carrer de València 427; mains €9-13; ⊙1pm-midnight; ✈; Ⓜ Sagrada Família) dodges the crowds and does excellent tacos.

★ Top Tip

Buy tickets online to beat the frequently dispiriting queues.

Gaudí devised a temple 95m long and 60m wide, able to seat 13,000 people, with a central tower 170m high above the transept (representing Christ) and another 17 of 100m or more. The 12 along the three facades represent the Apostles, while the remaining five represent the Virgin Mary and the four evangelists. With his characteristic dislike for straight lines (there were none in nature, he said), Gaudí gave his towers swelling outlines inspired by the weird peaks of the holy mountain Montserrat outside Barcelona and encrusted them with a tangle of sculpture that seems an outgrowth of the stone.

At Gaudí's death, only the crypt, the apse walls, one portal and one tower had been finished. Three more towers were added by 1930, completing the northeast (Nativity) facade. In 1936 anarchists burned and smashed the interior, including workshops, plans and models. Work began again in 1952, but controversy has always clouded progress. Opponents of the continuation of the project claim that the computer models based on what little of Gaudí's plans survived the anarchists' ire have led to the creation of a monster that has little to do with Gaudí's plans and style. It is a debate that appears to have little hope of resolution. Like or hate what is being done, the fascination it awakens is undeniable.

Even before reaching completion, some of the oldest parts of the church, especially the apse, have required restoration work.

Interior & the Apse

Inside, work on roofing over the church was completed in 2010. The roof is held up by a forest of extraordinary angled pillars.

As the pillars soar toward the ceiling, they sprout a web of supporting branches, creating the effect of a forest canopy. The tree image is in no way fortuitous – Gaudí envisaged such an effect. Everything was thought through, including the shape and placement of windows to create the mottled effect one would see with sunlight pouring through the branches of a thick forest. The pillars are made of four different types of stone. They vary in colour and load-bearing strength, from the soft Montjuïc stone pillars along the lateral aisles through to granite, dark grey basalt and finally burgundy-tinged Iranian porphyry for the key columns at the intersection of the nave and transept. The stained glass, divided in shades of red, blue, green and ochre, creates a hypnotic, magical atmosphere when the sun hits the windows. Tribunes built high above the aisles can host two choirs: the main tribune up to 1300 people and the children's tribune up to 300.

Nativity Facade

The Nativity Facade is the artistic pinnacle of the building, mostly created under Gaudí's personal supervision. You can climb high up inside some of the four towers by a combination of lifts and narrow spiral staircases – a vertiginous experience. These tower tours cost extra and must be prebooked online. Do not climb the stairs if you have cardiac or respiratory problems. The towers are destined to hold tubular bells capable of playing complex music at great volume. Their upper parts are decorated with mosaics spelling out 'Sanctus, Sanctus, Sanctus, Hosanna in Excelsis,

The cathedral's ceiling

Amen, Alleluia'. Asked why he lavished so much care on the tops of the spires, which no one would see from close up, Gaudí answered: 'The angels will see them'.

Three sections of the portal represent, from left to right, Hope, Charity and Faith. Among the forest of sculpture on the Charity portal you can see, low down, the manger surrounded by an ox, an ass, the shepherds, kings and angel musicians. Some 30 different plant species from around Catalonia are reproduced here and the faces of the many figures are taken from plaster casts of local people and the occasional one made from a corpse in the local morgue.

★ Did You Know?

Unfinished it may be, but La Sagrada Família attracts over 4.5 million visitors a year and is Spain's most visited monument.

STEFAN CIOATA/GETTY IMAGES ©

Directly above the blue stained-glass window is the archangel Gabriel's Annunciation to Mary. At the top is a green cypress tree, a refuge in a storm for the white doves of peace dotted over it. The mosaic work at the pinnacle of the towers is made from Murano glass, from Venice.

To the right of the facade is the curious Claustre del Roser, a Gothic-style minicloister tacked on to the outside of the church (rather than the classic square enclosure of the great Gothic church monasteries). Once inside, look back to the intricately decorated entrance. On the lower right-hand side you'll notice the sculpture of a reptilian devil handing a terrorist a bomb. Barcelona was regularly rocked by political violence and bombings were frequent in the decades prior to the civil war. The sculpture is one of several on the 'temptations of men and women'.

Passion Facade

The southwest Passion Facade, on the theme of Christ's last days and death, was built between 1954 and 1978 based on surviving drawings by Gaudí, with four towers and a large, sculpture-bedecked portal. The sculptor, Josep Subirachs, worked on its decoration from 1986 to 2006. He did not attempt to imitate Gaudí; rather, he produced angular, controversial images of his own. The main series of sculptures, on three levels, are in an S-shaped sequence, starting with the Last Supper at the bottom left and ending with Christ's burial at the top right.

To the right, in front of the Passion Facade, the Escoles de Gaudí is one of his simpler gems. Gaudí built this as a children's school, creating an original, undulating roof of brick that continues to charm architects to this day. Inside is a re-creation of Gaudí's modest office as it was when he died and explanations of the geometric patterns and plans at the heart of his building techniques.

☑ When to Go

There are always people visiting the Sagrada Família, but if you can get there when it opens, you'll find fewer crowds.

A Hidden Portrait

Careful observation of the Passion Facade will reveal a special tribute from sculptor Josep Subirachs to Gaudí. The central sculptural group (below Christ crucified) shows, from right to left, Christ bearing his cross, Veronica displaying the cloth with Christ's bloody image, a pair of soldiers and, watching it all, a man called the evangelist. Subirachs used a rare photo of Gaudí, taken a couple of years before his death, as the model for the evangelist's face.

Glory Facade

The Glory Facade is under construction and will, like the others, be crowned by four towers – the total of 12 representing the Twelve Apostles. Gaudí wanted it to be the most magnificent facade of the church. Inside will be the narthex, a kind of foyer made up of 16 'lanterns', a series of hyperboloid forms topped by cones. Further decoration will make the whole building a microcosmic symbol of the Christian church, with Christ represented by a massive 170m central tower above the transept and the five remaining planned towers symbolising the Virgin Mary and the four evangelists.

Museu Gaudí

Open the same times as the church, the Museu Gaudí, below ground level, includes interesting material on Gaudí's life and other works, as well as models and photos of La Sagrada Família. You can see a good example of his plumb-line models that showed him the stresses and strains he could get away with in construction. A

> ### ❶ What to Wear
> La Sagrada Família has an advertised policy of not admitting those in baseball caps, sleeveless tops or shorts. It isn't always enforced, but it's best not to take the risk. See-through clothing, low necklines and exposed backs/midriffs are also not permitted, and any skirts must be at least midthigh in length.

side hall towards the eastern end of the museum leads to a viewing point above the simple crypt in which the genius is buried. The crypt, where Masses are now held, can also be visited from the Carrer de Mallorca side of the church.

What's Nearby?

Església de les Saleses   Church

(Map p254; ☎93 458 76 67; Passeig de Sant Joan 90; ⊙10am-1pm & 5-7pm Mon-Sat, 10am-2pm Sun; Ⓜ Verdaguer) A singular neo-Gothic effort, this church is interesting because it was designed by Joan Martorell i Montells (1833–1906), Gaudí's architecture professor. Raised in 1878–85 with an adjacent convent (badly damaged in the civil war and now a school), it offers hints of what was to come with Modernisme, with his use of brick, mosaics and stained glass.

Museu del Disseny de Barcelona

Palau Macaya
Palace

(Map p254; ☏93 457 95 31; www.obrasocial-lacaixa.org/de/centros/palau-macaya; Passeig de Sant Joan 108; ☉9am-2pm & 4-8pm Mon-Fri; Ⓜ Verdaguer) FREE Palau Macaya is one of Barcelona's great Catalan Modernisme gems, but one of its least well known. Its architect was Josep Puig i Cadafalch, who also designed Casa Amatller (p55) and Casa de les Punxes (p78). The facade is impressive, with decorative windows and intricate paintwork, but the interior is where this palace really comes to life, with its grand entrance, open courtyard decked in colourful tiles and a delicately carved marble staircase.

Museu del Disseny de Barcelona
Museum

(☏93 256 68 00; www.museudeldisseny.cat; Plaça de les Glòries Catalanes 37; permanent/temporary exhibitions adult €6/4.40, child €4/3, combination tickets adult/child €8/5.50, free from 3pm Sun & 1st Sun of the month; ☉10am-8pm Tue-Sun; Ⓜ Glòries) Barcelona's design museum lies inside a monolithic contemporary building with geometric facades and a rather brutalist appearance that's nicknamed *la grapadora* (the stapler) by locals. Inside, it houses a dazzling collection of ceramics, decorative arts and textiles, and is a must for anyone interested in the design world.

MSTEPANPHOTOGRAPHER/SHUTTERSTOCK ©

La Rambla

Barcelona's most famous street is both a tourist magnet and a window into Catalan culture, with arts centres, theatres and intriguing architecture. The middle is a broad pedestrian boulevard, crowded daily with a wide cross-section of society. A stroll here is pure sensory overload, with souvenir hawkers, buskers, pavement artists and living statues part of the ever-changing street scene.

Great For...

ℹ Need to Know

Map p250; Ⓜ Catalunya, Liceu, Drassanes

★ **Top Tip**

Keep an eye on your belongings and wear backpacks on your front. Pickpockets find easy pickings along this stretch.

History

La Rambla takes its name from a seasonal stream (derived from the Arabic word for sand, *raml*) that once ran here. From the early Middle Ages, it was better known as the Cagalell (Stream of Shit) and lay outside the city walls until the 14th century. Monastic buildings were then built and, subsequently, mansions of the well-to-do from the 16th to the early 19th centuries. Unofficially, La Rambla is divided into five sections, which explains why many know it as Las Ramblas.

La Rambla de Canaletes

The section of La Rambla north of Plaça de Catalunya is named after the **Font de Canaletes**, an inconspicuous turn-of-the-20th-century drinking fountain, the water of which supposedly emerges from what were once known as the springs of Canaletes. It used to be said that *barcelonins* 'drank the waters of Les Canaletes'. Nowadays, people claim that anyone who drinks from the fountain will return to Barcelona, which is not such a bad prospect. Delirious football fans gather here to celebrate whenever the city's principal team, FC Barcelona, wins a cup or league title.

La Rambla dels Estudis

La Rambla dels Estudis, from Carrer de la Canuda running south to Carrer de la Portaferrissa, was formerly home to a twittering bird market, which closed in 2010 after 150 years in operation.

Palau de la Virreina

Església de Betlem

Just north of Carrer del Carme, this **church** (Map p250; ☏93 318 38 23; www.mdbetlem.net; Carrer d'en Xuclà 2; ⊘8.30am-1.30pm & 6-9pm; Ⓜ Liceu) was constructed in baroque style for the Jesuits in the late 17th and early 18th centuries to replace a church destroyed by fire in 1671. Fire was a bit of a theme for this

---

★ **Top Tip**

La Rambla is at its best first thing in the morning, before the cruise ships disgorge their passengers.

★ **Did You Know?**

La Rambla saw plenty of action during the civil war. In *Homage to Catalonia*, George Orwell vividly described the avenue gripped by revolutionary fervour.

---

site: the church was once considered the most splendid of Barcelona's baroque offerings, but leftist arsonists torched it in 1936.

Palau Moja

Looming over the eastern side of La Rambla, **Palau Moja** (☏93 316 27 40; https://palaumoja.com; Carrer de Portaferrissa 1; ⊘10am-9pm, cafe 9.30am-midnight Mon-Fri, 11am-midnight Sat & Sun; Ⓜ Liceu) **FREE** is a neoclassical building dating from the second half of the 18th century. Its clean, classical lines are best appreciated from across the other side of the street. These days it is a centre for Catalan heritage: its well-stocked information centre doubles as a ticket office for various attractions, and a large gift shop.

La Rambla de Sant Josep

From Carrer de la Portaferrissa to Plaça de la Boqueria, what is officially called La Rambla de Sant Josep (named after a now nonexistent monastery) is lined with flower stalls, which give it the alternative name La Rambla de les Flors.

Palau de la Virreina

The Palau de la Virreina is a grand 18th-century rococo mansion (with some neoclassical elements) housing an arts/entertainment information and ticket office run by the Ajuntament. Built by Manuel d'Amat i de Junyent, the captain general of Chile (a Spanish colony that included the Peruvian silver mines of Potosí), it is a rare example of postbaroque building in Barcelona. In a series of exhibition rooms, including the bulk of the 1st floor, it houses the **Centre de la Imatge** (☏93 316 10 00; www.ajuntament. barcelona.cat/lavirreina; ⊘noon-8pm Tue-Sun; Ⓜ Liceu) **FREE**, the scene of rotating photo exhibitions.

✕ **Take a Break**

There are some decent eateries in the vicinity, including Café de l'Òpera (p134); however, the vast majority of cafes and restaurants along La Rambla are expensive, mediocre tourist traps.

Mosaïc de Miró

At Plaça de la Boqueria, where four side streets meet just north of Liceu metro station, you can walk all over a Miró – the colourful mosaic in the pavement, with one tile signed by the artist. Miró chose this site as it's near the house where he was born on the Passatge del Crèdit. The mosaic's bold colours and vivid swirling forms are instantly recognisable to Miró fans, though plenty of tourists stroll right over it without realising.

La Rambla dels Caputxins

La Rambla dels Caputxins, named after a former monastery, runs from Plaça de la Boqueria to Carrer dels Escudellers. The latter street is named after the potters' guild, founded in the 13th century, the members of which lived and worked here. On the western side of La Rambla is the Gran Teatre del Liceu (p196) and to the southeast is the entrance to the palm-shaded Plaça Reial. Below this point La Rambla gets seedier, with the occasional strip club and peep show.

La Rambla de Santa Mònica

The final stretch of La Rambla widens out to approach the Mirador de Colom overlooking Port Vell. La Rambla here is named after the Convent de Santa Mònica, which once stood on the western flank of the street and has since been converted into the Centre d'Art Santa Mònica.

What's Nearby?

Basílica de Santa Maria del Pi   Church

(Map p250; ☎93 318 47 43; www.basilicadelpi. cat; Plaça del Pi; adult/concession/child under 7yr €4/3/free; ☺10am-6pm; Ⓜ Liceu) This striking 14th-century church is a classic of Catalan Gothic, with an imposing facade, a wide interior and a single nave. The simple decor in the main sanctuary contrasts with the gilded chapels and exquisite stained-glass windows that bathe the interior in ethereal light. The beautiful rose window above its entrance is one of the world's largest. Occasional concerts are staged here (classical guitar, choral groups and chamber orchestras).

Centre d'Art Santa Mònica   Arts Centre

(Map p250; ☎93 567 11 10; http://artssanta monica.gencat.cat; La Rambla 7; ☺11am-9pm Tue-Sat, 11am-5pm Sun; Ⓜ Drassanes) **FREE** The Convent de Santa Mònica was converted into this cultural centre that mostly exhibits modern multimedia installations.

Antic Hospital de la Santa Creu   Historic Building

(Former Hospital of the Holy Cross; Map p249; Carrer de l'Hospital 56; ☺9am-10pm; Ⓜ Liceu) **FREE** Behind La Boqueria stands the Antic Hospital de la Santa Creu, which was once the city's main hospital. Founded in 1401, it functioned until the 1930s and was considered one of the best in Europe in its medieval heyday – it is famously the place where Antoni Gaudí died in 1926. Today it houses the **Biblioteca de Catalunya** and

Plaça Reial

the **Institut d'Estudis Catalans** (Institute for Catalan Studies; Map p249; ☎93 270 16 20; www.iec.cat; ⏰8am-8pm Mon-Fri Sep-Jul). The hospital's former chapel **La Capella** (Map p250; ☎93 256 20 44; http://lacapella. barcelona; ⏰noon-8pm Tue-Sat, 11am-2pm Sun & holidays) FREE shows temporary exhibitions.

Plaça Reial   Square

(Map p250; Ⓜ Liceu) One of the most photo-genic squares in Barcelona, and certainly its liveliest. Numerous restaurants, bars and nightspots lie beneath the arcades of 19th-century neoclassical buildings, with a buzz of activity at all hours.

Mirador de Colom   Viewpoint

Columbus Monument; ☎93 285 38 32; www.barce-lonaturisme.com; Plaça del Portal de la Pau; adult/child €6/4; ⏰8.30am-8.30pm; Ⓜ Drassanes) High above the traffic, Christopher Columbus keeps watch, pointing vaguely out to the Mediterranean from this Corinthian-style iron column built for the 1888 Universal Exhibition. Zip up 60m in a lift for a bird's-eye view of La Rambla and Barcelona's ports. You can also enjoy a wine tasting afterwards in the cellar underneath (€8 for lift and wine).

Via Sepulcral
Romana   Archaeological Site

(Map p250; ☎93 256 21 22; www.muhba.cat; Plaça de la Vila de Madrid; adult/child/concession €2/free/1.50; ⏰11am-2pm Tue, to 7pm Thu; Ⓜ Catalunya) Along Carrer de la Canuda, a block east of La Rambla, is a sunken garden containing exposed Roman tombs. A display in Spanish and Catalan explores burial customs.

☑ Don't Miss

The Rambla stroll, from Plaça de Catalunya to Plaça del Portal de la Pau, is 1.5km.

Mercat de la Boqueria (p50)

Barcelona's Food Markets

Visitors are spoiled for choice when it comes to Barcelona's temples that groan with tantalising produce. Huge crowds at La Boqueria have made it something of a victim of its own success, but shoppers still wonder at the endless bounty of fruits and vegetables, gleaming fish counters and pyramids of pungent cheeses. Further afield are standout markets like the recently overhauled iron-and-brick Mercat de Sant Antoni.

Great For...

ⓘ Need to Know

The market stalls themselves are far more vibrant in the morning than afternoon.

★ **Top Tip**

Ask permission before taking photographs of stall-holders and be sure to buy something from their stall.

MERCAT

St JOSEP

LA BOQUERIA

Mercat de la Boqueria   Market

(Map p250; ☑93 318 20 17; www.boqueria.
barcelona; La Rambla 91; ⊙8am-8.30pm Mon-
Sat; Ⓜ Liceu) Mercat de la Boqueria is possi-
bly La Rambla's most interesting building,
not so much for its Modernista-influenced
design – it was actually built over a long
period, from 1840 to 1914, on the site of the
former St Joseph Monastery – but for the
action of the food market within.

La Boqueria may have changed in
recent years, filled more with tourist-
enticing fruit-shake stalls and novelty
chocolates than typical Spanish produce,
but head towards the back and you'll
discover what it's really about: rich and
bountiful fruit and vegetable stands,
seemingly limitless varieties of sea critters, sausages, cheeses, meats (including

the finest Jabugo ham) and huge tubs of
fragrant olives.

According to some chronicles, there
has been a market on this spot since 1217,
and while today it is a tourist attraction
in its own right, locals do still try to shop
here.

Many of Barcelona's top restaurateurs
also come here for their produce, which
vouches for the quality of the market's
offerings. Nowadays it's no easy task to
get through the crowds to indicate the
slippery slab of sole you're after, or the
tempting piece of Asturian *queso de cabra*
(goat's cheese), so it's worth getting here
early.

La Boqueria is dotted with half-a-dozen
or so vibrant places to eat, which open
up at lunchtime. Whether you eat here or

Mercat de Sant Antoni

you're self-catering, it's worth trying some of Catalonia's gastronomical specialities, such as *bacallà salat* (dried salted cod), which usually comes in an *esqueixada* – a tomato, onion and black-olive salad with frisée lettuce; chargrilled *calçots* (a cross between a leek and an onion), whose insides are eaten as a messy whole; *cargols* (snails), a Catalan staple that is best eaten baked as *cargols a la llauna; peus de porc* (pig's trotters), which are often stewed with snails; and *percebes* (goose-necked barnacles) – much loved across northern Spain, these look like witches' fingers and are eaten with a garlic-and-parsley sauce.

✕ Take a Break

The markets have several excellent eating options within their walls.

GRAHAM LUCAS COMMONS/GETTY IMAGES ©

Mercat de Sant Antoni Market

(Map p249; ☑93 426 35 21; www.mercatdesant antoni.com; Carrer de Comte d'Urgell 1; ⊗8am-8pm Mon-Sat; Ⓜ Sant Antoni) Just beyond the western edge of El Raval is Mercat de Sant Antoni, a glorious old iron-and-brick building constructed between 1872 and 1882. The market recently underwent a nine-year renovation and reopened in 2018 with 250 stalls. It's a great place to stock up on seasonal produce or grab a bite in between browsing. The second-hand book market takes place alongside it on Sunday mornings.

Mercat de la Llibertat Market

(☑93 217 09 95; www.mercatsbcn.com; Plaça de la Llibertat 27; ⊗8am-8.30pm Mon-Fri, to 3pm Sat; Ⓜ Fontana, ℝ FGC Gràcia) Opened in 1888, the 'Market of Liberty' was covered over in 1893 by Francesc Berenguer i Mestres (1866–1914), Gaudí's long-time assistant, in typically fizzy Modernista style, employing generous whirls of wrought iron. It received a considerable facelift in 2009 but remains emblematic of the Gràcia district: full of life and fabulous fresh produce.

Mercat de l'Abaceria Central Market

(Map p254; ☑93 213 62 86; www.mercatabaceria. cat; Travessera de Gràcia 186; ⊗8am-2.30pm & 5-8.30pm Mon-Thu, to 8.30pm Fri, to 3pm Sat; Ⓜ Joanic) Dating from 1892, this sprawling iron-and-brick market is an atmospheric place to browse for fresh produce, cheeses, bakery items and more. There are also several food stalls where you can grab a quick bite on the cheap.

Mercat de Santa Caterina

For this fabulous market, see p110.

☑ Don't Miss

The marvels of the traditional seafood stalls.

Casa Batlló

Casa Batlló is one of the most extraordinary structures to emerge from Gaudí's fantastical imagination. From its playful facade to its revolutionary experiments in light and architectural form (straight lines are few and far between), this apartment block is one of the most beautiful buildings in this city where competition for such a title is fierce.

Great For...

❶ Need to Know

Map p254; 📞93 216 03 06; www.casabatllo.es; Passeig de Gràcia 43; adult/child €28.50/25.50; ⏱9am-9pm, last admission 8pm; ℳPasseig de Gràcia

★ **Top Tip**

Make a return visit after sunset to see the facade illuminated in all its glory.

Facade

To Salvador Dalí it resembled 'twilight clouds in water'. Others see a more-than-passing resemblance to the impressionist masterpiece *Water Lilies* by Claude Monet. A Rorschach blot for the imagination, Casa Batlló's facade is exquisite and whimsical, sprinkled with fragments of blue, mauve and green tiles, and studded with wave-shaped window frames and mask-like balconies.

Roof

Casa Batlló's roof, with the twisting chimney pots so characteristic of Gaudí's structures, is the building's grand crescendo. The eastern end represents Sant Jordi (St George) and the Dragon. The ceaseless curves of coloured tiles have the effect of making the building seem like a living being.

Sala Principal

The staircase wafts you up to the 1st floor, where everything swirls in the main salon: the ceiling twists into a whirlpool-like vortex around its sun-like lamp; the doors, window and skylights are dreamy waves of wood and coloured glass in mollusc-like shapes. The sense of light and space here is extraordinary thanks to the wall-length window onto Passeig de Gràcia.

Back Terrace

Opening onto an expansive L'Eixample patio, Casa Batlló's back terrace is like a fantasy garden in miniature. It's a place where flowerpots take on strange forms and where the accumulation of *trencadís* (broken ceramic pieces) – a mere 330 of them on the building's rear facade – has the effect of immersing you in a kaleidoscope.

Casa Batlló from Passeig de Gràcia

Apple of Discord

It is one of the three houses in the block between Carrer del Consell de Cent and Carrer d'Aragó that gave it the playful name Manzana de la Discòrdia (Block of Discord, which in Spanish also means Apple of Discord). The others are Puig i Cadafalch's Casa Amatller and Domènech i Montaner's Casa Lleó Morera. They were all renovated between 1898 and 1906.

In Greek mythology, the original Apple of Discord was tossed onto Mt Olympus by Eris (Discord), with orders that it be given to the most beautiful goddess, sparking jealousies that were the catalyst for the Trojan War.

☑ Don't Miss

Before going inside, look at the pavement. Each paving piece has stylised images of an octopus and a starfish, designs originally cooked up by Gaudí.

PHOTO: ALIONA/GETTY IMAGES©

What's Nearby?

Casa Amatller   Architecture

(Map p254; ☑93 216 01 75; www.amatller.org; Passeig de Gràcia 41; adult/child 1hr guided tour €24/12, 40min multimedia tour €19/9.50; ⊙10am-6pm; M Passeig de Gràcia) One of Puig i Cadafalch's most striking flights of Modernista fantasy, Casa Amatller combines Gothic window frames with a stepped gable borrowed from Dutch urban architecture. But the busts and reliefs of dragons, knights and other characters dripping off the main facade are pure caprice. The pillared foyer and staircase lit by stained glass are like the inside of some romantic castle. The building was renovated in 1900 for the chocolate baron and philanthropist Antoni Amatller (1851–1910).

Casa Lleó Morera   Architecture

(Map p254; Passeig de Gràcia 35; M Passeig de Gràcia) Domènech i Montaner's 1905 contribution to the Illa de la Discòrdia, with Modernista carving outside and a bright, tiled lobby in which floral motifs predominate, is perhaps the least odd-looking of the three main buildings on the block. Luxury fashion store Loewe (p163) is located here.

Fundació Antoni Tàpies   Gallery

(Map p254; ☑93 487 03 15; www.fundaciotapies. org; Carrer d'Aragó 255; adult/child €7/5.60; ⊙10am-7pm Tue-Thu & Sat, to 9pm Fri, to 3pm Sun; M Passeig de Gràcia) The Fundació Antoni Tàpies is both a pioneering Modernista building (completed in 1885) and the major collection of leading 20th-century Catalan artist Antoni Tàpies, who died in February 2012, aged 88. Known for his esoteric work, he left a powerful range of paintings and a foundation to promote contemporary artists. Admission includes an audio guide.

✕ Take a Break

Tapas 24 (☑93 488 09 77; www.carles abellan.com; Carrer de la Diputació 269; tapas €4-12; ⊙9am-midnight; 🛜; M Passeig de Gràcia), one of Barcelona's most innovative tapas bars, is open all day.

Museu Nacional d'Art de Catalunya

The flamboyant neobaroque silhouette of the Palau Nacional can be seen from across Barcelona. It houses a vast collection of mostly Catalan art, from the early Middle Ages to early 20th century.

Great For...

☑ **Don't Miss**

The fantastic assemblage of Romanesque frescoes from churches around Catalonia.

Romanesque Masterpieces

The Romanesque art section is considered the most important concentration of early medieval art in the world. Rescued from neglected country churches across northern Catalonia in the early 20th century, the collection consists of 21 frescoes, woodcarvings and painted altar frontals (low-relief wooden panels that were the forerunners of the elaborate altarpieces that adorned later churches). The insides of several churches have been re-created and the frescoes – in some cases fragmentary, in others extraordinarily complete and alive with colour – have been placed as they were when in situ.

The first of the two most striking frescoes, in Sala 7, is a magnificent image of Christ in Majesty painted around 1123. Based on the text of the Apocalypse, we see

MARTIN WILLIAMS/ALAMY STOCK PHOTO ©

❶ Need to Know

MNAC; Map p256; 📞 936 22 03 76; www.
museunacional.cat; Mirador del Palau Nacional;
adult/child €12/free, after 3pm Sat & 1st Sun of
month free, rooftop viewpoint only €2; ⏲10am-
8pm Tue-Sat, to 3pm Sun May-Sep, to 6pm Tue-
Sat, to 3pm Sun Oct-Apr; 🚌55, Ⓜ Espanya

✗ Take a Break

On the upper level, beautifully set Oleum
(p147) serves high-end Mediterranean
fare, with great city views.

★ Top Tip

The Articket pass gives discounts for six
museums (including MNAC).

Christ enthroned with the world at his feet.
He holds a book open with the words *Ego
Sum Lux Mundi* (I am the Light of the World)
and is surrounded by the four evangelists.
The images were taken from the apse of
the Església de Sant Climent de Taüll in
northwest Catalonia. Nearby in Sala 9 are
frescoes painted around the same time in
the nearby Església de Santa Maria de Taüll.
This time the central image taken from the
apse is of the Virgin Mary and Christ Child.
These images were not mere decoration,
but tools of instruction in the basics of
Christian faith for the local population. Try
to imagine yourself as an average medieval
citizen: illiterate, ignorant, fearful and in
most cases eking out a subsistence living.
These images transmitted the basic per-
sonalities and tenets of the faith and were
accepted at face value by most.

Gothic Collection

Opposite the Romanesque collection on
the ground floor is the museum's Gothic
art section. In these halls you can see
Catalan Gothic painting and works from
other Spanish and Mediterranean regions.
Look out especially for the work of Bernat
Martorell in Sala 32 and Jaume Huguet in
Sala 34. Among Martorell's works you'll find
images of the martyrdom of St Vincent and
St Llúcia. Huguet's *Consagració de Sant
Agustí,* in which St Augustine is depicted as
a bishop, is dazzling in its detail.

Cambò Bequest & the Thyssen-
Bornemisza Collection

As the Gothic collection draws to a close,
you pass through two separate and equally
eclectic private collections. The Cambó Bequest, donated by Francesc Cambó, spans

the history of European painting between the 14th century and the beginning of the 19th century. The Thyssen-Bornemisza Collection presents a selection of European painting and sculpture produced between the 13th and 18th centuries, on loan to the MNAC by the Museo Thyssen-Bornemisza in Madrid. The Thyssen-Bornemisza Collection's highlight is Fra Angelico's *Madonna of Humility*, whereas the Cambó Bequest holds wonderful works by masters Veronese, Titian and Canaletto. Cranach, El Greco, Rubens and even Gainsborough also feature, and the collection's finale includes works by Francisco de Goya.

Modern Catalan Art

On the next floor, the collection turns to modern art, mainly but not exclusively Catalan. This collection is arranged thematically: Modernisme, Noucentisme, Art and the Civil War and so on. Among the many highlights: an early Salvador Dalí painting *(Portrait of My Father)*, Juan Gris' collage-like paintings, the brilliant portraits of Marià Fortuny and 1930s call-to-arms posters against the Francoist onslaught. There are works by Modernista painters Ramon Casas and Santiago Rusiñol, as well as Catalan luminary Antoni Tàpies.

Also on show are items of Modernista furniture and decoration, which include a mural by Ramon Casas (the artist and Pere Romeu on a tandem bicycle) that once adorned the legendary bar and restaurant Els Quatre Gats.

Fresco Strippers

Among the little known curiosities within MNAC, in Sala 3 you'll find a video depicting

Poble Espanyol

the techniques used by the 'Fresco Strip-pers' to preserve the great Romanesque works. The Stefanoni brothers, Italian art restorers, brought the secrets of *strappo* (stripping frescoes from walls) to Catalonia in the early 1900s. The Stefanoni would cover frescoes with a sheet of fabric, stuck on with a glue made of cartilage. When dry, this allowed the image to be stripped off the wall and rolled up. For three years the Stefanoni roamed the Pyrenean country-side, stripping churches and chapels and sending the rolls back to Barcelona, where they were eventually put back up on walls and inside purpose-built church apses to reflect how they had appeared in situ.

★ Did You Know?

An emblematic building, the Palau Nacional was built for the 1929 World Exhibition and restored in 2005.

CATARINA BELOVA/SHUTTERSTOCK©

What's Nearby?

Museu d'Arqueologia de Catalunya
Museum

(MAC; Map p256; ☑93 423 21 49; www.mac barcelona.cat; Passeig de Santa Madrona 39-41; adult/child €5.50/free; ⊗9.30am-7pm Tue-Sat, 10am-2.30pm Sun; ☐55, ⓂPoble Sec) This archaeology museum, housed in what was the Graphic Arts Palace during the 1929 World Exhibition, covers Catalonia and other Spanish cultures. Items range from copies of pre-Neanderthal skulls to jewel-studded Visigothic crosses.

Museu Etnològic
Museum

(Map p256; ☑93 256 34 84; http://ajuntament. barcelona.cat/museuetnologic; Passeig de Santa Madrona 16-22; adult/child €5/free, 3-8pm Sun & 1st Sun of month free; ⊗10am-7pm Tue-Sat, to 8pm Sun; ☐55) This ethnology museum presents an intriguing permanent collection that delves into the rich heritage of Catalonia. Ex-hibits cover origin myths, religious festivals, folklore, and the blending of the sacred and the secular – along those lines, don't miss the Nativity scene with that quirky Catalan character *el caganer,* aka 'the crapper'.

Poble Espanyol
Cultural Centre

(Map p256; ☑93 508 63 00; www.poble-espanyol. com; Avinguda de Francesc Ferrer i Guàrdia 13; adult/child €14/7; ⊗9am-8pm Mon, to midnight Tue-Thu & Sun, to 3am Fri, to 4am Sat; ☐13, 23, 150, ⓂEspanya) This 'Spanish Village' is an intriguing scrapbook of Spanish architec-ture built for the Spanish crafts section of the 1929 World Exhibition. You can meander from Andalucía to Galicia in the space of a couple of hours, visiting surprisingly good copies of Spain's characteristic structures. The 117 buildings include 17 restaurants, cafes and bars, and 20 craft shops and workshops (for glass artists and other artisans), as well as souvenir stores.

★ Top Tip

Be sure to take in the fine view from the terrace just in front of the museum. It draws crowds around sunset.

Fundació Joan Miró

Joan Miró, the city's best-known 20th-century artistic progeny, bequeathed this art foundation to his home town in 1971. Its light-filled buildings are crammed with seminal works.

Great For...

☑ Don't Miss

The central highlights of the collection, Miró's masterworks in Rooms 18 and 19.

Sert's Temple to Miró's Art

Designed by Josep Lluís Sert, this shimmering white temple to one of Spain's artistic luminaries is considered one of the world's most outstanding museum buildings. The architect designed it after spending many of Franco's dictatorship years in the USA as the head of the School of Design at Harvard University. The foundation rests amid the greenery of the mountains and holds the greatest single collection of Miró's work, containing around 220 of his paintings, 180 sculptures, some textiles and more than 8000 drawings spanning his entire life. Only a small portion is ever on display.

Collection

The exhibits give a broad impression of Miró's artistic development. The first

Personnage by Joan Miró (1970)

❶ Need to Know

Map p256; 📞93 443 94 70; www.fmirobcn.org; Parc de Montjuïc; adult/child €12/free; ⏰10am-8pm Tue, Wed, Fri & Sat, to 9pm Thu, to 3pm Sun Apr-Oct, 10am-6pm Tue, Wed & Fri, to 9pm Thu, to 8pm Sat, to 3pm Sun Nov-Mar; 🚌55, 150, 🚇Paral·lel

✕ Take a Break

The museum has a restaurant and terrace bar. Nearby, La Font del Gat (p147) has high-end Catalan cuisine.

★ Top Tip

Pay €5 for the multimedia guide, with commentary and background information.

couple of rooms (11 and 12) hold various works, including a giant tapestry in his trademark primary colours. Along the way, you'll pass *Mercury Fountain,* by Alexander Calder, a rebuilt work that was originally built for the 1937 Paris Fair and represented Spain at the Spanish Republic's Pavilion. Room 13, a basement space called Espai 13, leads you downstairs to a small room for temporary exhibitions.

After Room 13, climb back up the stairs and descend to two other basement rooms, 14 and 15. Together labelled Homenatge a Joan Miró (Homage to Joan Miró), this space is dedicated to photos of the artist, a 15-minute video on his life and a series of works from some of his contemporaries, including Henry Moore, Antoni Tàpies, Eduardo Chillida, Yves Tanguy, Fernand Léger and others.

Returning to the main level, you'll find Room 16, the Sala Joan Prats, with works spanning the early years until 1919. Here, you can see how the young Miró moved away, under surrealist influence, from his relative realism (for instance his 1917 painting *Ermita de Sant Joan d'Horta*, with obvious Fauvist influences) toward his own unique style that uses primary colours and morphed shapes symbolising the moon, the female form and birds.

This theme is continued upstairs in Room 17, the Sala Pilar Juncosa (named after his wife), which covers his surrealist years of 1932 to 1955. Rooms 18 and 19 contain masterworks of the years 1956 to 1983 and Room 20 has a series of paintings done on paper. Room 21 hosts a selection of the private Katsuta collection of Miró works from 1914 to 1974. Room 22 rounds off the permanent exhibition with some major paintings and bronzes from the 1960s and '70s. The museum library contains Miró's personal book collection.

Garden

Outside on the eastern flank of the museum is the Jardí de les Escultures, a small garden with various pieces of modern sculpture. The green areas surrounding the museum, together with the garden, are perfect for a picnic in the shade after a hard day's sightseeing.

What's Nearby?

L'Anella Olímpica & Estadi Olímpic   Area
(Map p256; www.estadiolimpic.cat; Avinguda de l'Estadi; 🚌13, 150) **FREE** L'Anella Olímpica

(Olympic Ring) is the group of installations built for the main events of the 1992 Olympics. They include the Piscines Bernat Picornell, where the swimming and diving events were held, and the Estadi Olímpic, which is open to the public when it's not in use for sporting events or concerts.

Estadi Olímpic
Lluís Companys   Stadium
(Map p256; 🕿93 426 20 89; www.estadiolimpic. cat; Passeig Olímpic 15-17; ⏰8am-8pm May-Sep, 10am-6pm Oct-Apr; 🚌13, 150) **FREE** The Estadi Olímpic was the main stadium of Barcelona's Olympic Games. If you saw the Olympics on TV, the 60,000-capacity stadium may seem surprisingly small. So might the Olympic flame holder into which an archer spectacularly fired a flaming arrow during the opening ceremony. The stadium was opened in 1929 and restored for the 1992 Olympics.

Estadi Olímpic Lluís Companys

Museu Olímpic i de l'Esport Museum

(Map p256; ☎93 292 53 79; www.museuolimpicbcn.cat; Avinguda de l'Estadi 60; adult/child €5.80/free; ⏲10am-8pm Tue-Sat, to 2.30pm Sun Apr-Sep, 10am-6pm Tue-Sat, to 2.30pm Sun Oct-Mar; 🚌55, 150) The Museu Olímpic i de l'Esport is an information-packed interactive sporting museum. After picking up tickets, you wander down a ramp that snakes below ground level and is lined with multimedia displays on the history of sport and the Olympic Games, starting with the ancients. Visitors can also get the chance to run against US sprint champion Carl Lewis in a simulator.

Castell de Montjuïc Fortress

(Map p256; ☎93 256 44 40; http://ajuntament.barcelona.cat/castelldemontjuic; Carretera de Montjuïc 66; adult/child €5/3, after 3pm Sun & all day 1st Sun of month free; ⏲10am-8pm Mar-Oct, to 6pm Nov-Feb; 🚌150, 🚡Telefèric de Montjuïc, Castell de Montjuïc) This forbidding *castell* (castle or fort) dominates the southeastern heights of Montjuïc and enjoys commanding views over the Mediterranean. It dates, in its present form, from the late 17th and 18th centuries. For most of its dark history, it has been used to watch over the city and as a political prison and killing ground.

JOHANNESS/SHUTTERSTOCK ©

Teleférico del Puerto Cable Car

(Map p256; ☎93 441 48 20; www.telefericodebarcelona.com; Avinguda de Miramar; one way/return €11/16.50; ⏲10.30am-8pm Jun–mid-Sep, to 7pm Mar-May & mid-Sep–Oct, 11am-5.30pm Nov-Feb; 🚌150) The quickest way from the beach to the mountain is via the cable car that runs between Torre de Sant Sebastiá in Barceloneta and the Miramar stop on Montjuïc. From Estació Parc Montjuïc, the separate **Telefèric de Montjuïc** (Map p256; ☎93 328 90 03; www.telefericdemontjuic.cat; Avinguda de Miramar 30; adult/child one way €8.40/6.60; ⏲10am-9pm Jun-Sep, to 7pm Mar-May & Oct, to 6pm Nov-Feb; 🚌55, 150) cable car carries you to the Castell de Montjuïc via the mirador (lookout point).

MUHBA Refugi 307 Historic Site

(Map p256; ☎93 256 21 00; http://ajuntament.barcelona.cat/museuhistoria; Carrer Nou de la Rambla 175; adult/child incl tour €3.50/free; ⏲tours in English 10.30am Sun; Ⓜ Paral·lel) Part of the Museu d'Història de Barcelona (MUHBA), this shelter dates back to the days of the Spanish Civil War. Barcelona was the city most heavily bombed from the air during the war and had more than 1300 air-raid shelters. Local citizens started digging this one in March 1937. Compulsory tours are conducted in English at 10.30am, Spanish at 11.30am and Catalan at 12.30pm on Sunday. Reserve ahead as places are limited.

Take a Break

Enjoy a picnic in the shady sculpture garden or head to the ornamental Jardins de Mossèn Cinto de Verdaguer (p127).

Vaulted ceiling over the nave

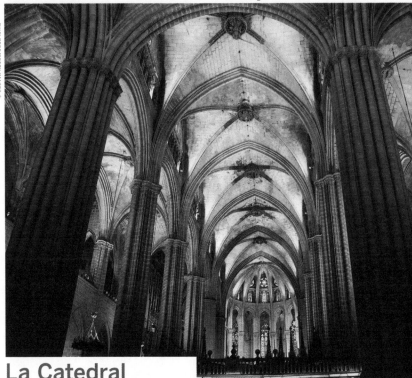

PIXELPROF/GETTY IMAGES ©

La Catedral

The richly decorated Gothic main facade of Barcelona's central place of worship, laced with gargoyles and stone intricacies, sets it quite apart from other churches in Barcelona.

Great For...

☑ Don't Miss

The *claustre* and its 13 geese, plus the views from the roof.

The key treasure of the Barri Gòtic, the cathedral was built between 1298 and 1460, though the facade was added in 1870.

Interior

The interior is a broad, soaring space divided into a central nave and two aisles by lines of elegant, slim pillars. The cathedral was one of the few churches in Barcelona spared by the anarchists in the civil war, so its ornamentation, never overly lavish, is intact.

Coro

In the middle of the central nave is the late-14th-century, exquisitely sculpted timber *coro* (choir stalls). The coats of arms on the stalls belong to members of the Barcelona chapter of the Order of the Golden Fleece. Emperor Carlos V presided over the order's meeting here in 1519.

La Catedral from Plaça de la Seu

GENNADY STETSENKO/SHUTTERSTOCK ©

Plaça d'Antoni Maura
Via Laietana
Plaça de la Seu
La Catedral
C de Jaume I
Jaume I

❶ Need to Know

Map p250; ☎93 342 82 62; www.catedralbcn. org; Plaça de la Seu; donation €7 or choir €3, roof €3; ☉worshipping 8.30am-12.30pm & 5.45-7.30pm Mon-Fri, 8.30am-12.30pm & 5.15-8pm Sat, 8.30am-1.45pm & 5.15-8pm Sun, tourist visits 12.30-7.45pm Mon-Fri, 12.30-5.30pm Sat, 2-5.30pm Sun; Ⓜ Jaume I

✕ Take a Break

A couple of minutes' walk away, Els Quatre Gats (p137) makes for an architecturally splendid pit stop.

★ Top Tip

Pay the 'donation entrance' to avoid the crowds and appreciate the building's splendour in relative peace.

Crypt

A broad staircase before the main altar leads you down to the crypt, which contains the tomb of Santa Eulàlia, one of Barcelona's two patron saints and more affectionately known as Laia. The reliefs on the alabaster sarcophagus recount some of her tortures and, along the top strip, the removal of her body to its present resting place.

Sant Crist de Lepant

In the first chapel on the right from the northwest entrance, the main Crucifixion figure above the altar is Sant Crist de Lepant. It is said Don Juan's flagship bore it into battle at Lepanto and that the figure acquired its odd stance by dodging an incoming cannonball. Left from the main entrance is the baptismal font where, according to one story, six Native Americans

brought to Europe by Columbus after his first voyage of accidental discovery were bathed in holy water.

Roof

For a bird's-eye view (mind the poop) of medieval Barcelona, visit the cathedral's roof and tower by taking the lift (€3) from the Capella de les Animes del Purgatori near the northeastern transept.

Claustre

From the southwest transept, exit by the partly Romanesque door (one of the few remnants of the present church's predecessor) to the leafy *claustre* (cloister), with its fountains and flock of 13 geese. The geese supposedly represent the age of Santa Eulàlia at the time of her martyrdom and have, generation after generation, been squawking here since medieval days. One of the cloister chapels commemorates 930 priests, monks and nuns killed during the civil war.

In the northwest corner of the cloister is the **Capella de Santa Llúcia** (⊘8am-7.15pm Mon-Fri, to 8pm Sat & Sun), one of the few reminders of Romanesque Barcelona (although the interior is largely Gothic). Originally it was the chapel for the adjacent Bishop's Palace.

Casa de l'Ardiaca

Upon exiting the Capella de Santa Llúcia, wander across the lane into the 16th-century **Casa de l'Ardiaca** (Arxiu Històric; ☑93 256 22 55; https://ajuntament.barcelona.cat; Carrer de Santa Llúcia 1; ⊘9am-8.45pm Mon-Fri, 10am-8pm Sat Oct-Jul, 10am-7pm Aug & Sep) **FREE**, which houses the city's archives. Stroll around the supremely serene courtyard, cooled by

trees and a fountain; it was renovated by Lluis Domènech i Montaner in 1902, when the building was owned by the lawyers' college. Domènech i Montaner also designed the postal slot, which is adorned with swallows and a tortoise said to represent the swiftness of truth and the plodding pace of justice. You can get a good glimpse at a stout Roman wall in here. Upstairs, you can look down into the courtyard and across to La Catedral.

Palau Episcopal

Across Carrer del Bisbe is the 17th-century **Palau Episcopal** (Palau del Bisbat, Bishop's Palace; Carrer del Bisbe). Virtually nothing remains of the original 13th-century structure. The Roman city's northwest gate was here and you can see the lower segments of the Roman towers that stood on either side of

Palau del Lloctinent

the gate at the base of the Palau Episcopal and Casa de l'Ardiaca. In fact, the lower part of the entire northwest wall of the Casa de l'Ardiaca is of Roman origin – you can also make out part of the first arch of a Roman aqueduct.

What's Nearby?

Temple d'August
Ruins

(Map p250; ☎93 256 21 22; www.muhba.cat; Carrer del Paradis 10; ◷10am-7pm Tue-Sat, to 8pm Sun, to 2pm Mon; Ⓜ Jaume I) FREE Opposite

> ### ☑ Don't Miss
> Outside La Catedral there's always some kind of entertainment, from *sardana* dancing (Catalonia's folk dance) on weekends to periodic processions and open-air markets; street musicians are never far away.

EUGENE IVANOFF/SHUTTERSTOCK ©

the southeast end of La Catedral, narrow Carrer del Paradis leads towards Plaça de Sant Jaume. Inside No 10, an intriguing building with Gothic and baroque touches, are four columns and the architrave of Barcelona's main Roman temple, dedicated to Caesar Augustus and built to worship his imperial highness in the 1st century AD.

Museu Diocesà/ Gaudí Exhibition Center
Museum

(Map p250; Casa de la Pia Almoina; ☎93 268 75 82; www.gaudiexhibitioncenter.com; Plaça de la Seu 7; adult/concession/child under 8yr €15/12/free; ◷10am-6pm Nov-Mar, to 7pm Apr, May & Oct, to 8pm Jun-Sep; Ⓜ Jaume I) Next to Le Catedral, the Diocesan Museum has a handful of exhibits on Gaudí (including a fascinating documentary on his life and philosophy) on the upper floors. There's also a sparse collection of medieval and Romanesque religious art, usually supplemented by a temporary exhibition or two.

Palau del Lloctinent
Historic Site

(Map p250; Carrer dels Comtes; ◷palace 10am-7pm daily, exhibition 10am-7pm Tue-Sun; Ⓜ Jaume I) FREE This converted 16th-century palace has a peaceful courtyard worth wandering through. Have a look upwards from the main staircase to admire the extraordinary timber *artesonado,* a sculpted ceiling made to seem like the upturned hull of a boat. Temporary exhibitions, usually related in some way to the archives, are often held here.

Roman Walls
Ruins

(Map p250; Ⓜ Jaume I) From Plaça del Rei it's worth a detour to see the two best surviving stretches of Barcelona's Roman walls, which once boasted 78 towers (as much a matter of prestige as of defence). One section is on the southern side of Plaça de Ramon Berenguer el Gran, with the Capella Reial de Santa Àgata atop. The other is a little further south, by the northern end of Carrer del Sots-Tinent Navarro.

LUKASZ SZWAJ/SHUTTERSTOCK ©

Park Güell

Park Güell is where Gaudí turned his hand to landscape gardening. It's a strange, enchanting place, where this iconic Modernista's passion for natural forms really took flight.

Great For...

☑ **Don't Miss**

The undulating tiled bench with views across the city.

A City Park

Park Güell originated in 1900, when Count Eusebi Güell bought the tree-covered hill-side of El Carmel (then outside Barcelona) and hired Gaudí to create a miniature city of houses for the wealthy, surrounded by landscaped grounds. The project was a commercial flop and was abandoned in 1914 – but not before Gaudí had created, in his inimitable manner, steps, a plaza, two gatehouses and 3km of roads and walks.

In 1922 the city bought the estate for use as a public park. The park became a Unesco World Heritage Site in 2004. The idea was based on the English 'garden cities', much admired by Güell, hence the spelling of 'Park'.

Just inside the main entrance on Carrer d'Olot, immediately recognisable by the two Hansel-and-Gretel gatehouses, is the

Dragon Stairway

ARCHER ALL SQUARE/SHUTTERSTOCK ©

ⓘ Need to Know

Map p254; 📞93 409 18 31; www.parkguell. cat; Carrer d'Olot 7; adult/child €8.50/6; ⏱8am-9.30pm May-Aug, to 8.30pm Apr, Sep & Oct, to 6.15pm Nov–mid-Feb, to 7pm mid-Feb–Mar; 🚌24, 92, Ⓜ Lesseps, Vallcarca

✕ Take a Break

It's a spectacular picnic setting, but bring supplies with you as there's nowhere to stock up nearby.

★ Top Tip

Go first thing in the morning or late in the day to beat the worst of the crowds.

park's Centre d'Interpretació, in the Pavelló de Consergeria, which is a typically curvaceous former porter's home that hosts a display on Gaudí's building methods and the history of the park. There are superb views from the top floor.

Much of the park is still wooded, but it's laced with pathways. The best views are from the cross-topped Turó del Calvari in the southwest corner.

Sala Hipóstila

The steps up from the entrance, guarded by a mosaic dragon-lizard (a copy of which you can buy in many central souvenir shops), lead to the Sala Hipóstila (aka the Doric Temple). This forest of 88 stone columns – some leaning like mighty trees bent by the weight of time – was originally intended as a market.

To the left curves a gallery, the twisted stonework columns and roof of which give the effect of a cloister beneath tree roots – a motif repeated in several places in the park. On top of the Sala Hipóstila is a broad open space. Its centrepiece is the Banc de Trencadís, a tiled bench curving sinuously around its perimeter, which was designed by one of Gaudí's closest colleagues, architect Josep Maria Jujol (1879–1949).

With Gaudí, however, there is always more than meets the eye. This giant platform was designed as a kind of catchment area for rainwater washing down the hillside. The water is filtered through a layer of stone and sand and it drains down through the columns to an underground cistern.

Casa-Museu Gaudí

The spired house above and to the right of the entrance is the **Casa-Museu Gaudí** (☑93 219 38 11; www.casamuseugaudi.org; Park Güell, Carretera del Carmel 23a; adult/child €5.50/free; ☺9am-8pm Apr-Sep, 10am-6pm Oct-Mar), where Gaudí lived for almost the last 20 years of his life (1906–26). It contains furniture he designed (including items that once lived in La Pedrera, Casa Batlló and Casa Calvet) along with other memorabilia. The house was built in 1904 by Francesc Berenguer i Mestres as a prototype for the 60 or so houses that were originally planned here.

Admission

The park is extremely popular and an entrance fee is imposed on the central area containing most of its attractions. Access is limited to a certain number of people every half-hour – book ahead online (and you'll also save on the admission fee).

What's Nearby?

Gaudí Experience   Museum

(☑93 285 44 40; www.gaudiexperiencia.com; Carrer de Larrard 41; adult/child €9/7.50; ☺10.30am-7pm Apr-Sep, 11.30am-4pm Oct-Mar; MLesseps) The Gaudí Experience is a fun-filled Disney-style look at the life and work of Barcelona's favourite son, just a stone's throw from Park Güell. There are models of his buildings and whizz-bang interactive exhibits and touchscreens, but the highlight is the stomach-churning 4D presentation in its tiny screening room. Not recommended for the frail or children aged under six years.

Barcelona from Turó de la Rovira

Turó de la Rovira   Viewpoint

(Bunkers del Carmel; ☎93 256 21 22; www.
museuhistoria.bcn.cat; Carrer de Marià Labèrnia;
⊙museum 4.30-8.30pm Wed, Fri & Sat, 10.30am-
2.30pm & 4.30-8.30pm Sun; ☐V17, 119) FREE
For magnificent city views well off the
beaten path, head to the neighbourhood
of El Carmel and ascend the hill known as
Turó de la Rovira to the Bunkers del Carmel
viewpoint. Above the weeds and dusty hillside, you'll find old concrete platforms that
were once part of anti-aircraft battery during the Spanish Civil War (postwar, it was a
shanty town until the early 1990s, and has

> ★ **Top Tip**
>
> One-hour guided tours in multiple
> languages, including English, take place
> year-round and cost €7 (plus park
> admission); prebook online.

MAREK STEPAN/ALAMY STOCK PHOTO ©

lain abandoned since then). There's a small
information centre and museum down
inside the bunkers themselves.

Casa Vicens   Museum

(☎93 547 59 80; www.casavicens.org; Carrer de
les Carolines 20-26; adult/child €16/14, guided
tour per person additional €3; ⊙10am-8pm Apr-
Sep, 10am-3pm Mon, 10am-7pm Tue-Sun Oct-
Mar, last admission 1hr 20min before closing;
Ⓜ Fontana) A Unesco-listed masterpiece,
Casa Vicens was first opened regularly to
the public in 2017. The angular, turreted
1885-completed private house created
for stock and currency broker Manuel
Vicens i Montaner was Gaudí's inaugural
commission, when the architect was just
30 years old. Tucked away west of Gràcia's main drag, the richly detailed facade
is awash with ceramic colour and shape.
You're free to wander through at your own
pace but 30-minute guided tours (available in English) bring the building to life.

As was frequently the case, Gaudí
sought inspiration from the past, in this
case the rich heritage of building in the
Mudéjar-style brick, typical in those
parts of Spain reconquered from the
Moors. Mudéjar architecture was created
by those Arabs and Berbers allowed
to remain in Spain after the Christian
reconquests.

The renovated building is accessible for
visitors with limited mobility (including
wheelchairs). Temporary exhibitions are
mounted alongside permanent displays
covering the building's history. Allow time
for a drink at the cafe in the garden.

> ✕ **Take a Break**
>
> Before or after making the trip up to
> the park, stop off at La Panxa del Bisbe
> (p148) for deliciously creative tapas and
> good wines.

Camp Nou

A pilgrimage site for football fans from around the world, Camp Nou, home to FC Barcelona, is one of the sport's most hallowed grounds. While you should do your utmost to attend a live match, the museum and stadium tour offered by the Camp Nou Experience is also a must for football fans.

Great For...

ⓘ Need to Know

☎ 902 189900; www.fcbarcelona.com; Carrer d'Arístides Maillol; Ⓜ Palau Reial

★ Top Tip

No need to wait in line – buy tour tickets from vending machines at Gate 9.

FC Barcelona

FC Barcelona, or 'Barça', is a name that resounds around the world to such a degree that it has become an ambassador for the region of Catalunya; it is a club deeply associated with Catalans and even Catalan nationalism. The team was long a rallying point when other aspects of Catalan culture were suppressed. The club openly supported Catalonia's drive towards autonomy in 1918, and in 1921 the club's statutes were drafted in Catalan. The pro-Catalan leanings of the club and its siding with the republic during the Spanish Civil War earned reprisals from the government. Club president Josep Sunyol was murdered by Franco's soldiers in 1936 and the club building was bombed in 1938.

In 1968 club president Narcís de Carreras uttered the now famous words, El

Barça: *més que un club* (more than a club), which became the team's motto and emphasised its role as an anti-Franco symbol and catalyst for change in the province and beyond. Today FC Barça is one of the world's most admired teams, with membership at around 140,000 in recent years.

Museum

Camp Nou Stadium Tour & Museum (Gate 9, Avinguda de Joan XXII near Carrer de Martí i Franquès I; adult/child self-guided tour €29.50/23.50, guided tour €50/35; ◷9.30am-7.30pm mid-Apr to mid-Oct, 10am-6.30pm Mon-Sat, to 2.30pm Sun mid-Oct to mid-Apr) begins in FC Barcelona's museum, which provides a high-tech view into the club. Massive touchscreens allow visitors to explore arcane aspects of the legendary team. You can also watch videos of particularly artful goals. Displays delve into

FC Barcelona crest at Camp Nou

the club's history, its social commitment and connection to Catalan identity, and in-depth stats of on-field action. Sound installations include the club's anthem (with translations in many languages) and the match-day roar of the amped-up crowds.

The museum's highlights are the photo section, the goal videos and the views out over the stadium. You can admire the golden boots (in at least one case, literally) of outstanding goal scorers of the past and learn about the greats who have played for the club over the years, including Cruyff, Maradona, Ronaldinho, Kubala and many others. A special area is devoted to Lionel Messi, generally considered to be the world's greatest current footballer.

✕ Take a Break

There are some open-air eating spots inside the gates, but outside the stadium.

SCOTT113/SHUTTERSTOCK ©

Stadium

Gazing out across Camp Nou is an experience in itself. The stadium, built in 1957 and enlarged for the 1982 World Cup, is one of the world's biggest, holding almost 100,000 people. After renovations that will last until 2023 (the stadium will remain open throughout), Camp Nou will have a capacity of 106,000.

The stadium tour takes in the visiting team's dressing room, then heads out through the tunnel and onto the edge of the pitch. You'll also get to visit the press room and the commentary boxes. A Player's Experience ticket (adult/child €139/90) allows you to visit the FC Barcelona dressing room and includes two free photos, a virtual experience and a leaving gift. Set aside at least 1½ hours.

Getting to a Game

Tickets to FC Barcelona matches are available at Camp Nou, online (through FC Barcelona's official website) and through various city locations, including tourist offices – the **main office** (☑93 285 38 34; www.barcelonaturisme.com; Plaça de Catalunya 17-S, underground; ⊘8.30am-9pm; ⋈Catalunya) is a centrally located option – and FC Botiga stores. Tickets can cost anything from €29 to upwards of €250, depending on the seat and match. On match days the ticket windows are open at Gate 9 (11am until kick-off match days) and Gate 14 (from 9am to 1.30pm). Tickets for matches with Real Madrid are extremely difficult to come by.

If you attend a game, go early so you'll have ample time to find your seat (this stadium is massive) and soak up the atmosphere.

You will almost definitely find scalpers lurking near the ticket windows. They are often club members and can sometimes get you in at a significant reduction. Don't pay until you are safely seated.

☑ Don't Miss

A live match, or if not, the museum's footage of the team's best goals.

BRIAN KINNEY/ALAMY STOCK PHOTO ©

La Pedrera

This undulating beast is a madcap Gaudí masterpiece, built from 1905 to 1910 as a combined apartment and office block. Formally called Casa Milà after the businessman who commissioned it, the building is better known as La Pedrera (the Quarry) because of its uneven grey stone facade, which ripples around the corner of Carrer de Provença.

Great For...

❶ Don't Miss
The marvellous roof.

History

Pere Milà had married the older – and far richer – Roser Guardiola, the widow of Josep Guardiola, and he clearly knew how to spend his new wife's money. When commissioned to design this apartment building, Gaudí wanted to top anything else done in L'Eixample. La Pedrera was conceived as an apartment block, and Gaudí's approach to space and light and his blurring of the dividing line between decoration and functionality are astounding. Milà was one of the city's first car owners and Gaudí built a parking space into the building, itself a first.

Facade

The natural world was one of the most enduring influences on Gaudí's work, and La Pedrera's undulating grey stone facade

Roof terrace

CATALUNYA LA PEDRERA FOUNDATION ©

❶ Need to Know

Map p254; Casa Milà; 📞93 214 25 76; www. lapedrera.com; Passeig de Gràcia 92; adult/ child €25/14; ⏰9am-8.30pm & 9-11pm Mar-Oct, 9am-6.30pm & 7-9pm Nov-Feb; Ⓜ Diagonal

✕ Take a Break

La Bodegueta Provença (Map p254; 📞93 215 17 25; www.provenca.labodegueta. cat; Carrer de Provença 233; tapas €6-15, mains €10-16; ⏰7am-1.45am Mon-Fri, 8am-1.45am Sat, 1pm-12.45am Sun; 📶; 🚆FGC Provença) serves first-rate tapas and wines by the glass.

★ Top Tip

For a few extra euros, a 'Premium' ticket means you don't have to queue.

evokes a cliff-face sculpted by waves and wind. The wave effect is emphasised by elaborate wrought-iron balconies that bring to mind seaweed washed up on the shore. The lasting impression is of a building on the verge of motion.

Roof Terrace

Gaudí's blend of mischievous form with ingenious functionality is evident on the roof, with its clusters of chimneys, stairwells and ventilation towers that rise and fall atop the structure's wave-like contours like giant medieval knights. Some are unadorned, others are deco-rated with *trencadís* (ceramic fragments) and even broken *cava* bottles. The deep patios, which Gaudí treated like interior facades, flood the apartments with natural light.

Gaudí wanted to put a tall statue of the Virgin Mary up here – but the Milà family said no, fearing it might make the building a target for anarchists, Gaudí resigned from the project in disgust.

Espai Gaudí

With 270 gracious parabolic arches, the Espai Gaudí feels like the fossilised ribcage of some giant prehistoric beast. At one point, 12 arches come together to form a palm tree. Watch out also for the strange optical effect of the mirror and hanging sculpture on the eastern side.

Apartment

Below the attic, the apartment (El Pis de la Pedrera) spreads out. Bathed in evenly distributed light, twisting and turning with the building's rippling distribution, the labyrinthine apartment is Gaudí's vision of domestic bliss. In the ultimate nod to flexible living, the apartment has no load-bearing walls: the interior walls could thus be moved to suit the inhabitants' needs.

What's Nearby?

Casa de les Punxes — Architecture

(Casa Terrades; Map p254; ☎93 018 52 42; www.casadelespunxes.com; Avinguda Diagonal 420; adult/child audioguide tour €12.50/10, guided tour €20/16; ⏰9am-7pm; MDiagonal) Puig i Cadafalch's Casa Terrades, completed in 1905, is better known as the Casa de les Punxes (House of Spikes) because of its pointed turrets. Resembling a medieval castle, the former apartment block is the only fully detached building in L'Eixample,

and was declared a national monument in 1976. Since 2017 it has been open to the public. Visits take in its stained-glass bay windows, handsome iron staircase and rooftop. Guided tours in English lasting one hour depart at 4pm.

Museu Egipci — Museum

(Map p254; ☎93 488 01 88; www.museuegipci.com; Carrer de València 284; adult/child €12/5; ⏰10am-8pm Mon-Sat, to 2pm Sun mid-Jun–mid-Sep & Dec, shorter hours rest of year; MPasseig de Gràcia) Hotel magnate Jordi Clos has spent much of his life collecting ancient Egyptian artefacts, brought together in this private museum. It's divided into different thematic areas (the pharaoh, religion, funerary practices, mummification, crafts etc) and houses an interesting variety of exhibits.

Casa de les Punxes

Basílica de la Puríssima Concepció i Assumpció Nostra Senyora
Church

(Map p254; ☎93 457 65 52; www.parroquia concepciobcn.org; Carrer d'Aragó 299; ◷7.30am-1pm & 5-9pm Mon-Sat, 7.30am-2pm & 5-9pm Sun, shorter hours Aug; Ⓜ Girona) One hardly expects to run into a medieval church on the grid-pattern streets of the late-19th-century city extension, yet that is just what this is. Transferred stone by stone from the old centre in 1871–88, this 14th-century church has a pretty 16th-century cloister with a peaceful garden.

Fundació Suñol
Gallery

(Map p254; ☎93 496 10 32; www.fundaciosunol. org; Passeig de Gràcia 98; adult/child €4/2; ◷11am-2pm & 4-8pm Mon-Fri, 4-8pm Sat; Ⓜ Diagonal) Rotating exhibitions of portions of this private collection of mostly 20th-century art (some 1200 works in total) offer anything from Man Ray's photography to sculptures by Alberto Giacometti. Over two floors, you are most likely to run into works by Spanish artists – anyone from Picasso to Jaume Plensa – along with a sprinkling of international artists.

☑ **Don't Miss**

La Pedrera is also a music venue, including for jazz concerts held on Friday and Saturday evenings on the roof terrace.

DIEGO FIORE/SHUTTERSTOCK ©

Museu Picasso

*Picasso's itchy feet and his extra-
ordinary artistic output mean that
his works fill several museums in
Europe. Though his best-known works
aren't here, the setting alone, in five
contiguous medieval stone mansions,
makes the Museu Picasso unique.
The pretty courtyards, galleries and
staircases preserved in these buildings
are as delightful as the collection inside.*

Great For...

ℹ Need to Know

Map p250; ☎93 256 30 00; www.museupicas-
so.bcn.cat; Carrer de Montcada 15-23; adult/
concession/under 16yr permanent collection
& temporary exhibit €14/7.50/free, 6-9.30pm
Thu & 1st Sun of month free; ⊘9am-7pm Tue,
Wed & Fri-Sun, to 9.30pm Thu; Ⓜ Jaume I

★ **Top Tip**

Queues here can be very long; the people strolling to the front booked online. Be them.

The permanent collection is housed in Palau Aguilar, Palau del Baró de Castellet and Palau Meca, all dating to the 14th century. The 18th-century Casa Mauri, built over medieval remains (even some Roman leftovers have been identified), and the adjacent 14th-century Palau Finestres accommodate temporary exhibitions. The first three of these buildings are particularly splendid.

History of the Museum

Allegedly it was Picasso himself who proposed the museum's creation to his friend and personal secretary Jaume Sabartés, a Barcelona native, in 1960. Three years later, the 'Sabartés Collection' opened, since a museum bearing Picasso's name would have been met with censorship –

Picasso's opposition to the Franco regime was well known. The Museu Picasso we see today opened in 1983. It originally held only Sabartés' personal collection of Picasso's art and a handful of works hanging at the Barcelona Museum of Art, but the collection gradually expanded with donations from Salvador Dalí and Sebastià Junyer Vidal, among others, though most artworks were bequeathed by Picasso himself. His widow, Jacqueline Roque, also donated 41 ceramic pieces and the *Woman With Bonnet* painting after Picasso's death.

Sabartés' contribution and years of service are honoured with an entire room devoted to him, including Picasso's famous Blue Period portrait of Sabartés wearing a ruff.

Museum interior

Collection

This collection concentrates on the artist's formative years, yet there is enough material from subsequent periods to give you a thorough impression of the man's versatility and genius. Above all, you come away feeling that Picasso was the true original, always one step ahead of himself (and everyone else, of course) in his search for new forms of expression. The collection includes more than 3500 artworks, largely pre-1904, which is apt considering the artist spent his formative creative years in Barcelona.

It is important, however, not to expect a parade of his well-known works or even

works representative of his best-known periods. The holdings at the museum reflect Picasso's years in Barcelona and elsewhere in Spain, and what makes this collection truly impressive – and unique among the many Picasso museums around the world – is the way in which it displays his extraordinary talent at such a young age. Faced with the technical virtuosity of a painting such as *Ciència i Caritat* (Science and Charity), for example, it is almost inconceivable that such a work could have been created by the hands of a 15-year-old. Some of his self-portraits and the portraits of his parents, which date from 1896, are also evidence of his precocious talent.

PIG3/SHUTTERSTOCK ©

Las Meninas through the Prism of Picasso

From 1954 to 1962 Picasso was obsessed with the idea of researching and 'rediscovering' the greats, in particular Velázquez. In 1957 he created a series of renditions of the Velázquez masterpiece *Las meninas* (The Ladies-in-Waiting), now displayed in rooms 12 to 14. It is as though Picasso has looked at the original Velázquez painting through a prism reflecting all the styles he had worked through until then, creating his own masterpiece in the process. This is a wonderful opportunity to see *Las meninas* in its entirety in this beautiful space.

Ceramics

What is also special about the Museu Picasso is its showcasing of his work in lesser-known media. The last rooms contain engravings and some 40 ceramic pieces completed throughout the latter years of his unceasingly creative life. You'll see plates and bowls decorated with simple, single-line drawings of fish, owls and other animal shapes, typical of Picasso's daubing on clay.

What's Nearby?

Parc de la Ciutadella Park

(Map p250; Passeig de Picasso; ☺10am-10.30pm; ♿; Ⓜ Arc de Triomf) Come for a stroll, a picnic, a visit to the zoo or to inspect Catalonia's regional parliament, but don't miss a visit to this, the most central green lung in the city. Parc de la Ciutadella is perfect for winding down.

Museu de Cultures del Món Museum

(Map p250; ☏93 256 23 00; http://museu culturesmon.bcn.cat; Carrer de Montcada 12; adult/concession/under 16yr €5/3.50/free, temporary exhibitions vary, 3-8pm Sun & 1st Sun of month free; ☺10am-7pm Tue-Sat, to 8pm Sun; Ⓜ Jaume I) The Palau Nadal and the Palau Marquès de Llió, which once housed the Museu Barbier-Mueller and the Museu Tèxtil respectively, reopened in 2015 as the site of the new Museum of World Cultures. Exhibits from private and public collections, including many from the Museu Etnològic on Montjuïc, take the visitor on a trip through the ancient cultures of Africa, Asia, the Americas and Oceania. There's a combined ticket with the Museu Egipci (p78) and Museu Etnològic (p59) for €12.

✕ Take A Break

Euskal Etxea (p140) is a formidably good spot for authentic Basque *pintxos* (tapas).

Castell dels Tres Dragons Architecture

(Castle of the Three Dragons; Parc de la Ciutadella; Ⓜ Arc de Triomf) Along the Passeig de Picasso side of Parc de la Ciutadella are several buildings constructed for, or just before, the Universal Exhibition of 1888. The Castell dels Tres Dragons is an engaging, medieval-looking caprice. It long housed the Museu de Zoologia, which is now in the Fòrum area.

El Born Centre de Cultura i Memòria Historic Building

(Map p250; ☏93 256 68 51; http://elborncultura imemoria.barcelona.cat; Plaça Comercial 12; centre free, exhibition spaces adult/concession/ child under 16yr €6/4.20/free; ☺10am-8pm Tue-Sun; Ⓜ Jaume I) Launched in 2013 as part of the events held for the tercentenary of the

Parc de la Ciutadella fountain

Catalan defeat in the War of the Spanish Succession, this cultural space is housed in the former Mercat del Born, a handsome 19th-century structure of slatted iron and brick. Excavation in 2001 unearthed remains of whole streets flattened to make way for the much-hated *ciutadella* (citadel) – these are now displayed on the exposed subterranean level.

Carrer de Montcada Street

(Map p250; M Jaume I) An early example of town planning, this medieval high street was driven towards the sea from the road that in the 12th century led northeast from the city walls. It was the city's most coveted address for the merchant classes. The great mansions that remain today mostly date from the 14th and 15th centuries.

CEZARY WOJTKOWSKI/SHUTTERSTOCK ©

Walking Tour: Hidden Treasures in the Barri Gòtic

This scenic walk will take you back in time, from the early days of Roman-era Barcino through to the medieval era.

Start: La Catedral
Distance: 1.5km
Duration: 1½ hours

Classic Photograph: The Gothic main facade of La Catedral

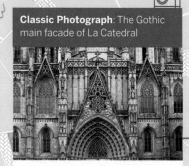

1 Before entering the cathedral, look at the three Picasso friezes on the building facing the square. Next, wander through the magnificent **La Catedral** (p65).

2 Pass through the city gates; turn right into **Plaça de Sant Felip Neri**. The shrapnel-scarred church was damaged by pro-Franco bombers in 1938.

3 Track west to the looming 14th-century **Basílica de Santa Maria del Pi** (p46), famed for its magnificent rose window.

4 Follow the curving road to pretty **Plaça Reial** (p47). Flanking the fountain are Gaudí-designed lamp posts.

C d'en Roca

C del Petritxol

La Rambla de Sant Josep

Plaça del Pi

Plaça de St Josep Oriol

3 Plaça de Sant Josep Oriol

C del Cardenal Casañas

La Rambla

C de la Boqueria

C d'en Quintana

Plaça de la Boqueria

Ⓜ Liceu

C de n'Arolés

C de Sant Pau

La Rambla dels Caputxins

C de la Unió

Ⓝ 0 _____ 180 m
0 _____ 0.1 miles

7 The final stop is picturesque **Plaça del Rei**. The former palace today houses a superb history museum, with significant Roman ruins.

6 Cross Plaça de Sant Jaume and turn left after Carrer del Bisbe. You'll pass the entrance to a ruined **Temple d'August** (p67), a ruined Roman temple with four columns hidden in a small courtyard.

5 Head into El Call, the medieval Jewish quarter. Here you'll find the **Sinagoga Major** (Map p250), one of Europe's oldest synagogues.

✕ Take a Break

In the heart of El Call, **Alcoba Azul** (p134) is atmospheric.

Rambla de Mar promenade

Barcelona's Waterfront

Since the late 20th century, Barcelona's formerly industrial waterfront has experienced a dramatic transformation, with sparkling beaches and seaside bars and restaurants, elegant sculptures, a 4.5km-long boardwalk, ultramodern high-rises and yacht-filled marinas. The gateway to the Mediterranean is the gridlike neighbourhood of Barceloneta, an old-fashioned fishing quarter full of traditional seafood restaurants.

Great For...

❶ Need to Know

Metro Línia 4 serves all the beaches; get Línia 3 to Drassanes for the Museu Marítim.

★ **Top Tip**

The main swimming season is from May to mid-September, when water temperatures can reach 24°C.

Museu Marítim
Museum

(🖉 93 342 99 20; www.mmb.cat; Avinguda de les Drassanes; adult/child €10/5, free from 3pm Sun; ⊗10am-8pm; Ⓜ Drassanes) The city's maritime museum occupies Gothic shipyards – a remarkable relic from Barcelona's days as the seat of a seafaring empire. Highlights include a full-scale 1970s replica of Don Juan of Austria's 16th-century flagship, fishing vessels, antique navigation charts and dioramas of the Barcelona waterfront.

In the courtyard is a life-sized replica of the *Ictíneo I*, one of the world's first submarines. It was invented and built in 1858 by Catalan polymath Narcis Monturiol. The cafe here has outdoor seating and a decent *menú del día* (daily set menu) at lunchtime. The entrance fee also includes a visit to the three-mast schooner **Pailebot Santa Eulàlia** (adult/child €3/1, free with Museu Marítim ticket; ⊗10am-8.30pm Tue-Sun Apr-Oct, to 5.30pm Tue-Sun Nov-Mar; Ⓜ Drassanes) on Moll de la Fusta.

Rambla de Mar
Waterfront

(off Passeig de Colom; Ⓜ Drassanes) The city's authorities extended the world-famous La Rambla thoroughfare out into the sea in the early 2000s, connecting the city with the reclaimed port area of Port Vell. Seeming to float above the water, it offers elevated marina views.

L'Aquàrium
Aquarium

(🖉 93 221 74 74; www.aquariumbcn.com; Moll d'Espanya; adult/child €20/15, dive from €150; ⊗10am-9.30pm Jul & Aug, shorter hours Sep-Jun; Ⓜ Drassanes) It's hard not to shudder at the sight of a shark gliding above you, displaying its toothy, wide-mouthed grin.

El Peix sculpture by Frank Gehry, Passeig Marítim de la Barceloneta

But this, the 80m shark tunnel, is the highlight of one of Europe's largest aquariums. It has the world's best Mediterranean collection and plenty of colourful fish from as far off as the Red Sea, the Caribbean and the Great Barrier Reef. All up, some 11,000 creatures of 450 species reside here.

Back in the shark tunnel, which you reach after passing a series of themed fish tanks with everything from bream to sea horses, various species of shark (white tip, sand tiger, black tip and sandbar) flit around you, along with a host of other critters, from flapping rays to creepy Mediterranean moray. An interactive

---

☑ Don't Miss

The replica of Don Juan of Austria's flagship in the Museu Marítim.

SPATULETAIL/SHUTTERSTOCK ©

zone, Planeta Aqua, is host to a family of Humboldt penguins from Chile and a tank of rays and guitarfish that you watch close up. Explora is a dedicated children's area with activities spread over three themed environments.

Underwater adventurers can cage dive in the main tank with the sharks, or scuba dive with a valid dive certificate.

Museu d'Història de Catalunya   Museum

(Museum of the History of Catalonia; ☏93 225 47 00; www.mhcat.cat; Plaça de Pau Vila 3; adult/child €4.50/3.50, last Tue of the month Oct-Jun free; ⏱10am-7pm Tue & Thu-Sat, to 8pm Wed, to 2.30pm Sun; Ⓜ Barceloneta) Inside the Palau de Mar, this worthwhile museum takes you from the Stone Age through to the early 1980s. It is a busy hotchpotch of dioramas, artefacts, videos, models, documents and interactive bits: all up, an entertaining exploration of 2000 years of Catalan history. Signage is in Catalan and Spanish.

Passeig Marítim de la Barceloneta   Waterfront

(Ⓜ Barceloneta, Ciutadella Vila Olímpica) On Barceloneta's seaward side are the first of Barcelona's beaches, which are hugely popular on summer weekends. The broad Passeig Marítim de la Barceloneta, a 1.25km promenade from Barceloneta to Port Olímpic, is a favourite with strollers and runners, with cyclists zipping by on a separate path nearby.

Platja de la Barceloneta   Beach

(www.barcelona.cat; Ⓜ Barceloneta) Just east of its namesake neighbourhood, Barceloneta's golden-sand beach is beloved by sunseekers, and has ample eating and drinking options just inland when you need a bit of refreshment.

✕ Take a Break

Barceloneta is chock-full of appealing seafood restaurants.

Main hall

Palau Güell

This extraordinary neo-Gothic mansion, one of few major buildings of that era raised in the old city, is a magnificent example of the early days of Gaudí's fevered architectural imagination.

Great For...

☑ Don't Miss

The music room, the basement stables and the tiled chimney pots.

Gaudí & Güell

Gaudí built this palace off La Rambla (p42) in the late 1880s for his wealthy patron, the industrialist Eusebi Güell. Although sombre compared with some of his later whimsy, the Palau is still a characteristic riot of materials and styles (Gothic, Islamic, art nouveau). After the civil war the police tortured political prisoners in the basement, but the building was then abandoned, leading to its long-term disrepair. It was finally reopened in 2012 after several years of refurbishment.

Building

The ground floor was once the coach house, and the basement, with squat mushroom-shaped brick pillars, is where the horses were stabled. Back upstairs

JULIANS2000/SHUTTERSTOCK ©

❶ Need to Know

Map p250; ☎93 472 57 75; www.palauguell.
cat; Carrer Nou de la Rambla 3-5; adult/
concession/child under 10yr incl audio guide
€12/9/free, 1st Sun of month free; ☉10am-
8pm Tue-Sun Apr-Oct, to 5.30pm Nov-Mar;
Ⓜ Drassanes

✖ Take a Break

Nearby **Cañete** (Map p250; ☎93 270 34
58; www.barcanete.com; Carrer de la Unió
17; tapas from €4.50, sharing plates €9-25;
☉1pm-midnight Mon-Sat; ☎; ⓂLiceu) has
upmarket tapas.

★ Top Tip

Book online to avoid the queue and
ensure you visit at your preferred time.

is the elaborate wrought iron of the main
doors from the splendid vestibule and
the grand staircase lined with sandstone
columns. Up another floor are the main hall
and its annexes; check out the rosewood
coffered ceilings and the gallery behind
trelliswork, from where the family could spy
on their guests as they arrived.

Central to the structure is the magnificent music room with a rebuilt organ
played during opening hours; the choir
would sing from the mezzanine up on the
other side. Alongside the alcove containing the organ is another that opened
out to become the family chapel, with
booths to seat nobility and, above them,
the servants. The main hall is a parabolic
pyramid – each wall an arch stretching
up three floors and coming together to

form a dome, giving a magnificent sense
of space in what is a surprisingly narrow
building, constructed on a site of just 500
sq metres.

Above the main floor are the family
rooms, which are sometimes labyrinthine
and dotted with piercings of light or
grand, stained-glass windows. The bright,
diaphanous attic used to house the servants' quarters, but now houses a detailed
exhibition on the history and renovation of
the building. The roof is a tumult of tiled
mosaics and fanciful chimney pots. The
audio guide (included) is worth getting
not only for the detailed description of
the architecture, but also for the pieces of
music and its photographic illustrations
(on screen) of the Güell family's life.

MACBA

Designed by Richard Meier and opened in 1995, MACBA (Museu d'Art Contemporani de Barcelona) has become the city's foremost contemporary art centre, with captivating exhibitions for the serious art lover.

Great For...

☑ Don't Miss

The permanent collection dedicated to 20th-century Spanish and Catalan art.

The ground and 1st floors of this great white bastion of contemporary art are generally given over to exhibitions from the gallery's own collections. There are some 3000 pieces centred on three periods: post-WWII; around 1968; and the years since the fall of the Berlin Wall in 1989, right up until the present day.

Permanent Collection

The permanent collection is on the ground floor and dedicates itself to Spanish and Catalan art from the second half of the 20th century, with works by Antoni Tàpies, Joan Brossa and Miquel Barceló, among others, though international artists, such as Paul Klee, Bruce Nauman and John Cage, are also represented.

The rest of the gallery, across two floors, is dedicated to temporary visiting exhibitions

❶ Need to Know

Map p249; Museu d'Art Contemporani de Barcelona; ☑93 412 08 10; www.macba. cat; Plaça dels Àngels 1; adult/concession/ child under 14yr €10/8/free, 4-8pm Sat free; ◷11am-7.30pm Mon & Wed-Fri, 10am-8pm Sat, 10am-3pm Sun & holidays; Ⓜ Universitat

✗ Take a Break

Modernista Casa Almirall (p177) is a stunning nearby bar, perfect for a cold beer.

Top Tip

Unlike most Barcelona museums, MACBA is open on Mondays.

that are almost always challenging and intriguing. MACBA's 'philosophy' is to do away with the old model of a museum where an artwork is a spectacle and to create a space where art can be viewed critically, so the exhibitions are usually tied in with talks and events. If you're after some serious brain candy, MACBA is your place.

Fringe Attractions

The library and auditorium stage regular concerts, talks and events, all of which are either reasonably priced or free. The extensive art bookshop is fantastic for stocking up on art and art theory books, as well as quirky gifts and small design objects.

Outside, the spectacle is as intriguing as it is inside. While skateboarders dominate the space south of the museum (considered one of Europe's great skateboard

locations), you may well find kids enjoying a game of cricket in Plaça de Joan Coromines.

What's Nearby?

Centre de Cultura Contemporània de Barcelona   Gallery

(CCCB; Map p249; ☑93 306 41 00; www.cccb.org; Carrer de Montalegre 5; adult/concession/child under 12yr for 1 exhibition €6/4/free, 2 exhibitions €8/6/free, Sun 3-8pm free; ◷11am-8pm Tue-Sun; Ⓜ Universitat) A complex of auditoriums, exhibition spaces and conference halls opened here in 1994 in what had been an 18th-century hospice, the Casa de la Caritat. The courtyard, with a vast glass wall on one side, is spectacular. With 4500 sq metres of exhibition space in four separate areas, the centre hosts a constantly changing program of exhibitions, film cycles and other events.

Basílica del Sagrat Cor de Jesús (p99)

Tibidabo Mountain

Framing the north end of the city, the forest-covered mountain of Tibidabo, which tops out at 512m, is the highest peak in Serra de Collserola. Aside from the superb views from the top, highlights include an 8000-hectare park, an old-fashioned amusement park, a telecommunications tower with viewing platform, and a looming basilica, visible from many parts of the city.

Great For...

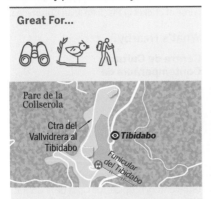

Parc de la Collserola

Ctra del Vallvidrera al Tibidabo

⊙ **Tibidabo**

Funicular del Tibidabo

ℹ Need to Know

See Getting There (p100) for transport details

★ **Top Tip**

Pack a picnic and make a day of it, staying for sunset cocktails at a bar with a view.

Tibidabo gets its name from the devil, who, trying to tempt Christ, took him to a high place and said in Latin: '*Haec omnia tibi dabo si cadens adoraberis me*' (All this I will give you if you fall down and worship me).

Parc de Collserola

Barcelonins needing an escape from the city without heading far seek out this extensive, 80-sq-km park in the hills. It's a great place to hike and bike and go for picnics. Pick up a map from one of the information centres (such as the Carretera de l'Església 92 location, close to the Baixador de Vallvidrera FGC train station).

The park has a smattering of country chapels (some Romanesque), the ragged ruins of the 14th-century Castellciuro castle in the west, various lookout points and, to the north, the 15th-century Can Coll, a grand farmhouse. It's used as an environmental education centre where you can see how richer farmers lived from the 17th to 19th centuries. You can also learn about one of Barcelona's great 19th-century writers at the **Vil·la Joana** (☏93 256 21 00; www.museuhistoria.bcn.cat; Carretera de l'Església 104; ☉10am-2pm Thu, to 7pm Sat, Sun & holidays; ⒭FGC Baixador de Vallvidrera) **FREE**. This historic villa is where Catalonia's revered writer Jacint Verdaguer lived in the final days of his life before his death on 10 July 1902. Displays pay homage to Verdaguer's legacy and his impact on literature in Catalonia and beyond.

Torre de Collserola

Sir Norman Foster designed the 288m-high **Torre de Collserola** (☏93 406 93 54; www.torredecollserola.com; Carretera de Vallvidrera al

Parc d'Atraccions

Tibidabo; adult/child €5.60/3.30; ⏲hours vary, closed Jan & Feb; 🚌111, 🚟Funicular de Vallvidrera) telecommunications tower, which was completed in 1992. An external glass lift whisks you to the visitors' observation area, 115m up, from where there are some magnificent views – extending up to 70km on a clear day. All of Barcelona's TVs and radios receive transmissions from here, and repeater stations across Catalonia are also controlled from this tower.

Parc d'Atraccions

The reason most *barcelonins* come up to Tibidabo is for some thrills at **Parc d'Atraccions** (📞93 211 79 42; www.tibidabo.cat; Plaça de Tibidabo 3-4; adult/child €28.50/10.30; ⏲closed

> **☑ Don't Miss**
>
> A break-from-the-city stroll in the Parc de Collserola.

SHILER/SHUTTERSTOCK ©

Jan & Feb; 🚌T2A, 🚟Funicular del Tibidabo), close to the top funicular station. Here you'll find whirling high-speed rides and a high-tech 4D cinema, as well as old-fashioned amusements including an old steam train and the Museu d'Autòmats, with automated puppets dating as far back as 1880. Check the website for seasonal opening times.

Basílica del Sagrat Cor de Jesús

Above Tibidabo's top funicular station, this landmark **basilica** (Basilica of the Sacred Heart of Jesus; 📞93 417 56 86; www.templotibidabo.es; Plaça de Tibidabo; lift €3.50; ⏲11am-6pm; 🚌T2A, 🚟Funicular del Tibidabo) is meant to be Barcelona's answer to Paris' Sacré-Cœur. Built from 1902 to 1961 with some Modernista influence, it's certainly as visible as its Parisian counterpart and even more vilified by aesthetes. It's actually two churches, one on top of the other. The top one is surmounted by a giant statue of Christ and has a lift to take you to the roof for the panoramic (and often wind-chilled) views.

Stargazing

Inaugurated in 1904, the Modernista **Observatori Fabra** (📞93 417 57 36; www.fabra.cat; Carretera del Observatori; tours €3, night observation €15-25; ⏲tours 11am-2pm Sun, night observation by reservation Fri & Sat Oct-Jun; 🚇FGC Avinguda Tibidabo), 415m above sea level, is still a functioning scientific foundation. On certain evenings visitors can observe the stars through its grand old telescope (check the website for the latest schedule). Visits, generally in Catalan or Spanish, must be prebooked. From mid-June to mid-September, **Sopars amb Estrelles** (Dinner under the Stars; 📞93 327 01 21; www.sternalia.com; meal & observatory packages €73-126; ⏲8.30pm-midnight Tue-Sun mid-Jun–mid-Oct; 🔦👪) offers an evening of high-end dining and astronomy.

> **✕ Take a Break**
>
> Grab a drink with a view at Mirablau (p191) by the funicular.

Gran Hotel La Florida

Hemingway is among the guests to have stayed at this magnificent 1920s-built **hotel** (☏93 259 30 00; www.hotellaflorida. com; Carretera de Vallvidrera al Tibidabo 83-93; d/f/ste from €235/345/495; [P][❄][🛜][💺]; [🖥]111), which only received its first guests in the 1950s and had a designer makeover this century. Amenities include indoor and outdoor swimming pools, a spa and two restaurants. Its location atop Tibidabo provides jaw-dropping views. Public areas are lined with original works by local artists.

Getting There

To reach the basilica and amusement park, take an FGC train to Avinguda Tibidabo. Outside Avinguda Tibidabo station, hop on the *tramvia blau*, which runs past fancy Modernista mansions to Plaça del Doctor Andreu (one way €5.50, 15 minutes, every 15 or 30 minutes 10am to 7.30pm daily late June to early September, 10am to 6.15pm Saturday, Sunday and holidays early September to late June; hours can vary). Bus 196 runs the same route. From Plaça del Doctor Andreu the Tibidabo funicular railway climbs to the top of the hill (return €7.70, five minutes). Departures start around 10am and run every 15 minutes until shortly after the Parc d'Atraccions' closing time. Start queuing well before the funicular stops running, as places are limited.

An alternative is bus T2A, the 'Tibibús', from Plaça de Catalunya to Plaça de Tibidabo (€3, 30 minutes, every 30 to 50 minutes on Saturday, Sunday and holidays March to December, and hourly from 10.15am Monday to Friday late June to early September).

For Parc de Collserola, take an FGC train to Baixador de Vallvidrera. Alternatively, you can stop one station earlier at Peu del Funicular and ride to the top via the Funicular Vallvidrera.

Bus 111 runs between Tibidabo and Vallvidrera (passing in front of the Torre de Collserola).

What's Nearby?

Bellesguard — Architecture

(☏93 250 40 93; www.bellesguardgaudi.com; Carrer de Bellesguard 20; adult/child €9/7.20; ⏱10am-3pm Tue-Sun; [🚊]FGC Avinguda Tibidabo) This Gaudí masterpiece was rescued from obscurity and opened to the public in 2013. Built between 1900 and 1909, this private residence (still owned by the original Guilera family) has a castle-like appearance with crenellated walls of stone and brick, narrow stained-glass windows, elaborate ironwork and a soaring turret mounted by a Gaudían cross. It's a fascinating work that combines both Gothic and Modernista elements.

Guided tours in English (€16 per person) take place on weekends at 11am. At other times, you can visit the interior of the build-

Bellesguard interior

ing and the grounds with an audio guide that gives historical background.

The downside: it's a long walk to a train station, though many buses pass near (including bus 22 from Plaça de Catalunya). Be sure to call before making the trek out – Bellesguard sometimes closes for private events.

Parc de la Creueta del Coll   Park

(Passeig de la Mare de Déu del Coll 77; ⏰10am-9pm Apr-Oct, to 7pm Nov-Mar; 🚌92, 129, N5, Ⓜ Penitents) A favourite with families, this refreshing public park has a meandering lake pool for splashing in, along with swings, showers and a snack bar. The park is set inside a deep crater left by long years of stone quarrying, and has an enormous concrete sculpture, *Elogio del agua* (In Praise of Water) by Eduardo Chillida, suspended

on one side. The pool closes outside of summer.

Enter from Carrer Mare de Déu del Coll, a 1km walk east from the Penitents metro station.

☑ **Don't Miss**

Views of the city and Tibidabo extend from the hilly trails.

★ **Did You Know?**

Tibidabo is the setting for one of Spain's best-loved rock songs, 'Cadillac solitario', by legendary local singer Loquillo and his band Los Trogloditas.

ALBUM/ALAMY STOCK PHOTO ©

Museu-Monestir de Pedralbes

Dating from medieval times, this atmospheric convent is now a museum of monastic life. Perched at the top of busy Avinguda de Pedralbes in what was once unpeopled countryside, the monastery remains a divinely quiet corner of Barcelona and is full of architectural treasures. Adjoining the monastery is the sober church, an excellent example of Catalan Gothic.

Great For...

ℹ Need to Know

☎93 256 34 34; http://monestirpedralbes. bcn.cat; Baixada del Monestir 9; adult/child €5/free, after 3pm Sun free; ⊘10am-5pm Tue-Fri, to 7pm Sat, to 8pm Sun Apr-Sep, 10am-2pm Tue-Fri, to 5pm Sat & Sun Oct-Mar; 🚌63, 68, 75, 78, H4, V5, 🚊FGC Reina Elisenda

★ **Top Tip**

To make the most of your visit, be sure to pick up an audio guide, which gives crucial historical details.

Cloister & Chapel

The architectural highlight is the large, elegant, three-storey cloister, a jewel of Catalan Gothic, built in the early 14th century. Following its course to the right, stop at the first chapel, the Capella de Sant Miquel, the murals of which were completed in 1346 by Ferrer Bassá, one of Catalonia's earliest documented painters. A few steps on is the ornamental grave of Queen Elisenda, who founded the convent. Curiously, it's divided in two: the side in the cloister shows her dressed as a penitent widow, while the other part, an alabaster masterpiece inside the adjacent church, shows her dressed as queen.

Refectory & Sleeping Quarters

As you head around the ground floor of the cloister, you can peer into the restored refectory, kitchen, stables, stores and a reconstruction of the infirmary – all giving a good idea of convent life. Eating in the refectory must not have been a whole lot of fun, judging by the inscriptions around the walls exhorting *Silentium* (Silence) and *Audi Tacens* (Listen and Keep Quiet). Harder still must have been spending one's days in the cells on the ground and 1st floors in a state of near-perpetual prayer and devotional reading.

Upstairs is a grand hall that was once the *dormidor* (sleeping quarters). It was lined with tiny night cells, but they were long ago removed. Today a modest collection of the monastery's art, especially Gothic devotional works, and furniture grace this space. Most is by largely unknown Catalan artists, with some 16th-century Flemish works, and was acquired thanks to the considerable wealth of the convent's mostly upper-class nuns.

CosmoCaixa

Parc de l'Orenata

A little-visited park lies just behind the Museu-Monestir de Pedralbes. Set amid woodlands, the compact oak- and pine-filled Parc de l'Orenata has fine lookouts and the ruins of an old castle. On weekends, families arrive for short

★ Did You Know?

The monastery's different rooms are grouped around the three-storey Gothic cloister and include the chapel, dormitory, refectory, kitchen, infirmary, storerooms, abbey room and chapter house.

☑ Don't Miss

Ferrer Bassá's murals, the three-storey Gothic cloister or the refectory's admonishing inscriptions.

FRANTIC00/SHUTTERSTOCK ©

rides on a mini locomotive. To get here, take the stairs leading past the monastery, and continue uphill along Carrer de Montevideo.

What's Nearby?

CosmoCaixa
Museum

(Museu de la Ciència; ☎93 212 60 50; www. cosmocaixa.com; Carrer d'Isaac Newton 26; adult/child €4/free, guided tours from €2, planetarium €4; ☺10am-8pm; ☐60, 196) Kids (and the young at heart) are fascinated by displays at this science museum. The single greatest highlight is the re-creation of more than 1 sq km of flooded Amazon rainforest (Bosc Inundat). More than 100 species of Amazon flora and fauna (including anacondas, colourful poisonous frogs, and capybaras) prosper in this unique, living diorama in which you can even experience a tropical downpour.

In another original section, the Mur Geològic, seven great chunks of rock (90 metric tons in all) have been assembled to create a Geological Wall.

Exhibits cover many fascinating areas of science, from fossils to physics, and from the alphabet to outer space. Interactive exhibits such as the Planetari (Planetarium) cost extra. Aside from the Planetarium, which has multilingual commentary, many exhibits are in Catalan and Spanish. Various guided tours are available.

Outside, you can stroll through the extensive Plaça de la Ciència, whose modest garden flourishes with Mediterranean flora.

✕ Take a Break

A kilometre northeast, next door to Sarrià's pretty 18th-century church, cheery **Santamasa** (☎93 676 35 74; www. santamasarestaurant.com; Carrer Major de Sarrià 97; dishes €7-13; ☺8am-midnight Mon-Fri, 9am-midnight Sat & Sun; ☐FGC Reina Elisenda) is open all day.

Palau de la Música Catalana

This concert hall is a high point of Barcelona's Modernista architecture: a symphony in tile, brick, sculpted stone and stained glass conceived as a temple for the Catalan Renaixença (Renaissance).

Built by Lluís Domènech i Montaner between 1905 and 1908 for the Orfeó Català musical society, the *palau* (palace) was built with the help of some of the best Catalan artisans of the time, in the cloister of the former Convent de Sant Francesc. Since 1990 it has undergone several major changes.

Facade

The *palau,* like a peacock, shows off much of its splendour on the outside. Take in the principal facade with its mosaics, floral capitals and the sculpture cluster representing Catalan popular music.

Interior

Wander inside the foyer and restaurant areas to admire the spangled, tiled pillars. Best of all, however, is the richly colourful

Great For...

☑ Don't Miss

The principal facade's mosaics and columns and the foyer and pillars in the restaurant.

Stained-glass dome

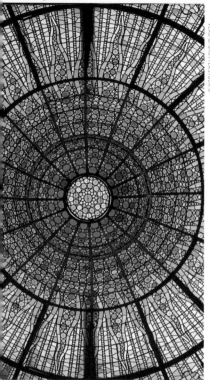

❶ Need to Know

Map p254; ☎93 295 72 00; www.palaumusica.
cat; Carrer de Palau de la Música 4-6; adult/
concession/under 10yr €20/11/free; ☺guid-
ed tours 10am-3.30pm Sep-Jun, to 6pm Easter
& Jul, 9am-6pm Aug; Ⓜ Urquinaona

✕ Take a Break

Le Cucine Mandarosso (☎93 269 07
80; www.lecucinemandarosso.com; Carrer de
Verdaguer i Callís 4; mains €12-14; ☺1.30-
4pm & 9pm-midnight Tue-Sat, 1.30-4.30pm
& 9pm-midnight Sun; Ⓜ Urquinaona) is good
for Italian comfort food.

★ Top Tip

Prebook tours online if visiting in
summer.

auditorium upstairs, with its ceiling of
blue-and-gold stained glass and shimmering skylight that looks like a giant,
crystalline, downward-thrusting nipple.
Above a bust of Beethoven on the stage
towers a wind-blown sculpture of Wagner's
valkyries (Wagner was top of the Barcelona charts at the time it was created). This
can only be savoured on a guided tour or
by attending a performance – either is
highly recommended. Tour tickets can be
bought up to a week in advance by phone
or online. Space is limited to a maximum
of 55 people.

Performances

This is the city's most traditional **venue** (tickets from €18; ☺box office 9.30am-9pm Mon-Sat,
10am-3pm Sun) for classical and choral music,
although it has a wide-ranging program,
including flamenco, pop and – particularly
– jazz. Just being here for a performance is
an experience. Sip a preconcert tipple in the
foyer, its tiled pillars all a-glitter.

Controversial History

The original Modernista creation, now a
World Heritage Site, did not meet with
universal approval in its day. The doyen
of Catalan literature, Josep Pla, did not
hesitate to condemn it as 'horrible', but
few share his sentiments today. Montaner
himself was also in a huff. He failed to
attend the opening ceremony in response
to unsettled bills.

In 2009 the *palau* was at the centre
of a fraud scandal, as its president, who
subsequently resigned, admitted to having
siphoned off millions of euros of funds.

Casa Gispert (p111)

Foodie Trails in La Ribera

Gourmands and gastronomes will be thoroughly beguiled by the choice in La Ribera, home to a fabulous market and gourmet shops offering all sorts of delicacies. It's almost impossible to walk into its enticing pedestrian zone and come out without having tried, tasted or bought something.

Great For...

ⓘ Need to Know

Buying cooked meats and meat products? The Spanish phrase for 'vacuum pack' is *'envasar al vacío'*.

★ **Top Tip**

Start your day at the market; it's at its best in the morning.

Mercat de Santa Caterina   Market

(Map p250; ☑93 319 57 40; www.mercatsanta
caterina.com; Avinguda de Francesc Cambó 16;
⏲7.30am-3.30pm Mon, Wed & Sat, to 8.30pm Tue,
Thu & Fri, closed afternoons Jul & Aug; ⓂJaume
I) Come shopping for your tomatoes at this
extraordinary-looking produce market,
designed by Enric Miralles and Benedetta
Tagliabue to replace its 19th-century predecessor. Finished in 2005, it is distinguished
by its kaleidoscopic and undulating roof, held
up above the bustling produce stands, restaurants, cafes and bars by twisting slender
branches of what look like grey steel trees.

Museu de la Xocolata   Museum

(☑93 268 78 78; www.museuxocolata.cat; Carrer
del Comerç 36; adult/concession/child under 7yr
€6/5/free; ⏲10am-8pm Mon-Sat & 10am-3pm
Sun mid-Jun–mid-Sep, 10am-7pm Mon-Sat & 10am-
3pm Sun mid-Sep–mid-Jun; ♿; ⓂArc de Triomf)

Mercat de Santa Caterina

Chocoholics have a hard time containing
themselves in this museum dedicated to the
fundamental foodstuff – especially when
faced with displays of cocoa-based treats in
the cafe at the exit. The displays trace the
origins of chocolate, its arrival in Europe and
the many myths associated with it.

Kids and grown-ups can join guided
tours (from €7.50) and occasionally take
part in chocolate-making and tasting sessions, especially at weekends.

Hofmann Pastisseria   Food

(Map p250; ☑93 268 82 21; www.hofmann-bcn.
com; Carrer dels Flassaders 44; ⏲9am-2pm &
3.30-8pm Mon-Thu, 9am-2pm & 3.30-8.30pm Fri
& Sat, to 2.30pm Sun; ⓂBarceloneta) With its
painted wooden cabinets, this bite-sized
gourmet patisserie, linked to the prestigious
Hofmann cooking school, has an air of time-
lessness. Choose between jars of delicious

jams, the renowned croissants (in various flavours) and more dangerous pastries, or an array of cakes and other sweet treats.

Casa Gispert
Food

(Map p250; ☑ 93 319 75 35; www.casagispert. com; Carrer dels Sombrerers 23; ⊗ 10am-8.30pm Mon-Sat; Ⓜ Jaume I) The wonderful, atmospheric and wood-fronted Casa Gispert has been toasting nuts and selling all manner of dried fruit since 1851. Pots and jars piled high on the shelves contain an unending variety of crunchy titbits: some roasted, some honeyed, all of them moreish. Your order is shouted over to the till, along with the price, in a display of old-world accounting.

> ☑ **Don't Miss**
> The Mercat de Santa Caterina: what a place.

AGF SRL/ALAMY STOCK PHOTO ©

La Botifarreria
Food

(Map p250; ☑ 93 319 91 23; www.labotifarreria. com; Carrer de Santa Maria 4; ⊗ 8.30am-2.30pm & 5-8.30pm Mon-Sat; closed Aug; Ⓜ Jaume I) Although this delightful deli sells all sorts of goodies, the mainstay is an astounding variety of handcrafted sausages – the *botifarra*. Not just the regular pork variety either – these sausages are stuffed with anything from green pepper and whisky to apple curry.

El Magnífico
Coffee

(Map p250; ☑ 93 319 60 81; www.cafeselmag nifico.com; Carrer de l'Argenteria 64; ⊗ 9am-5pm Mon-Fri; Ⓜ Jaume I) Coffee beans have been roasted here since the early 20th century. The variety of coffee (and tea) is remarkable – and the aromas hit you as you walk in.

Vila Viniteca
Wine

(Map p250; ☑ 90 232 77 77; www.vilaviniteca.es; Carrer dels Agullers 7; ⊗ 8.30am-8.30pm Mon-Sat; Ⓜ Jaume I) One of the best wine stores in Barcelona (and there are a few...), this place has been searching out the best local and imported wines since 1932. On a couple of November evenings it organises what has become an almost riotous wine-tasting event in Carrer dels Agullers, at which cellars from around Spain present their new wines.

Olisoliva
Food

(Map p250; ☑ 93 268 14 72; www.olisoliva.com; Mercat de Santa Caterina; ⊗ 9.30am-3.30pm Mon, Wed & Sat, to 7pm Tue, to 8pm Thu-Fri; Ⓜ Jaume I) Inside the Mercat de Santa Caterina, this simple, glassed-in store is stacked with olive oils and vinegars from all over Spain. Taste some of the products before deciding.

Sans i Sans
Drinks

(Map p250; ☑ 93 310 25 18; www.sansisans.com; Carrer de l'Argenteria 59; ⊗ 10am-8pm Mon-Sat; Ⓜ Jaume I) This exquisite tea shop is run by the same people who run El Magnífico across the road.

> ★ **Did You Know?**
> The design of the roof is from a photo of a fruit and veg stall, blown up to huge scale.

Entrance from Plaça del Rei

MARC SOLER/ALAMY STOCK PHOTO ©

Museu d'Història de Barcelona

This fascinating Barri Gòtic museum takes you back through the centuries to the foundations of Roman Barcino. It has an impressive display of archaeology and wandering around the city's underground is most intriguing.

At the museum, you'll stroll amid extensive ruins of the town that flourished here following its founding by Emperor Augustus around 10 BC. Equally impressive is the setting inside the former Palau Reial Major (Grand Royal Palace), among the key locations of medieval princely power in Barcelona.

Casa Padellàs

Enter through Casa Padellàs, just south of Plaça del Rei. Casa Padellàs was built for a 16th-century noble family in Carrer dels Mercaders and moved here, stone by stone, in the 1930s. It has a courtyard typical of Barcelona's late-Gothic and baroque mansions, with a graceful external staircase up to the 1st floor. Today it leads to a restored Roman tower and a section of Roman wall (the exterior of which faces Plaça Ramon

Great For...

☑ **Don't Miss**

The public laundry and the winemaking stores.

Exhibitions above the ruins

LUCAS VALLECILLOS/ALAMY STOCK PHOTO ©

ⓘ Need to Know

MUHBA; Map p250; ☎93 256 21 00; www.
museuhistoria.bcn.cat; Plaça del Rei; adult/
concession/child €7/5/free, 3-8pm Sun & 1st
Sun of month free; ⊙10am-7pm Tue-Sat, to
8pm Sun; Ⓜ Jaume I

★ Top Tip

Entry includes admission to other
MUHBA-run sites, such as Domus de
Sant Honorat (p115).

✕ Take a Break

Stop by La Granja (p134) for a hot chocolate and another glimpse of Roman
walls.

de Berenguer el Gran), as well as a section
of the house set aside for temporary
exhibitions.

Underground Ruins

Below ground is a remarkable walk
through about 4 sq km of excavated
Roman and Visigothic Barcelona. After
the display on the typical Roman *domus*
(villa), you reach a public laundry (outside
in the street were containers for people
to urinate into, as the urine was used as
disinfectant). You pass more laundries
and dyeing shops, a 6th-century public
cold-water bath and more dye shops. As
you hit the Cardo Minor (a main street),
you turn right then left and reach various
shops dedicated to the making of *garum*.
This paste, a favourite food across the
Roman Empire, was made of mashed-up
fish intestines, eggs and blood. Occasionally prawns, cockles and herbs were
added to create other flavours. Further on
are fish-preserve stores. Fish were sliced
up (and all innards removed for making
garum), laid in alternate layers using salt
for preservation, and sat in troughs for
about three weeks before being ready for
sale and export.

Next come remnants of a 6th- to 7th-
century church and episcopal buildings,
followed by wine-making stores, with
ducts for allowing the must to flow off, and
ceramic, round-bottomed *dolia* for storing
and ageing wine. Ramparts then wind
around and upward, past remains of the
gated patio of a Roman house, the medieval
Palau Episcopal (Bishops' Palace) and into
two broad vaulted halls with displays on
medieval Barcelona.

In Columbus' Footsteps

You eventually emerge at a hall and ticket office set up on the north side of Plaça del Rei. To your right is the Saló del Tinell, the banqueting hall of the royal palace and a fine example of Catalan Gothic (built 1359–70). Its broad arches and bare walls give a sense of solemnity that would have made an appropriate setting for Fernando and Isabel to hear Columbus' first reports of the New World. The hall is sometimes used for temporary exhibitions, which may cost extra and mean that your peaceful contemplation of its architectural majesty is somewhat obstructed.

Chapel

As you leave the *saló* you come to the 14th-century Capella Reial de Santa Àgata, the palace chapel. Outside, a spindly bell tower rises from the northeast side of Plaça del Rei. Inside, all is bare except for the 15th-century altarpiece and the magnificent *techumbre* (decorated timber ceiling). The altarpiece is considered to be one of Jaume Huguet's finest surviving works.

Out to the Square

Head down the fan-shaped stairs into Plaça del Rei and look up to observe the Mirador del Rei Martí (lookout tower of King Martin), built in 1555, long after the king's death. It is part of the Arxiu de la Corona d'Aragón; the magnificent views over the old city are now enjoyed only by a privileged few.

Palau de la Generalitat

What's Nearby?

Palau de la
Generalitat
Historic Building

(Map p250; http://presidencia.gencat.cat; Plaça de Sant Jaume; ⊘2nd & 4th weekends of month Sep-Jul; Ⓜ Jaume I) Early-15th-century Palau de la Generalitat is open on limited occasions – one-hour guided tours on the second and fourth weekends of the month, plus open-door days. The most impressive of its ceremonial halls is the Saló de Sant Jordi (Hall of St George), named after the region's patron saint. To see inside, book online.

Marc Safont designed the original Gothic main entrance on Carrer del Bisbe.

✕ Take a Break

For microbrews and vegan burgers check out Cat Bar (p139) in El Born.

KRZYSZTOF DYDYNSKI/LONELY PLANET ©

The modern main entrance on Plaça de Sant Jaume is a late-Renaissance job with neoclassical leanings. If you wander by in the evening, squint up through the windows into the Saló de Sant Jordi and you will get some idea of the sumptuousness of the interior.

Normally you will have to enter from Carrer de Sant Sever. The first rooms you pass through are characterised by low vaulted ceilings. From here you head upstairs to the raised courtyard known as the Pati dels Tarongers, a modest Gothic orangery (open about once a month for concert performances of the palace's chimes). The 16th-century Sala Daurada i de Sessions, one of the rooms leading off the patio, is a splendid meeting hall illuminated by huge chandeliers. Renaissance Saló de Sant Jordi is still more imposing; its murals were added last century, and many an occasion of pomp and circumstance takes place here. Finally, you descend the staircase of the Gothic Pati Central to leave by what was originally the building's main entrance.

Domus de
Sant Honorat
Archaeological Site

(Map p250; ☎93 256 21 22; www.museuhistoria. bcn.cat; Carrer de la Fruita 2; adult/concession/child €2/1.50/free, 1st Sun of month free; ⊘10am-2pm Sun; Ⓜ Jaume I) The remains of a Roman *domus* (town house) have been unearthed and opened to the public. The house (and vestiges of three small shops) lies close to the Roman forum and the owners were clearly affluent. In addition to providing an idea of daily Roman life through these remains, the location also contains six medieval grain silos installed during the period when this was the Jewish quarter, El Call.

The whole site is housed in the mid-19th-century Casa Morell. So, in an unusual mix, one gets a glimpse of three distinct periods in history in the same spot.

Basílica de Santa Maria del Mar

At one end of Passeig del Born stands the apse of Barcelona's finest Catalan Gothic church, Santa Maria del Mar (Our Lady of the Sea). Its construction started in 1329, with Berenguer de Montagut and Ramon Despuig as the architects. Famously, the parishioners themselves gave up their time to help construct the church, particularly the stevedores from the nearby port.

Great For...

❶ Need to Know

Map p250; ☎93 310 23 90; www.santamaria delmarbarcelona.org; Plaça de Santa Maria; guided tour €10 1-5pm; ⊙9am-8.30pm Mon-Sat, from 10am-8pm Sun; Ⓜ Jaume I

★ Top Tip

Take a guided tour (offered 1pm to 5pm) to visit the roof terrace and crypt (€10).

Main Sanctuary

The pleasing unity of form and symmetry of the church's central nave and two flanking aisles owed much to the rapidity with which the church was built – a mere 54 years, which must be a record for a major European house of worship. The slender, octagonal pillars create an enormous sense of lateral space bathed in the light of stained glass.

The People's Church

Its construction started in 1329, with Berenguer de Montagut and Ramon Despuig as the architects in charge. During construction the city's *bastaixos* (porters) spent a day each week carrying on their backs the stone required to build the church from royal quarries in Montjuïc. Their memory lives on in reliefs of them in the main doors and stone carvings elsewhere in the church. The walls, the side chapels and the facades were finished by 1350, and the entire structure was completed in 1383.

Interior

The exterior gives an impression of sternness and, like many of the buildings in the old part of town, it suffers from the impossibility of an overall perspective – the narrow streets around it are restrictive and claustrophobic. It may come as a (pleasant) surprise then, to find a spacious and light interior – the central nave and two flanking aisles separated by slender octagonal pillars give an enormous sense of lateral space.

Barcelona Head by Roy Lichtenstein

The interior is almost devoid of imagery of the sort to be found in Barcelona's other large Gothic churches, but Santa Maria was lacking in superfluous decoration even before anarchists gutted it in 1909 and 1936.

Keep a look out for music recitals, often baroque and classical. From 1pm to 5pm (and 2pm to 5pm on Sundays), visitors must pay to enter and join a guided tour, which includes visits to the main church, museum, galleries and crypt.

✕ Take a Break

Admire the church's western facade with tapas and drinks at La Vinya del Senyor (p179).

☑ Don't Miss

The church's builders portrayed in memorial stone relief.

Old Flame

Opposite Basílica de Santa Maria del Mar's southern flank, an eternal flame burns brightly over an apparently anonymous sunken square. This is El Fossar de les Moreres (The Mulberry Cemetery), the site of a Roman cemetery. It's also where Catalan resistance fighters were buried after the siege of Barcelona ended in defeat in September 1714; it is for them that the flame burns.

What's Nearby?

Museu Europeu d'Art Modern   Museum

(MEAM; Map p250; ☑93 319 56 93; www.meam.es; Carrer Barra de Ferro 5; adult/concession/child under 10yr €9/7/free; ⊙10am-8pm Tue-Sun; Ⓜ Jaume I) The European Museum of Modern Art opened in the summer of 2011 in the Palau Gomis, a handsome 18th-century mansion around the corner from the Museu Picasso. The art within is strictly representational (the 'Modern' of the name simply means 'contemporary') and is mostly from young Spanish artists, though there are some works from elsewhere in Europe.

Barcelona Head   Sculpture

(Map p250; Passeig de Colom; Ⓜ Barceloneta) An icon by the waterfront, this eye-catching 15m-high primary-coloured sculpture was designed by famous American pop artist Roy Lichtenstein for the 1992 Olympics.

MARC SOLER/ALAMY STOCK PHOTO ©

GAGLIARDIPHOTOGRAPHY/SHUTTERSTOCK ©

Recinte Modernista de Sant Pau

Domènech i Montaner outdid himself as architect and philanthropist with the Modernista Hospital de la Santa Creu i de Sant Pau, renamed the 'Recinte Modernista' in 2014.

The Recinte Modernista de Sant Pau was long considered one of the city's most important hospitals but was repurposed, its various spaces becoming cultural centres, offices and something of a monument. The complex, including 16 pavilions – together with the Palau de la Música Catalana (p106), a joint Unesco World Heritage Site – is lavishly decorated and each pavilion is unique.

Domènech i Montaner wanted to create an environment that would also cheer up patients. Among artists who contributed statuary, ceramics and artwork was the prolific Eusebi Arnau.

Great For...

☑ **Don't Miss**

The re-creation of a 1920s hospital ward.

What's Nearby?
Birra 08 Brewery
(☏ 93 013 02 30; www.birra08.com; Carrer de La Llacuna 165; tour & tasting €30; ☺ by

Nau Bostik

ℹ️ Need to Know

📞 93 553 78 01; www.santpaubarcelona.org; Carrer de Sant Antoni Maria Claret 167; adult/child €14/free; 🕐 9.30am-6.30pm Mon-Sat, to 2.30pm Sun Apr-Oct, 9.30am-4.30pm Mon-Sat, to 2.30pm Sun Nov-Mar; Ⓜ Sant Pau/Dos de Maig

✕ Take a Break

There's a decent café here in the main pavilion.

★ Top Tip

Guided tours (adult/child €19/free) lasting 90 minutes are available in a variety of languages.

reservation 7.30pm; Ⓜ Clot) Book ahead for an evening tour (English available) of this organic brewery. Over the course of two hours, you'll taste the malt, hops and cereals and, better yet, the end product, with five samples all-up. Brews are named after Barcelona neighbourhoods, such as Barceloneta Blonde Ale or Clot Pale Ale; look out for them around town. It also runs courses where you can learn to brew your own beer (10am to 5pm Saturday; €80 including lunch and, yes, beer).

Nau Bostik   Arts Centre

(📞 616 364831; www.naubostik.com; Carrer Ferran Turné 1-11; 🕐 10am-10pm; Ⓜ La Sagrera) **FREE** Hip Nau Bostik is a must-visit for vintage lovers, and street-art fans in particular. Set in an old factory, it's a bit rough around the edges but is covered in murals by some

of Barcelona's best graffiti artists. The centre also hosts temporary exhibitions, as well as vintage and street food markets on some weekends. Head up to the roof terrace to see the huge mural by famous street artist Sixe Paredes.

Parc de la Pegaso   Park

(Carrer Gran de la Sagrera 179; Ⓜ Fabra i Puig) If you're looking for a bit of green in the northeast of the city, head to Parc de la Pegaso, a huge space filled with a variety of ponds, water features and lush walkways. It was designed by the architects Enric Batlle and Joan Roig, and built in 1986 on the site of the Pegaso truck factory, after which the park is named.

Statues of the Child Jesus

GUY MOBERLY/LONELY PLANET ©

Museu Frederic Marès

One of the wildest collections of historical curios lies inside this vast medieval complex, once part of the royal palace of the counts of Barcelona.

Great For...

☑ **Don't Miss**

Displays from the collector's cabinet.

The building housing the museum is an intriguing one. A rather worn coat of arms on the wall indicates that it was also, for a while, the seat of the Spanish Inquisition in Barcelona.

Sculpture

Frederic Marès i Deulovol (1893–1991) was a rich sculptor, traveller and obsessive collector. He specialised in medieval Spanish sculpture, huge quantities of which are displayed in the basement and on the ground and 1st floors – including some lovely polychrome wooden sculptures of the Crucifixion and the Virgin. Among the most eye-catching pieces is a reconstructed Romanesque doorway with four arches, taken from a 13th-century country church in the Aragonese province of Huesca.

Plaça de Sant Jaume

MISTERVLAD/SHUTTERSTOCK ©

❶ Need to Know

Map p250; ☎93 256 35 00; www.museu-mares.bcn.cat; Plaça de Sant lu 5; adult/concession/child €4.20/2.40/free, 3-8pm Sun & 1st Sun of month free; ⊙10am-7pm Tue-Sat, 11am-8pm Sun; Ⓜ Jaume I

✕ Take a Break

The museum's likeable summer cafe is the handiest place for refreshments.

★ Top Tip

The collections are dizzying, but tickets are valid for two separate visits within six months.

Collector's Cabinet

The top two floors comprise 'the collector's cabinet', a mind-boggling array of knick-knacks, including medieval weaponry, finely carved pipes, delicate ladies' fans, intricate 'floral' displays made of seashells and 19th-century daguerreotypes and photographs. A room that once served as Marès' study and library is now crammed with sculptures.

The shaded courtyard houses a pleasant summer cafe (Cafè de l'Estiu).

What's Nearby?

Plaça de Sant Jaume Square
(Map p250; Ⓜ Liceu, Jaume I) In the 2000 or so years since the Romans settled here, the area around this square (often remodelled), which started life as the forum, has been

the focus of Barcelona's civic life. This is still the central staging area for Barcelona's traditional festivals. Facing each other across the square are the seat of Catalonia's regional government, the Palau de la Generalitat (p115), on the north side, and the town hall, or **Ajuntament** (Casa de la Ciutat; ☎93 402 70 00; www.bcn.cat; Plaça de Sant Jaume; ⊙10am-2pm Sun) FREE to the south.

Palau Centelles Architecture
(Map p250; Baixada de Sant Miquel 8; Ⓜ Jaume I) A rare 15th-century gem, Palau Centelles is on the corner of Baixada de Sant Miquel. You can wander into the fine Gothic-Renaissance courtyard if the gates are open.

Walking Tour: More Modernisme in L'Eixample

Catalan modernism (Modernisme) abounds in the Barcelona's L'Eixample district. This walk introduces you to the movement's main form of expression: the architecture.

Start: Casa Calvert

Distance: 4km

Duration: 1 hour

5 Completed in 1912, **Casa Thomas** was one of Domènech i Montaner's earlier efforts; the wrought-iron decoration is magnificent.

4 Casa Comalat was built in 1911 by Salvador Valeri and has a Gaudi-inspired wavy roof and bulging balconies.

3 Puig i Cadafalch let his imagination loose on **Casa Serra** (1903–08), a neo-Gothic whimsy now home to government offices.

Verdaguer

Av Diagonal

L'EIXAMPLE

C de Còrsega
C del Rosselló
C de Mallorca

Plaça de Joan Carles I

Diagonal

Av Diagonal

C del Rosselló
Pg de Gràcia
C de Provença
C de Pau Claris
C de Roger de Llúria

Diagonal

C de Provença

Rambla de Catalunya
C de Mallorca

Passeig de Gràcia

Passeig de Gràcia

Pg de Gràcia

C d'Aragó

Jardins de la Reina Victòria

7 Puig i Cadafalch's **Palau Macaya** (1901) features the typical playful, pseudo-Gothic decoration that characterises many of the architect's projects.

0 — 400 m
0 — 0.2 miles

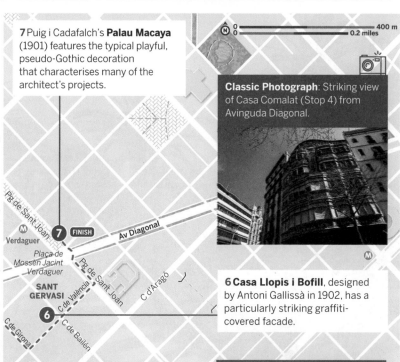

Classic Photograph: Striking view of Casa Comalat (Stop 4) from Avinguda Diagonal.

Pg de Sant Joan

7 **FINISH** Av Diagonal

M Verdaguer

Plaça de Mossèn Jacint Verdaguer

Pg de Sant Joan

C d'Aragó

SANT GERVASI

C de València

6

C de Girona

C de Bailèn

6 Casa Llopis i Bofill, designed by Antoni Gallissà in 1902, has a particularly striking graffiti-covered facade.

✕ Take a Break

It's worth seeking out **Casa Amalia** (p144) for hearty Catalan cooking.

2 Casa Enric Batlló, today part of the Comtes de Barcelona hotel, was completed in 1896 by Josep Vilaseca.

Gran Via de les Corts Catalanes

C de Casp

1 **START**

Via Laietana

Ronda de Sant Pere

Plaça de Joan Carles I

Urquinaona **M** d'Urquinaona

1 Antoni Gaudí's most conventional contribution to L'Eixample is **Casa Calvet**, built in 1900.

Jardí Botànic

IAKOV FILIMONOV/SHUTTERSTOCK ©

Gardens of Montjuïc

The hillside overlooking the centre and port is a gem. Exploring verdant Montjuïc on foot, along the numerous forest paths that zigzag through gardens, is one of Barcelona's great pleasures.

Great For...

☑ Don't Miss

The attractive watercourses of Jardins de Laribal.

Jardí Botànic   Gardens

(Map p256; www.museuciencies.cat; Carrer del Doctor Font i Quer 2; adult/child €3.50/free, after 3pm Sun & 1st Sun of month free; ☺10am-7pm Apr-Sep, to 5pm Oct-Mar; 🚌55, 150) This botanical garden is dedicated to Mediterranean flora and has a collection of some 40,000 plants and 1500 species, including many that thrive in areas with a climate similar to that of the Mediterranean, such as the Canary Islands, North Africa, Australia, California, Chile and South Africa.

Jardins de Laribal   Gardens

(Map p256; Passeig de Santa Madrona 2; ☺10am-sunset; 🚌55) **FREE** Opened in 1922, the Jardins de Laribal comprise a combination of terraced gardens linked by paths and stairways. The pretty sculpted watercourses along some of the stairways were inspired by Granada's palace of El Alhambra.

Jardins de Laribal

ALEXANDER SPATARI/GETTY IMAGES ©

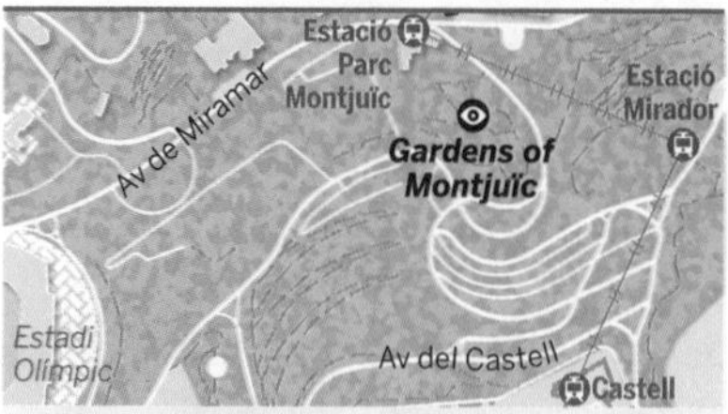

Need to Know

Getting up here by the Teleférico del Puerto (p63) is both quick and spectacular.

Take a Break

The museums have cafes, but this is real picnic territory.

★ Top Tip

It's worth being up here in the late afternoon; the sunsets can be spectacular.

Jardins de Mossèn Cinto de Verdaguer Gardens

(Map p256; http://ajuntament.barcelona.cat/ecologiaurbana; Avinguda Miramar 30; 10am-sunset; 55, 150) FREE These sloping gardens, near the Estació Parc Montjuïc Telefèric station, are home to various kinds of aquatic plants and bulbs – many of the 80,000 bulbs have to be replanted each year.

Jardins de Mossèn Costa i Llobera Gardens

(Map p256; http://ajuntament.barcelona.cat/ecologiaurbana;Carretera de Miramar 38; 10am-sunset; Transbordador Aeri, Miramar) FREE Above the thundering traffic of the main road to Tarragona, these gardens have a good collection of tropical and desert plants – including Europe's largest collection of cacti, with some species reaching over 5m in height.

Jardins de Joan Maragall Gardens

(Map p256; Avinguda dels Montanyans 48; 10am-3pm Sat & Sun; M Espanya) FREE Lovely but little visited, the lush lawns, ornamental fountains, photogenic sculptures and a neoclassical palace of this garden set it apart from the other green spaces on Montjuïc.

Jardins del Mirador Gardens

(Map p256; http://ajuntament.barcelona.cat/ecologiaurbana; Carretera de Montjuïc; 10am-sunset; Telefèric de Montjuïc, Mirador) FREE These gardens, opposite the Estació Mirador, offer expansive views over the port of Barcelona.

Jardins de Joan Brossa Gardens

(Map p256; Plaça de la Sardana; 10am-sunset; Telefèric de Montjuïc, Mirador) FREE Set on the site of a former amusement park, these gardens contain many Mediterranean species, from cypresses to pines and a few palms.

DINING OUT

From tapas to world-renowned restaurants

Dining Out

Barcelona has a celebrated food scene fuelled by a combination of world-class chefs, imaginative recipes and magnificent ingredients fresh from farms and the sea. Catalan culinary masterminds, like brothers Ferran and Albert Adrià, have become international icons, reinventing the world of haute cuisine, while classic old-world Catalan recipes continue to earn accolades in dining rooms and tapas bars across the city.

Traditional Catalan recipes showcase the great produce of the Mediterranean: fish, prawns, cuttlefish, clams, pork, rabbit, game, first-rate olive oil, peppers and loads of garlic. Classic dishes also feature unusual pairings, such as, fruit with fowl, cured ham with caviar, rabbit with prawns and goose with pears.

In This Section

Price Ranges & Tipping

The following price ranges represent the average cost of a main course:

€ less than €12

€€ €12–€20

€€€ over €20

A service charge is rarely included in the bill. Catalans and other Spaniards are not overwhelming tippers. If you are particularly happy, 5% on top is generally fine.

Useful Phrases

The bill please	*La cuenta, por favor*	la kwen·ta por fa·vor
I'd/We'd like ...	*Quería/queríamos ...*	ke·ria/ ke·ria·most
A dish of ... chicken	*Una de ... pollo*	oo·na de...po·yo
I'm allergic to ...	*Tengo alergía a ...*	ten·go al·er·hi·ya a
I don't eat ... meat	*No como ... carne*	no ko·mo kar·ne
Very good, thank you!	*¡Muy rico, gracias!*	Mwee ri·ko gra·thyas!

Classic Dishes

Calçots Barbecued leek/spring onion cross.

Escalivada Grilled and cooled sliced vegetables with oil.

Esqueixada Salad of salt cod with vegetables and beans.

Botifarra amb mongetes Pork sausage with white beans.

Cargols/Caracoles Snails, often stewed with rabbit.

Fideuà Like seafood paella, but with vermicelli noodles.

The Best...

Experience Barcelona's top restaurants and cafes

Tapas

El 58 (p141) French-owned space on the newly hip Rambla del Poblenou.

Quimet i Quimet (p145) Mouth-watering morsels served to a standing crowd.

Palo Cortao (p145) A buzzy Poble Sec option with outstanding sharing plates.

Pinotxo Bar (p138) Pull up a bar stool at this legendary Boqueria joint.

Tapas 24 (p143) Everyone's favourite gourmet tapas bar.

Cafes

Bar del Convent (p139; pictured) Great terrace in a former cloister.

Café Godot (p148) Friendly and easy-going, with tasty snacks and mains.

Federal (p134) Unnervingly hip, but the food is excellent and the service friendly.

La Granja (p134) Best place in town for a hot chocolate.

La Nena (p148) Kid-friendly cafe in Gràcia.

Catalan

Vivanda (p149) Magnificent Catalan cooking with year-round garden dining.

La Panxa del Bisbe (p148) Creative sharing plates on a quiet Gràcia street.

Cafè de l'Acadèmia (p136) High-quality dishes that never disappoint.

Can Culleretes (p136; pictured) The city's oldest restaurant, with great-value traditional dishes.

Bar Muy Buenas (p137) Catalan classics amid stunningly preserved 1920s decor.

Vegetarian & Vegan

Green Spot (p141; pictured) Designer dining room with dishes to match.

Aguaribay (p142) First-rate prix fixe lunches and a small but well-executed evening à la carte menu.

Cerería (p137) Pizzas and galettes in an old-fashioned setting.

Flax & Kale (p138) Vast, colourful salads and a truly creative approach.

Rasoterra (p137) Airy vegetarian charmer in Barri Gòtic.

Veggie Garden (p137) Inexpensive Indian-influenced fare beloved by a young crowd.

For Eating Like a Local

Mitja Vida (p149) Mouth-watering tapas and vermouth.

Can Lluís (p138) Loved by Catalans for its great-value daily *menú* (set menu).

Las Delicias (p147) A Sunday-morning classic, well located for a walk in Park Güell.

La Cova Fumada (p140) Fight for a table at this scruffy little joint with outstanding food.

Taverna El Glop (p148) A buzzing neighbourhood spot in Gràcia.

Brunch

Federal (p145) Excellent brunches and a small roof terrace.

En Aparté (p139) French restaurant serving tasty brunch dishes.

Milk (p134) Serves brunch until 4.30pm daily.

Benedict (p134) The clue is in the name, but there's more besides.

Copasetic (p143) Vintage-filled cafe with weekend brunch.

Seafood

Barraca (p142) A sparkling waterfront restaurant with unique and flavour-rich seafood combinations.

Can Majó (p143) Fine seafood in a pleasant outdoor setting.

Can Ros (p142) A family-run Barceloneta classic.

Can Maño (p140) An unfussy place with great dishes at low prices.

Lonely Planet's Top Choices

Disfrutar (p144) An avant-garde venue that is consistently one of Barcelona's most talked-about restaurants.

Tickets (p147) The celebrated restaurant of Albert Adrià, showcasing Barcelona's best *nueva cocina española* (Spanish nouvelle cuisine).

Tapas 24 (p143) Carles Abellan creates some of Barcelona's best tapas.

La Cova Fumada (p140) Cramped, noisy, but unmissable tapas restaurant, open at lunch only.

Restaurant 7 Portes (p142) An elegant spot that's famed for its delectable paella.

⊗ La Rambla & Barri Gòtic

Federal
Cafe €

(Map p250; ☎93 280 81 71; www.federalcafe.es; Passatge de la Pau 11; mains €7-10; ⊙9am-midnight Mon-Thu, to 1am Fri & Sat, to 5.30pm Sun; ☎; M Drassanes) Don't be intimidated by the industrial chic, the sea of open MacBooks or the stack of design mags – this branch of the Poble Sec Federal mothership is incredibly welcoming, with healthy, good-value food. Set in a lovely, quiet square, it's best known for its Australian-inspired brunches, such as baked eggs with feta and chorizo.

La Plata
Tapas €

(Map p250; ☎93 315 10 09; www.barlaplata.com; Carrer de la Mercè 28; tapas €2.50-5; ⊙10am-3.15pm & 6.15-11pm Mon-Sat; M Jaume I) Tucked away in a narrow lane near the waterfront, La Plata is a humble but well-loved bodega that serves just four plates: *pescadito frito* (small fried fish), *butifarra* (sausage), anchovies and tomato salad. Add in the drinkable, affordable wines (€1.20 per glass) and vermouth, and you have the makings of a fine pre-dinner tapas spot.

Milk
International €

(Map p250; ☎93 268 09 22; www.milkbarcelona. com; Carrer d'en Gignàs 21; mains €9-12; ⊙9am-2am Thu-Mon, to 2.30am Fri & Sat; ☎; M Jaume I) Also known as an enticing cocktail spot, Irish-run Milk plays a key role in providing Barcelona night owls with morning-after brunches (served till 4.30pm). Avoid direct sunlight and tuck into pancakes, eggs Benedict and other hangover dishes in a cosy lounge-like setting complete with ornate wallpaper, framed prints on the wall and cushion-lined seating. The musical selection is also notable.

La Granja
Cafe €

(Map p250; ☎93 302 69 75; Carrer dels Banys Nous 4; ⊙9am-9pm Mon-Sat, from 9.30am Sun; ☎; M Jaume I) This cafe, dating from 1872, serves thick, rich cups of chocolate with doughy, sugar-covered churros, as well as speciality coffees, herbal teas and other pastries. A section of Roman wall is visible at the back.

Benedict
Brunch €

(Map p250; ☎93 250 75 11; www.benedictbcn. com; Carrer d'en Gignás 23; mains €10-11; ⊙9am-4pm Mon-Wed, 9am-4pm & 7pm-2.30am Thu-Fri, 9am-2.30am Sat & Sun; ☎; M Jaume I) As the name suggests, brunch is the main event at friendly little Benedict, with eggs prepared every which way, pancakes and the option of a full English fry-up. There's also a list of house-made burgers, omelettes and sandwiches. In the evening various tapas are served, such as Mexican-style plantain chips, tacos and fried green tomatoes.

Caelum
Cafe €

(Map p250; ☎93 302 69 93; www.caelum barcelona.com; Carrer de la Palla 8; ⊙10am-8.30pm Mon-Sun; ☎; M Liceu) Centuries of heavenly gastronomic tradition from across Spain are concentrated in this exquisite medieval space in the heart of the city. The ground-floor cafe is a dainty setting for decadent cakes and pastries, while descending into the underground chamber with its stone walls and flickering candles is like a trip into the Middle Ages.

Wherever you decide to sit, you'll also pass through the shop that sells sweets made by nuns in convents across the country – the marzipan from Toledo is irresistible.

Alcoba Azul
Mediterranean €

(Map p250; ☎93 302 81 41; Carrer de Salamó Ben Adret 14; mains €6-10; ⊙noon-midnight Mon-Thu, to 2.30am Fri & Sat, 6pm-midnight Sun; ☎; M Jaume I) Peel back the centuries inside this remarkably atmospheric watering hole, with medieval walls, low ceilings, wooden floors and flicker- ing candles. Grab one of the seats in the quaint square out front or slide into one of the table booths inside, where you can enjoy good wines by the glass, satisfying plates of goat-cheese-stuffed peppers, salads and *tostas* (sandwiches).

Cafè de l'Òpera
Cafe €

(Map p250; ☎93 317 75 85; www.cafeoperabcn. com; La Rambla 74; ⊙8.30am-2.30am; ☎; M Liceu) Opposite the Gran Teatre del Liceu is La Rambla's most traditional cafe. Operating since 1929 and still popular with opera- goers, it is pleasant enough for an early evening libation or, in the morning, coffee and croissants. Head upstairs for a seat overlooking the busy boulevard, and try the house speciality, the *cafè de l'Òpera* (coffee with chocolate mousse).

Salterio

Cafe €

(Map p250; 📞93 302 50 28; www.facebook.com/teteriasalterio; Carrer de Salomó Ben Adret 4; ⏰noon- 1.30am; 📶; Ⓜ Jaume I) A wonderfully photo- genic, candlelit spot tucked down a tiny lane in El Call, Salterio serves Turkish coffee, authentic Moroccan mint teas and pots of milky, sweet spiced chai, amid stone walls, incense and ambient Middle Eastern music. If hunger strikes, try the *sardo* (grilled flat-bread covered with pesto, cheese or other toppings).

Čaj Chai

Cafe €

(Map p250; 📞93 301 95 92; www.cajchai.com; Carrer de Salomó Ben Adret 12; ⏰10.30am-10pm; Ⓜ Jaume I) Inspired by Prague's bohemian tearooms, this bright and buzzing cafe in the heart of the old Jewish quarter is a tea connoisseur's paradise, stocking around 200 teas from China, India, Korea, Japan, Nepal, Morocco and beyond. It's a much-loved local haunt.

Granja La Pallaresa

Cafe €

(Map p250; 📞93 302 20 36; Carrer del Petritxol 11; ⏰9am-1pm & 4-9pm Mon-Sat, 9am-1pm & 5-9pm Sun; 📶; Ⓜ Liceu) An old-school cafe filled with both locals and visitors, specialising in crispy churros with thick hot chocolate. It also sells plates of whipped cream, pastries and *ensaimadas* (sweet bread swirls dusted with icing sugar) from Mallorca.

La Vinateria del Call

Spanish €€

(Map p250; 📞93 302 60 92; www.lavinateria delcall.com; Carrer Salomó Ben Adret 9; raciones €7-12; ⏰7.30pm-1am; 📶; Ⓜ Jaume I) In a magical setting in the former Jewish quarter, this tiny jewel-box of a wine bar serves up tasty Iberian dishes, including Galician octopus, cider-cooked chorizo and the Catalan *escalivada* (roasted peppers, aubergine and onions) with anchovies. Portions are small and made for sharing, and there are more than 160 varieties of wine to choose from.

Els Quatre Gats (p137)

🍴 Top Tapas Plates

If you opt for tapas, it is handy to recognise some of the common items:

bombes/bombas large meat-and-potato croquettes

boquerons/boquerones white anchovies in vinegar – delicious and tangy

carxofes/alcachofas artichokes

gambes/gambas prawns, either done *al all/al ajillo* (with garlic), or *a la plantxa/plancha* (grilled)

navalles/navajas razor clams

patates braves/patatas bravas potato chunks bathed in a slightly spicy tomato sauce, sometimes mixed with mayonnaise

pop a feira/pulpo a la gallega tender boiled octopus with paprika

truita de patates/tortilla de patatas potato-filled omelette; one with vegetables is a *tortilla de verduras*

xampinyons/champiñones mushrooms

Patatas bravas
SALPARADIS/GETTY IMAGES ©

Cafè de l'Acadèmia — Catalan €€

(Map p250; ☎93 319 82 53; Carrer dels Lledó 1; mains €8-20; ⏰1-3.30pm & 8-11.30pm Mon-Fri; 🛜; Ⓜ Jaume I) Expect a mix of traditional Catalan dishes with the occasional creative twist. At lunchtime, local city hall workers pounce on the *menú del día* (€16). In the evening it is rather more romantic, as low lighting emphasises the intimacy of the beamed ceiling and stone walls. On warm days you can also dine in the pretty square at the front.

Belmonte — Tapas €€

(Map p250; ☎93 310 76 84; Carrer de la Mercè 29; tapas €4-10, mains €13-14; ⏰8pm-midnight Tue-Thu, 1-3.30pm & 8pm-midnight Fri & Sat; 🛜; Ⓜ Jaume I) This tiny tapas joint in the southern reaches of the Barri Gòtic whips up beautifully prepared small plates – including an excellent *truita* (tortilla), rich *patatons a la sal* (salted new potatoes with *romesco* sauce) and tender *carpaccio de pop* (octopus carpaccio). Wash it down with the house-made *vermut* (vermouth).

Ocaña — International €€

(Map p250; ☎93 676 48 14; www.ocana.cat; Plaça Reial 13; mains €12-18; ⏰cafe 11am-8pm daily, restaurant 8pm-midnight Thu-Sun, bar 3.30pm-2.30am Thu & Fri, to 3am Sat & Sun; 🛜; Ⓜ Liceu) A flamboyant but elegantly designed space with high ceilings, chandeliers and plush furnishings, Ocaña blends late-night carousing with serious eating. It's a casual cafe, restaurant and cocktail bar in one, serving everything from tapas and burgers to seafood and rice dishes. You can enjoy a cocktail at Moorish-inspired Apotheke downstairs, or out on the Plaça Reial terrace.

Can Culleretes — Catalan €€

(Map p250; ☎93 317 30 22; www.culleretes.com; Carrer d'en Quintana 5; mains €7.50-19; ⏰1.30-4pm & 8-10.45pm Tue-Sat, 1.30-4pm Sun; 🛜; Ⓜ Liceu) Founded in 1786, Barcelona's oldest restaurant is still going strong, with tourists and locals flocking here to enjoy its rambling interior, old-fashioned tile-filled decor and enormous helpings of traditional Catalan food, including fresh seafood and sticky stews. From Tuesday to Friday there is a fixed three-course lunch menu for €24 or €32.

Opera Samfaina — Catalan €€

(Map p250; ☎93 481 78 71; www.operasamfaina. com; La Rambla 51; mains €11-15, Odissea tasting menu adult/child under 12yr €33/20; ⏰noon-midnight Wed-Fri, 1pm-midnight Sat & Sun; Ⓜ Liceu) A surreal sensory experience deep in the bowels of the Liceu opera house. Enter through the Vermuteria, a tenebrous tapas bar, and then either head to the Odissea – a shared table, surrounded by audiovisuals – for a tasting menu of traditional Catalan dishes; or down to the Opera Prima, a dreamlike labyrinth of wine and tapas bars and psychedelic installations.

Cererı́a
Vegetarian €€

(Map p250; ☏ 93 301 85 10; Baixada de Sant Miquel 3; mains €8-11; ☺ 1-11pm Tue-Sat, to 6pm Sun; 🌐🍴; Ⓜ Jaume I) Black-and-white marble floors, a smattering of old wooden tables and ramshackle displays of musical instruments lend a certain bohemian charm to this vegetarian restaurant. The menu changes according to the season, but expect dishes, such as stuffed courgettes, coconut curry with cous cous and quesadillas filled with mushrooms in white wine. Vegan options too.

Rasoterra
Vegetarian €€

(Map p250; ☏ 93 318 69 26; www.rasoterra.cat; Carrer del Palau 5; small plates €8-14, lunch menu €15.50, tasting menu €32; ☺ 1-4pm & 7-11pm Wed-Sun; 🌐🍴; Ⓜ Jaume I) Slow Food advocates at Rasoterra cook up first-rate vegetarian dishes in a Zen-like setting – tall ceilings, low-playing jazz and fresh flowers on the tables. The creative, globally influenced menu changes regularly and might feature red corn tacos with mushrooms and avocado, mozzarella with crispy capers and preserved lemon, or violet potato and chickpea curry. Good vegan and gluten-free options too.

Koy Shunka
Japanese €€€

(Map p250; ☏ 93 412 79 39; www.koyshunka. com; Carrer de Copons 7; tasting menu €89-132; ☺ 1.30-3pm & 8.30-11pm Tue-Sat, 1.30-3pm Sun; Ⓜ Urquinaona) Down a narrow lane north of the cathedral, Koy Shunka opens a portal to exquisite dishes from the East – mouth-watering sushi, sashimi, seared Wagyu beef and flavour-rich seaweed salads are served alongside inventive cooked fusion dishes such as steamed clams with sake or tempura of scallops and king prawns with Japanese mushrooms. Don't miss the house speciality of tender *toro* (tuna belly).

Els Quatre Gats
Catalan €€€

(Map p250; ☏ 93 302 41 40; www.4gats.com; Carrer de Montsió 3; mains €17-65; ☺ 1-4pm & 7pm-1am; Ⓜ Urquinaona) Once the lair of

Barcelona's Modernista artists, Els Quatre Gats is a stunning example of the movement, inside and out, with its colourful tiles, geometric brickwork and wooden fittings. The restaurant is not quite as thrilling as its setting, but you can just have a coffee and a croissant in the cafe (open from 9am to 1am) at the front.

✪ El Raval

Granja M Viader
Cafe €

(Map p250; ☏ 93 318 34 86; www.granjaviader. cat; Carrer d'en Xuclà 6; ☺ 9am-1.15pm & 5-9.15pm Mon-Sat; Ⓜ Liceu) For more than a century, people have been coming here for hot chocolate with whipped cream (ask for a *suís*) ladled out in this classically Catalan milk bar. In 1931, the Viader clan invented Cacaolat, a bottled chocolate milk drink, with iconic label design. The interior here is delightfully old fashioned and the atmosphere always lively.

Veggie Garden
Vegan €

(Map p249; ☏ 93 180 23 34; https://veggie gardengroup.com; Carrer dels Àngels 3; mains €6.50-10; ☺ 12.30-11.30pm; 🍴; Ⓜ Liceu) The crowd at this vegan haunt is so young and woke you'd be forgiven for thinking you were in a student canteen, but don't let that stop you. Sit amid bright murals while charming staff serve a ridiculously good-value Indian-influenced menu including thalis, curries, salads, veggie burgers and pastas. There's another branch over on Gran Via de les Corts Catalanes.

Bar Muy Buenas
Catalan €

(Map p249; ☏ 93 807 28 57; http://muybuenas. cat; Carrer del Carme 63; mains €9-15; ☺ 1-3.30pm & 8-11pm Sun-Thu, 1-4pm & 8-11.30pm Fri & Sat; Ⓜ Liceu) Modernista classic Muy Buenas has been a bar since 1928, and wears its past proudly with stunning and sinuous original woodwork, etched-glass windows and a marble bar. Though the cocktails are impressive, these days it's more restaurant than bar, expertly turning out traditional Catalan dishes such as *esqueixada* (salad of shredded salted cod) and *fricandó* (pork and vegetable stew).

🍽 New Catalan Cuisine

Avant-garde chefs have made Catalonia famous throughout the world for their food laboratories, their commitment to food as art and their crazy riffs on the themes of traditional local cooking.

Here the notion of gourmet cuisine is deconstructed as chefs transform liquids and solid foods into foams, create 'ice cream' of classic ingredients by means of liquid nitrogen, freeze-dry foods to make concentrated powders and employ spherification to create unusual and artful morsels. This alchemical cookery is known as molecular gastronomy, and invention is the keystone of this technique.

Diners may encounter olive oil 'caviar', 'snow' made of gazpacho with anchovies, jellified Parmesan turned into spaghetti, and countless other concoctions.

The dining rooms themselves also offer a reconfiguration of the five-star dining experience. Restaurateurs generally aim to create warm and buzzing spaces, with artful design flourishes, and without the stuffiness and formality typically associated with high-end dining.

Molecular-gastronomy ceviche
AGE FOTOSTOCK/ALAMY STOCK PHOTO ©

Sésamo   Vegetarian €

(Map p249; 📞 93 441 64 11; Carrer de Sant Antoni Abat 52; mains €9-13; ⏰7pm-midnight Tue-Sun; 🛜🌿; Ⓜ Sant Antoni) Widely held to be one of the best veggie restaurants in the city, Sésamo is a cosy, fun place. The menu is mainly tapas, and most people go for the seven-course tapas menu (€25, wine included, minimum two people), but there are a few more substantial dishes. Nice touches include the home-baked bread and cakes.

Pinotxo Bar   Tapas €€

(Map p250; 📞93 317 17 31; www.pinotxobar.com; Mercat de la Boqueria, La Rambla 89; mains €9-17; ⏰6.30am-4pm Mon-Sat; Ⓜ Liceu) Pinotxo is arguably La Boqueria's, and even Barcelona's, best tapas bar. The ever-charming owner, Juanito, might serve up chickpeas with pine nuts and raisins, a soft mix of potato and spinach sprinkled with salt, soft baby squid with cannellini beans, or a quivering cube of caramel-sweet pork belly.

Flax & Kale   Health Food €€

(Map p249; 📞93 317 56 64; http://teresacarles. com/fk; Carrer dels Tallers 74b; mains €13-18; ⏰9am-11.30pm Mon-Fri, from 9.30am Sat & Sun; 🛜🌿; Ⓜ Universitat) Occupying a huge yet elegant space, Flax & Kale describes itself as a 'healthy flexitarian restaurant', meaning 80% of its menu is plant-based, 20% comprises oily fish, and there's an all-round emphasis on nutrition. Gluten-free and vegan options abound, and dishes include salmon mini-burgers and Panang red curry.

El Quim   Tapas €€

(Map p250; 📞93 301 98 10; http://elquimde laboqueria.com; Mercat de la Boqueria; mains €16-24; ⏰noon-4pm Mon & Wed, 8am-4pm Tue & Thu, 8am-5pm Fri & Sat; Ⓜ Liceu) This classic counter bar in the Mercat de la Boqueria is ideal for trying traditional Catalan dishes such as fried eggs with baby squid (the house speciality) or *escalivada* (smoky grilled vegetables). Daily specials are prepared using whatever is in season, and might include artichoke chips or sautéed wild mushrooms.

Can Lluís   Catalan €€

(Map p249; 📞93 441 11 87; www.restaurantcan lluis.cat; Carrer de la Cera 49; mains €10-22; ⏰1-4pm & 8.30-11.30pm Mon-Sat; Ⓜ Sant Antoni) Three generations have kept this spick-and-span old-time classic in business since 1929. Beneath the olive-green beams in the back dining room you can see the spot where an anarchist's bomb went off in 1946, killing the then owner. The restaurant is still going strong, however, with excellent seafood dishes and a good *menú del día* (€11.50).

Suculent
Catalan €€€

(Map p250; ☑93 443 65 79; https://suculent. com; Rambla del Raval 45; tasting menus €48-80; ☺1-4pm & 8-11.30pm Wed-Sun; ☎; ⓂLiceu) Celebrity chef Carles Abellan adds to his stable with this old-style bistro, which showcases the best of Catalan cuisine. From the prawn ceviche to the steak tartare over grilled bone marrow, only the best ingredients are used. There is no à la carte, just three different tasting menus to choose from.

La Barra del Suculent next door is more of a cocktail bar, but still offers updated versions of traditional tapas.

⊗ La Ribera

Paradiso/
Pastrami Bar
Cocktail Bar €

(Map p250; ☑639 310671; www.rooftopsmokehouse.com; Carrer de Rera Palau 4; mains €7-9; ☺7pm-1.15am Sun-Thu, to 2.15am Fri & Sat; ☎; ⓂBarceloneta) A kind of Narnia-in-reverse, Paradiso is fronted with a snowy-white space, not much bigger than a wardrobe, with pastrami sandwiches and other home-cured delights. But this is only the portal – pull open the huge wooden fridge door, and step through into a glam, sexy speakeasy of a cocktail bar guaranteed to raise the most world-weary of eyebrows.

Bar del Convent
Cafe €

(☑93 256 50 17; www.bardelconvent.com; Plaça de l'Acadèmia; ☺10am-9pm Tue-Sat; ⚇; ⓂArc de Triomf) Alongside the Gothic arches of what remains of the Sant Agusti convent cloister is this pleasant cafe-bar. It's particularly good for people with children – kids often play football in the cloister grounds, and there are children's books and toys in the cafe itself. You can also enter at Carrer del Comerç 36 through James Turrell's light installation.

En Aparté
French €

(☑93 269 13 35; www.enaparte.es; Carrer de Lluís el Piadós 2; mains €8-13; ☺10am-1am Mon-Thu, to 2am Fri & Sat, to 12.30am Sun; ☎; ⓂArc de Triomf) A great low-key place to eat good-quality French food, just off the quiet Plaça de Sant Pere. The restaurant is small but spacious, with sewing-machine tables and vintage details, and floor-to-ceiling windows that bring in some wonderful early-afternoon sunlight.

Cat Bar
Vegan €

(Map p250; www.catbarcat.com; Carrer de la Bòria 17; mains €6-9; ☺1-11pm Wed-Sat, 1-5pm Sun; ☎☑; ⓂJaume I) This small joint may be reminiscent of a local student bar, but it serves the best vegan burgers in the city. The selection includes a spicy Mexican burger with jalapeños, a nut burger with pesto and spinach, and a hemp burger with pickles. There's also a range of artisanal vegan beers and a gluten-free dish of the day.

Bormuth
Tapas €

(Map p250; ☑93 310 21 86; www.facebook.com/bormuthbarcelona; Carrer del Rec 31; tapas €4-10; ☺12.30pm-1.30am Sun-Thu, to 2.30am Fri & Sat; ☎; ⓂJaume I) Bormuth is a popular tapas bar clad in bare brick and recycled wood. It serves favourites from around Spain, including *pimientos de Padrón* (fried green peppers) and *buñelos de bacalao* (cod fritters). There is also homemade vermouth, a speciality, on tap.

Mag by El Magnífico
Cafe €

(Map p250; ☑93 488 57 86; www.facebook.com/magbyelmagnifico; Carrer de Grunyí 10; ☺10am-6pm Fri & Sat, from 11am Sun; ⓂJaume I) One of Barcelona's best coffee roasters, **El Magnífico** (☑93 319 60 81; www.cafeselmagnifico.com; Carrer de l'Argenteria 64; ☺9am-5pm Mon-Fri), now has its own cafe, so you can sit down and enjoy a cup. It's a hip space with bare stone walls, soft leather chairs and huge coffee roasting machines. Pair your freshly roasted blends with the decadent flaky pastries

from the nearby **Hofmann Pastisseria**
(☎93 268 82 21; www.hofmann-bcn.com; Carrer
dels Flassaders 44; ⏰9am-2pm & 3.30-8pm
Mon-Thu, 9am-2pm & 3.30-8.30pm Fri & Sat, to
2.30pm Sun; ⓂBarceloneta).

Bar del Pla   Tapas €€
(Map p250; ☎93 268 30 03; www.bardelpla.cat;
Carrer de Montcada 2; mains €12-16; ⏰noon-11pm
Mon-Thu, to midnight Fri & Sat; Ⓡ; ⓂJaume I) A
bright and occasionally rowdy place, with
glorious Catalan tiling, a vaulted ceiling and
bottles of wine lining the walls. The tapas
at informal Bar del Pla are traditionally
Spanish, but the riffs on a theme display
an assured touch. Try the ham croquettes,
Wagyu burger, T-bone steak or marinated
salmon, yoghurt and mustard.

Casa Delfín   Catalan €€
(Map p250; ☎93 319 50 88; www.casadelfin
restaurant.com; Passeig del Born 36; mains €12-
18; ⏰noon- midnight Sun-Thu, to 1am Fri & Sat;
Ⓡ; ⓂJaume I) One of Barcelona's culinary
delights, Casa Delfín is everything you dream
of when you think of Catalan (and Mediterranean) cooking. Start with salt-strewn *Padrón*
peppers, moving on to plump anchovies
from L'Escala in the Costa Brava, then tackle
suquet de los pescadores (traditional Catalan
fish stew; €14.50, minimum two people).

Cal Pep   Tapas €€
(Map p250; ☎93 310 79 61; www.calpep.com;
Plaça de les Olles 8; mains €13-20; ⏰7.30-11.30pm
Mon, 1-3.45pm & 7.30-11.30pm Tue-Sat, closed
last 3 weeks Aug; ⓂBarceloneta) It's getting
a foot in the door of this legendary tapas
and seafood restaurant that's the problem
– there can be queues out into the square.
And if you want one of the five tables out the
back, you'll need to call ahead. Most people
are happy elbowing their way to the bar for
some of the tastiest seafood tapas in town.

Euskal Etxea   Tapas €€
(Map p250; ☎93 310 21 85; www.euskaletxea
taberna.com; Placeta de Montcada 1; pintxos €2.10,
mains €14-26; ⏰bar 10am-12.30am Sun-Thu, to
1am Fri & Sat, restaurant 1-4pm Sun-Thu, 1-5pm &
7pm-midnight Fri & Sat; Ⓡ; ⓂJaume I) Barcelona

has plenty of Basque and pseudo-Basque
tapas bars, but this is the real deal, captur-
ing the feel of San Sebastián better than
many of its newer competitors. Choose
your *pintxos* (Basque tapas), sip *txakoli*
(Basque white wine) and keep the tooth-
picks so the staff can count them up for
your bill. There's also a restaurant section
serving main meals.

✪ Barceloneta, the Waterfront & El Poblenou

Can Maño   Seafood €
(Carrer del Baluard 12; mains €7-15; ⏰8-11pm
Mon, 8.30am-4pm & 8-11pm Tue-Fri, 8.30am-4pm
Sat; ⓂBarceloneta) It may look like a dive, but
you'll need to be prepared to wait before
being squeezed in at a packed table for a
raucous night of *raciones* (full-plate-size
tapas serving) over a bottle of cloudy white
turbio (Galician wine) at this family-run
stalwart. The seafood is abundant, with
first-rate squid, prawns and fish served at
rock-bottom prices.

La Cova Fumada   Tapas €
(☎93 221 40 61; Carrer del Baluard 56; tapas
€4-12; ⏰9am-3.15pm Mon-Wed, 9am-3.15pm &
6-8.15pm Thu & Fri, 9am-1pm Sat; ⓂBarceloneta)
There's no sign and the setting is decid-
edly downmarket, but this tiny, buzzing
family-run tapas spot always packs in a
crowd. The secret? Mouth-watering *pulpo*
(octopus), calamari, sardines, *bombas*
(meat and potato croquettes served with
aioli) and grilled *carxofes* (artichokes)
cooked in the open kitchen. Everything is
amazingly fresh.

Minyam   Seafood €€
(☎93 348 36 18; www.facebook.com/minyam
cisco; Carrer de Pujades 187; tapas €2-10, mains
€15-25; ⏰12.30pm-midnight Tue-Thu, to 2am Fri
& Sat, to 5pm Sun; 🛦; ⓂPoblenou) Billowing
with smoke beneath a tajine-like metal
lid, smouldering herbs infuse the rice of
Minyam's signature Vulcanus (smoked
seafood paella with squid ink). Tapas
dishes at this stylish, contemporary El

Poblenou restaurant are equally inventive and include asparagus fritters, oysters with sea urchin and lemon, fried anchovies and prawn tortillas. Crayons and paper are provided for kids.

Can Recasens   Catalan €€

(☑93 300 81 23; www.facebook.com/can recasens; Rambla del Poblenou 102; mains €8-21; ☺restaurant 8pm-1am; delicatessen 9.30am-1.30pm & 5pm-1am Mon-Fri, 9.30am-2pm & 5pm-1am Sat; Ⓜ Poblenou) One of El Poblenou's most romantic settings, Can Recasens hides a warren of warmly lit rooms full of oil paintings, flickering candles, fairy lights and baskets of fruit. The food is outstanding, with a mix of salads, smoked meats, fondues, and open sandwiches topped with delicacies like wild mushrooms and Brie, *escalivada* (grilled vegetables) and Gruyère, and spicy chorizo. There's live jazz every second Wednesday.

El 58   Tapas €€

(Le cinquante huit; ☑93 601 39 03; www.facebook. com/el58poblenou; Rambla del Poblenou 58; tapas €4-12; ☺1.30-11pm Tue-Sat, to 4pm Sun; Ⓜ Poblenou) This French-Catalan place serves imaginative, beautifully prepared tapas dishes: grilled turbot with romesco sauce and asparagus, scallop ceviche, sausage and chickpea stew, and duck magret. Solo diners can take a seat at the marble-topped front bar. The back dining room with its exposed brick walls, industrial light fixtures and local artworks is a lively place for a long meal.

Green Spot   Vegetarian €€

(Map p250; ☑93 802 55 65; www.encompania delobos.com/en/the-green-spot; Carrer de la Reina Cristina 12; mains €13-16.50; ☺1pm-midnight Mon-Thu & Sun, to 2am Fri & Sat; ☑; Ⓜ Barceloneta) Fried cauliflower with tamarind and mint sauce, quesadillas with kimchi and avocado, Ethiopian curry with injera bread, sweet potato tagliatelle with macadamia and black truffle sauce, and buckwheat pizza with cashew cheese and asparagus are among the inventive

🍽️ Seafood Heaven

There is a wealth of restaurants specialising in seafood. Not surprisingly, Barceloneta, which lies near the sea, is packed with eateries of all shapes and sizes doling out decadent paellas, cauldrons of bubbling molluscs, grilled catches of the day and other delights. Nearest the sea, you'll find pricier open-air places with Mediterranean views, while those on the main drag of Passeig Joan de Borbó mainly serve tourists. Instead, plunge into the narrow lanes to find the real gems, including bustling family-run places that serve first-rate plates at great prices.

Seafood paella
HLPHOTO/SHUTTERSTOCK ©

vegetarian, vegan and gluten-free dishes presented in a stylish, minimalist dining room with vaulted ceilings. Live music plays on Thursday evenings.

L'Òstia   Tapas €€

(☑93 221 47 58; www.facebook.com/barceloneta; Plaça de la Barceloneta 1; tapas €2.50-10, mains €9-16; ☺10am-11.45pm; ☎; Ⓜ Barceloneta) On a charming hidden square, this neighbourhood bar opens to a terrace facing Barceloneta's beautiful baroque church Església de Sant Miquel del Port. Tapas reflect the area's heritage but also come with fusion twists like seafood pappardelle or marinated sardines with orange. Wines are primarily Catalan; the sangría is some of the best around. A heated marquee sets up on the terrace in winter.

Aguaribay   Vegetarian €€
(☑93 300 37 90; www.aguaribay-bcn.com; Carrer del Taulat 95; mains €12-13; ⊘1-4pm Mon-Wed, 1-4pm & 8.30-11pm Thu, 1-4pm & 8-11.30pm Fri & Sat, 1-4.30pm Sun; ☑; MLlacuna) ✿ Polished Aguaribay serves a small well-executed à la carte menu by night: rice noodles with crispy tofu and peanut sauce, green lasagne with goat's cheese, and seasonal vegetables with rich black rice, along with craft beers and biodynamic wines. At lunchtime, stop in for the daily fixed price lunch specials. All ingredients are organic; vegan and gluten-free options abound.

Restaurant 7 Portes   Seafood €€€
(Map p250; ☑93 319 30 33; https://7portes.com; Passeig d'Isabel II 14; mains €19-32; ⊘1pm-1am; ☎; MBarceloneta) Founded in 1836 as a cafe and converted into a restaurant in 1929, 7 Portes has a grand setting beneath the cloisters, and exudes an old-world atmosphere with its wood panelling, tiles, mirrors and plaques naming luminaries – such as Orson Welles – who have passed through. Paella is the speciality, or try the *gran plat de marisc* ('big plate of seafood').

Can Solé   Seafood €€€
(☑93 221 50 12; http://restaurantcansole.com; Carrer de Sant Carles 4; mains €17-53; ⊘1-4pm & 8-11pm Tue-Thu, 1-4pm & 8.30-11pm Fri & Sat, 1-4pm Sun; MBarceloneta) Behind imposing wooden doors, this elegant restaurant with white-clothed tables and white-jacketed waiters has been serving seafood since 1903, and is now run by the fourth generation of owners. Freshly landed seafood stars in traditional dishes such as *arròs caldòs* (rice broth with squid and langoustines) and *zarzuela* (casserole with ground almonds, saffron, garlic, tomatoes, mussels, fish and white wine). Photos on the walls attest to the celebrities who have visited over the years.

La Barra de Carles Abellan   Seafood €€€
(☑93 760 51 29; www.carlesabellan.com/mis-restaurantes/la-barra; Passeig de Joan de Borbó 19; tapas €5-18, mains €22-36; ⊘1.30-4pm & 8-11pm Tue-Sat, 1.30-4pm Sun; MBarceloneta) Catalan chef Carles Abellán's stunning glass-encased, glossy-tiled restaurant celebrates seafood in tapas, such as pickled octopus and fried oyster with salmon roe. Even more show-stopping are the mains: grilled razor clams with *ponzu* citrus sauce, squid filled with spicy poached egg yolk, and stir-fried sea cucumber. Most seats are at long, communal counter-style tables, making it great for solo diners.

Torre d'Alta Mar   Mediterranean €€€
(☑93 221 00 07; www.torredealtamar.com; Torre de Sant Sebastià, Passeig de Joan de Borbó 88; mains €35-45, 7-/9-course menus €82/98, with wine €115/137; ⊘1-3.30pm & 7.30-11pm Tue-Thu, 1-3.30pm & 7.30-11.30pm Fri & Sat, 7.30-11pm Sun & Mon; ☐V15, 39, MBarceloneta) Head 75m skyward to the top of the 1929-built **Teleférico del Puerto** (p63) cable-car tower Torre de Sant Sebastià, and take a ringside seat for 360-degree views of the harbour, beaches, city and mountains. Menu highlights include salt-baked prawns, acorn-fed Iberian ham, and beef tartar with quail egg and mustard cream.

Can Ros   Seafood €€€
(☑93 221 45 79; www.canros.cat; Carrer del Almirall Aixada 7; mains €15-27; ⊘1-4pm & 7-11pm Tue-Sun; MBarceloneta) The fifth generation is now at the controls of this immutable seafood favourite, which first opened in 1908. In a restaurant where the decor is a reminder of simpler times, there's a straightforward guiding principle: juicy fresh fish cooked with a light touch.

Barraca   Seafood €€€
(☑93 224 12 53; www.tribuwoki.com; Passeig Marítim de la Barceloneta 1; mains €17-23; ⊘1-11.30pm; ☑; MBarceloneta) ✿ Opening to an elevated terrace, this buzzing space has mesmerising views over the Mediterranean – a key reference point in the all-organic dishes served here. Start off with a cauldron of chilli-infused clams, cockles and mussels before moving on to the lavish rice dishes. There are some good vegetarian options and it's one of Barcelona's few places serving vegan paella.

Pinotxo Bar (p138)

Can Majó   Seafood €€€

(☏93 221 54 55; www.canmajo.es; Carrer del
Almirall Aixada 23; mains €15-36; ⊙1-4pm &
8-11.30pm Tue-Sat, 1-4pm Sun; Ⓜ Barceloneta)
On a square across from the beachside
promenade, with outdoor tables and heat
lamps in winter, Can Majó has a long and
steady reputation for fine seafood, particularly its rice dishes and bountiful *suquets*
(fish stews). The bouillabaisse of fish and
seafood is succulent.

⊗ L'Eixample

Copasetic   Cafe €

(Map p249; ☏93 532 76 66; www.copasetic
barcelona.com; Carrer de la Diputació 55; mains
€6-13.50; ⊙10.30am- midnight Tue & Wed, to
1am Thu, to 2am Fri & Sat, to 5.30pm Sun; 🛜🖊;
Ⓜ Rocafort) Decked out with retro furniture,
Copasetic has a fun, friendly vibe. The
menu holds plenty for everyone, whether
your thing is eggs Benedict, wild-berry
tartlets or a fat, juicy burger. There are lots
of vegetarian, gluten-free and organic options, and superb (and reasonably priced)

weekend brunches. Lunch *menús* (Tuesday
to Friday) cost between €9.50 and €12.

Tapas 24   Tapas €

(Map p254; ☏93 488 09 77; www.carles
abellan.com; Carrer de la Diputació 269; tapas
€4-12; ⊙9am- midnight; 🛜; Ⓜ Passeig de
Gràcia) Hotshot chef Carles Abellán runs
this basement tapas haven known for its
gourmet versions of old faves. Highlights
include the *bikini* (toasted ham-and-cheese
sandwich – here the ham is cured and the
truffle makes all the difference) and zesty
boquerones al limón (lemon-marinated
anchovies). You can't book, and service can
be slow, but it's worth the wait.

Cremeria Toscana   Gelato €

(☏93 539 38 25; www.cremeriatoscana.es; Carrer
de Muntaner 161; ice cream €3-5.50; ⊙1pm-mid-
night Mon-Thu, to 1am Fri & Sat, noon-midnight Sun
Apr-Oct, 1-9pm Tue-Thu, to 11pm Fri & Sat, noon-
11pm Sun Nov-Mar; Ⓜ Hospital Clínic) At the most
authentic gelato outlet in town, all flavours
are natural and most are gluten-free. Along
with classic Italian choices such as creamy
stracciatella and wavy hazelnut *nocciola* are

more unusual offerings such as goat cheese and caramelised fig. Buy a cone or a tub.

Entrepanes Díaz
Sandwiches €€

(Map p254; ☎93 415 75 82; www.facebook.com/entrepanesdiaz; Carrer de Pau Claris 189; sandwiches €6-10, tapas €3-10; ☺1pm-midnight; ⓂDiagonal) Gourmet sandwiches, from roast beef to suckling pig or crispy squid with squid-ink aioli, are the highlight at this sparkling old-style bar, along with sharing plates of Spanish specialities such as sea urchins and prawn fritters or blood-sausage croquettes. Service is especially charming and B&W photos of Barcelona line the walls.

Casa Amalia
Catalan €€

(Map p254; ☎93 458 94 58; www.casamaliabcn.com; Passatge del Mercat 4-6; mains €9-20; ☺1-3.30pm & 9-10.30pm Tue-Sat, 1-3.30pm Sun; ⓂGirona) This very local split-level restaurant is popu-lar for its hearty Catalan cooking that uses fresh produce from the busy market next door. On Thursdays during winter it of-fers the mountain classic, *escudella* (Catalan stew). Otherwise, try light variations on local cuisine like the *bacallà al allioli de poma* (cod in apple-based aioli sauce). The three-course *menú del día* is a bargain at €15.50.

Lasarte
Modern European €€€

(Map p254; ☎93 445 32 42; www.restaurantlasarte.com; Carrer de Mallorca 259; mains €52-70; ☺1.30-3pm & 8.30-10pm Tue-Sat; ⓂDiagonal) One of the preeminent restaurants in Barcelona – and the city's first to gain three Michelin stars – Lasarte is overseen by lauded chef Martín Berasategui. From Duroc pig's trotters with quince to squid tartare with kaffir consommé, this is seriously sophisticated stuff, served in an ultra-contemporary dining room by waiting staff who could put the most overawed diners at ease.

Disfrutar
Modern European €€€

(☎93 348 68 96; www.disfrutarbarcelona.com; Carrer de Villarroel 163; tasting menus €150-190; ☺1-2.30pm & 8-9.30pm Mon-Fri; ⓂHospital Clínic) Disfrutar ('Enjoy' in Catalan) is among the city's finest restaurants, with two Michelin stars. Run by alumni of Ferran Adrià's

game-changing (now closed) El Bulli restaurant, nothing is as it seems, such as black and green olives that are actually chocolate ganache with orange-blossom water.

Mont Bar
Bistro €€€

(Map p254; ☎93 323 95 90; www.montbar.com; Carrer de la Diputació 220; tapas €4-14, mains €12.50-29; ☺1-4pm & 7-11.30pm Wed-Mon; ⓂUniversitat) Named for the owner's Val d'Aran hometown, this stylish wine-bar-style space with black-and-white floors, forest-green banquette and bottle-lined walls offers next-level cooking. Exquisite tapas (a pork-and-baby shrimp sandwich; French oyster with apple and beetroot) precede small-plate mains (tuna belly with pine-nut emulsion) and show-stopping desserts (Jerusalem artichoke and coffee taco). Reservations recommended.

Cinc Sentits
International €€€

(☎93 323 94 90; www.cincsentits.com; Carrer d'Entença 60; tasting menus €100-120; ☺1.30-3pm & 8.30-9.30pm Tue-Sat; ⓂRocafort) Enter the realm of the 'Five Senses' to indulge in a jaw-dropping tasting menu consisting of a series of small, experimental dishes (there is no à la carte, although dishes can be tweaked to suit requests). The use of fresh local produce, such as Costa Brava line-caught fish and top-quality Extremadura suckling pig, is key.

Speakeasy
International €€€

(☎93 217 50 80; www.drymartiniorg.com; Carrer d'Aribau 162; mains €18.50-28; ☺8-11.30pm Mon-Sat; ⒻFGC Provença) This clandestine restaurant with a tempting menu lurks behind the Dry Martini bar (p183). You will be shown a door through the open kitchen area to the 'storeroom', lined with hundreds of bottles of back-lit quality tipples.

Monvínic
Spanish €€€

(Map p254; ☎93 272 61 87; www.monvinic.com; Carrer de la Diputació 249; mains €16-36; ☺1.30-3.30pm & 8-10.30pm Tue-Fri, 8-10.30pm Mon & Sat; ⓂPasseig de Gracia) ✿ Opening to a leafy, ta-ble- filled garden, this is the *espacio culinario* of world-famous wine emporium **Monvínic** (☺1-11pm Tue-Fri, 7-11pm Mon & Sat). The menu offers elaborate confections, such as scallop with a mushroom velouté, beef sweetbreads with hazelnuts and potato confit, or rabbit stew. Its ingredients, wine and building materials are all sourced from Catalonia.

⊗ Montjuïc, Poble Sec & Sant Antoni

Federal   Cafe €

(Map p256; ☏93 187 36 07; www.federalcafe.es; Carrer del Parlament 39; mains €9-12; ⊗8am-11pm Mon-Thu, to 1am Fri, 9am-1am Sat, 9am-5.30pm Sun; ☢☑; Ⓜ Sant Antoni) On a stretch that now teems with cafes, Australian-run Federal was the trailblazer, with its good coffee (including a decent flat white) and superb brunches. Later in the day, healthy, tasty options span snacks (prawn toast, polenta chips with gorgonzola) to larger dishes like veggie burgers or grilled salmon with soba noodles. Head to the small, breezy roof terrace.

Quimet i Quimet   Tapas €€

(Map p256; ☏93 442 31 42; www.facebook.com/quimetyquimet; Carrer del Poeta Cabanyes 25; tapas €4-10, montaditos €3-4; ⊗noon-4pm & 7-10.30pm Mon-Fri, noon-4pm Sat, closed Aug; Ⓜ Paral·lel) Quimet i Quimet is a family-run business that has been passed down from generation to generation. There's barely space to swing a *calamar* (squid) in this bottle-lined, standing-room-only place, but it is a treat for the palate, with *montaditos* (tapas on a slice of bread) made to order.

Mano Rota   Bistro €€

(Map p256; ☏93 164 80 41; www.manorota.com; Carrer de la Creu dels Molers 4; mains €18-21; ⊗8-11.30pm Mon, 1-3.30pm & 8-11.30pm Tue-Sat; Ⓜ Poble Sec) Exposed brick, aluminium pipes, indus- trial light fittings and recycled timbers create a hip, contemporary setting for inspired bistro cooking at Mano Rota (which literally translates as 'broken hand' but is actually a Spanish idiom for consummate skill). Asian, South American and Mediterranean flavours combine in dishes such as beef rib with satay sauce or prawns with Peruvian peppers.

Lascar 74   Peruvian €€

(Map p256; ☏93 017 98 72; www.lascar.es; Carrer del Roser 74; mains €12-15; ⊗7pm-midnight Mon-Fri, 2pm-midnight Sat, 2-10pm Sun; Ⓜ Paral·lel) At this self-styled 'ceviche and pisco bar', oyster shooters with *leche de tigre* (traditional ceviche marinade) are served alongside exquisite Peruvian ceviches and renditions from Thailand, Japan and Mexico. Pisco sours are the real deal, frothy egg white and all.

Malamén   Catalan €€

(Map p256; ☏93 252 77 63; www.malamen.es; Carrer de Blai 53; mains €12-24; ⊗7.30pm-midnight Tue-Sun; Ⓜ Poble Sec) Carrer de Blai is lined with bars and restaurants, but Malamén towers above most for its elegant art-deco-inspired design, immaculate service and gourmet versions of Catalan classics. Its shortish menu offers confit tuna, dill and caper salad, juicy steak with creamed mushrooms and croquettes of the day; the wine list is equally concise.

Bodega 1900   Tapas €€

(Map p256; ☏93 325 26 59; www.bodega1900. com; Carrer de Tamarit 91; tapas €6-15; ⊗1-4pm & 7-10.30pm Tue-Sat; Ⓜ Poble Sec) Bodega 1900 mimics an old-school tapas and vermouth bar, but don't be fooled: this venture from the world-famous Adrià brothers creates gastronomic tapas such as 'spherified' reconstructed olives, or its *mollete de calamars*, probably the best squid sandwich in the world, hot from the pan and served with chipotle mayonnaise, kimchi and lemon zest.

Palo Cortao   Tapas €€

(Map p256; ☏93 188 90 67; www.palocortao. es; Carrer Nou de la Rambla 146; mains €10-17; ⊗8pm-1am Tue-Fri, 1-5pm & 8pm-1am Sat & Sun; Ⓜ Paral·lel) Contemporary Palo Cortao is renowned for its beautifully executed seafood and meat dishes, served at fair prices. Highlights include truffled free-range chicken cannelloni, octopus with white-bean hummus, squid with ink mayonnaise and tuna tataki tempura. Its long wooden bar with metal stools is ideal for solo diners. Friendly English-speaking staff can guide you through the menu and wine list.

Barcelona on a Plate

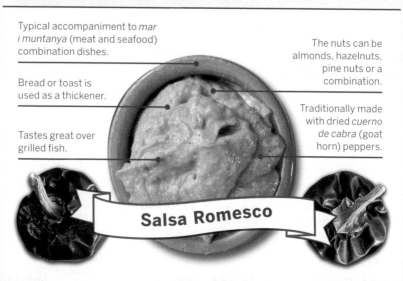

Typical accompaniment to *mar i muntanya* (meat and seafood) combination dishes.

Bread or toast is used as a thickener.

Tastes great over grilled fish.

The nuts can be almonds, hazelnuts, pine nuts or a combination.

Traditionally made with dried *cuerno de cabra* (goat horn) peppers.

Salsa Romesco

NITO/SHUTTERSTOCK ©

A Catalan Classic

This classic Catalan sauce pervades the region's cuisine, popping up in numerous dishes as an accompaniment to roasted vegetables, grilled meats and fish. It's a rich, garlicky, nutty combination based on peppers and tomatoes. A thickened version, *salvitxada*, is the de rigueur dipping accompaniment for the late-winter barbecues of *calçots*, the delicious leek-like onions beloved by Catalans.

Calcots with salsa romesco
ALEXANDRE AROCAS/SHUTTERSTOCK ©

Top Five Spots to Try Romesco

El 58 (p141) This French-Catalan place serves imaginative, beautifully prepared tapas dishes.

Vivanda (p149) Magnificent Catalan cooking with dishes showcasing seasonal fare.

Belmonte (p136) This tiny tapas joint in the southern reaches of Barri Gòtic whips up beautifully prepared small plates.

Casa Delfín (p140) A culinary delight, this place is everything you dream of when you think of Catalan (and Mediterranean) cooking.

Taverna El Glop (p148) The secret to this raucous restaurant is no-nonsense, slap-up meals.

Oleum — Mediterranean €€

(Map p256; ☎93 289 06 79; http://oleum-barcelona.com; 1st fl, Museu Nacional d'Art de Catalunya (MNAC); mains €16-25; ⏰12.30-4pm Tue-Thu & Sun, 12.30-4pm & 8.30-11pm Fri & Sat; ☐55, ⓂEspanya) Situated in the former throne room of the Palau Nacional, Oleum has soaring ceilings and gorgeous city views. The regularly changing Mediterranean menu is small but well executed. A meal here combines perfectly with a visit to the Museu Nacional d'Art de Catalunya (p56) where the restaurant resides (although no museum ticket is required to dine here).

La Font del Gat — Mediterranean €€

(Map p256; ☎93 289 04 04; Passeig de Santa Madrona 28; 3-course menu €16; ⏰10am-6pm Tue-Fri, noon-6pm Sat & Sun; ☐55) Set on the edge of the Jardins de Laribal, La Font del Gat's lovely, spacious terrace is dotted with orange trees and surrounded by greenery. It has a daily changing menu (there's no à la carte); dishes might include cinnamon-and-lemon- marinated chicken or grilled tuna with caper butter. There's always a vegetarian option such as vegetable and goat-cheese risotto.

Enigma — Gastronomy €€€

(Map p256; ☎616 696322; www.enigmaconcept.es; Carrer de Sepúlveda 38-40; tasting menu €220; ⏰7-9.30pm Tue-Fri, 1-2.30pm & 7-9.30pm Sat; ⓂEspanya) Resembling a 3D art installation, this conceptual offering from the famed Adrià brothers is a 40-course tour de force of cutting-edge gastronomy across six dining spaces. A meal takes 3½ hours and includes customised cocktail pairings (you can order additional drinks). There's a minimum of two diners; reserve months in advance. A €100 deposit per guest is required upon booking.

Tickets — Tapas, Gastronomy €€€

(Map p256; ☎93 292 42 52; www.ticketsbar.es; Avinguda del Paral·lel 164; tapas €3-30; ⏰6.30pm-midnight Tue-Fri, 1-3.30pm & 7pm-midnight Sat; ⓂPoble Sec) A flamboyant affair playing with circus images and theatre lights, this is one of the sizzling tickets in the restaurant world: a Michelin-starred tapas bar opened by Ferran Adrià, of the legendary (since closed) El Bulli, and his brother Albert. Bookings are only taken online 60 days in advance, but you can try calling for last-minute cancellations.

Martínez — Spanish €€€

(Map p256; ☎93 106 60 52; www.martinezbarcelona.com; Carretera de Miramar 38; mains €22-35; ⏰1-11pm; ☐150, 🚠Teleférico del Puerto) With a fabulous panorama over the city and port, Martínez is a standout among the lacklustre dining options atop Montjuïc. On warm days, head to the outdoor terrace for its signature rice and paella dishes (€34 to €77 for two). There are also oysters, calamari, fresh market fish and other seafood hits, plus *jamón* and grilled meat dishes.

⊗ Gràcia & Park Güell

Chivuo's — Burgers €

(☎93 218 51 34; www.chivuos.com; Carrer del Torrent de l'Olla 175; burgers €8.50-13.75; ⏰1-5pm & 7pm-midnight Mon-Sat; ⓂFontana) Burgers and craft beers make a fine pair at this buzzing den. A mostly local crowd comes for huge burgers (including veggie burger and Philly cheese steak) with house-made sauces – ordered with fluffy, golden-fried *fritas* (chips). Mostly Catalan and Spanish brews, including excellent offerings from Barcelona-based Edge Brewing, Catalan Brewery, Napar and Garage Beer, rotate on the eight taps.

Las Delicias — Spanish €

(☎93 429 22 02; www.barrestaurantedelicias.com; Carrer de Mühlberg 1; tapas €4-13, mains €9-14; ⏰10am-4pm Tue-Sun & 7-10.30pm Tue-Thu, 8-11pm Fri & Sat; ⓂEl Carmel, then bus 86) This welcoming restaurant on a hillside in El Carmel makes a fine add-on to an afternoon exploring either nearby Park Güell or the Bunkers del Carmel. There's a decent selection of tapas on offer as well as heartier grilled meat and seafood dishes. Standouts include classics such as *pulpo a gallega* (Galician-style octopus), *jamón ibérico* (cured Iberian ham) and fluffy paella.

La Nena
Cafe €

(Map p254; ☑93 285 14 76; https://la-nena-chocolate-cafe. business.site; Carrer de Ramon y Cajal 36; dishes €2-4.50; ⊙8.30am-10.30pm Mon-Fri, 9am-10.30pm Sat & from 9.30am Sun; ♿; MFontana) At this delightfully chaotic space, indulge in cups of *suïssos* (rich hot chocolate) served with a plate of heavy homemade whipped cream and *melindros* (spongy sweet biscuits), desserts and a few savoury dishes (including crêpes). You can also play the board games on the shelves.

Bar Bodega Quimet
Tapas €

(☑93 218 41 89; Carrer de Vic 23; tapas €3-11.50; ⊙10am-11.30pm Mon-Fri, noon-11.30pm Sat & Sun; MFontana) A remnant from a bygone age, this is a delightfully atmospheric spot, with old bottles lining the walls, marble tables and a burnished wooden bar. The list of tapas is almost exhaustive and it specialises in *conservas* (canned seafood), as well as fresh anchovies and octopus.

Café Godot
International €€

(Map p254; ☑93 368 20 36; www.cafegodot.com; Carrer de Sant Domènec 19; mains €10-18.50; ⊙10am-1am Mon-Fri, 11am-2am Sat & Sun; MFontana) A stylish space of exposed brick, timber and tiles, opening to a garden out back, Godot is a relaxing place with an extensive menu, ranging from white-wine-steamed mussels and duck confit with lentils and spinach to aubergine-and-onion-stuffed ravioli. Their weekend brunch menu features favourites such as eggs Benedict, avocado toast and fluffy banana pancakes.

La Panxa del Bisbe
Tapas €€

(Map p254; ☑93 313 70 49; Carrer del Torrent de les Flors 158; tapas €7.50-15, tasting menus €30-37; ⊙1.30-3.30pm & 8.30pm-midnight Tue-Sat; MJoanic) With low lighting and an minimalist interior, the 'Bishop's Belly' serves creative tapas that earn high praise from locals and visitors. Feast on prawn-stuffed courgette flowers, grilled octopus with green chilli and watermelon, and slow-roasted lamb with mint couscous. Top off the meal with a bottle of wine (by-the-glass options are more limited).

Taverna El Glop
Catalan €€

(Map p254; ☑93 213 70 58; www.elglop.com; Carrer de Sant Lluís 24; mains €8-20; ⊙1pm-midnight Mon-Fri, from 12.30pm Sat & Sun; MJoanic) This raucous restaurant is decked out in country Catalan fashion with gingham tablecloths and slap-up meals. The secret is hearty portions of simple dishes, such as *cordero a la brasa* (grilled lamb), *paella de pescado y marisco* (fish and seafood paella) and starters like *berenjenas rellenas* (stuffed aubergines).

Pepa Tomate
Tapas €€

(Map p254; ☑93 210 46 98; www.pepatomate grup.com; Plaça de la Revolució de Setembre de 1868 17; sharing plates €7-17; ⊙8pm-midnight Mon, from 9am Tue-Fri, from 10am Sat, from 11am Sun; ♿; MFontana) This casual tapas spot on Plaça de la Revolució de Setembre de 1868 is popular at all hours of the day. Fresh produce takes front and centre on the wide-ranging menu in dishes like fried green tomatoes, Andalucian baby squid, tandoori lamb tacos, Iberian pork or mushroom, croquettes, and carrot gazpacho in summer.

Con Gracia
Fusion €€€

(Map p254; ☑93 238 02 01; www.congracia.es; Carrer de Martínez de la Rosa 8; tasting menus €65, with wine €95; ⊙7-11pm Tue-Sat; MDiagonal) This teeny hideaway (seating about 20) is a hive of originality, producing delicately balanced Mediterranean cuisine with Asian touches. On offer is a regularly changing surprise tasting menu or the set 'traditional' one (both six courses), with dishes such as squid stuffed with *jamón ibérico* and black truffle, and sake-marinated tuna with walnut pesto. Book ahead.

Roig Robí
Catalan €€€

(Map p254; ☑93 218 92 22; www.roigrobi.com; Carrer de Sèneca 20; mains €21-36; ⊙1.30-4pm & 8.30-11.30pm Mon-Fri, 8.30-11.30pm Sat; P; MDiagonal) At this altar to refined traditional cooking, the seasonally changing menu serves as a showcase for beautifully presented creations with local, organic ingredients. Dishes may include sautéed wild mushrooms to start, followed by outstanding seafood rice dishes, salt-baked market-fresh fish or slow-roasted Pyrenees lamb. Call ahead to reserve a table on the vine-draped back patio.

Botafumeiro　　　　　Seafood €€€

(☑93 218 42 30; www.botafumeiro.es; Carrer Gran de Gràcia 81; mains €22-59; ☺1pm-1am; MFontana) This temple of Galician shellfish has long been a magnet for VIPs visiting Barcelona. You can bring the price down by sharing a few *medias raciones* (large tapas plates) to taste a range of marine offerings, followed by mains like spider crab pie, squid-ink paella or grilled spiny lobster.

✪ Camp Nou, Pedralbes & La Zona Alta

Mitja Vida　　　　　　Tapas €

(www.morrofi.cat; Carrer de Brusi 39; tapas €3-7; ☺6-11pm Mon-Thu, noon-4pm & 6-11pm Fri & Sat, noon-4pm Sun, closed Aug; ℝFGC Sant Gervasi) A young, fun, mostly local crowd gathers around the stainless-steel tapas bar of tiny Mitja Vida. It's a jovial eating and drinking spot, with good-sized portions of anchovies, calamari, smoked herring, cheeses and *mojama* (salt-cured tuna). The drink of choice is house-made vermouth.

Acontraluz　　　　Mediterranean €€

(☑93 203 06 58; www.acontraluz.com; Carrer del Milanesat 19; mains €15-25; ☺1.30-4pm & 8.30-11pm Mon-Sat, 1.30-4pm Sun; ℝFGC Les Tres Torres) This romantic, bougainvillea-draped, tree-filled garden, reached by an arbour, is the most magical place to dine. Salmon with a tangerine and tamarind emulsion, octopus with a parsnip purée and almonds, and carpaccio of veal with Parmesan, rocket and pine nuts are all outstanding choices.

Aspic　　　　　　　Cafe, Deli €€

(☑93 200 04 35; www.aspic.es; Avinguda de Pau Casals 24; dishes €10-20; ☺cafe 11am-1.30pm & 6-8.30pm Tue-Sat, 11am-4pm Sun, deli 9am-8pm Tue-Sat, to 4pm Sun, bar to midnight Tue-Sat, to 4pm Sun; ☺☑; ☐T1, T2, T3 Francesc Macià) Luxury ingredients (smoked salmon, premium charcuterie and cheeses, high-grade olive oils and carefully

chosen Spanish wines) are utilised at the flagship cafe of this Barcelona caterer in stunning dishes like local carrelet fish with cockle foam and broccoli purée. The attached deli is perfect for picking up items for a gourmet picnic in nearby Jardins del Poeta Eduard Marquina.

Vivanda　　　　　　Catalan €€

(☑93 203 19 18; www.vivanda.cat; Carrer Major de Sarrià 134; sharing plates €9-22; ☺1.30-3.30pm & 8.30-11pm Tue-Sat, 1.30-3.30pm Sun; ℝFGC Reina Elisenda) Diners are in for a treat with this menu designed by acclaimed Catalan chef Jordi Vilà. Changing dishes showcase seasonal fare, such as black rice with crayfish, and smoked salmon with hibiscus and cucumber. Hidden behind the restaurant is the tree-shaded terrace, which opens year-round – heat lamps are switched on in winter, and blankets and broth are distributed to diners.

La Balsa　　　　Mediterranean €€€

(☑93 211 50 48; www.labalsarestaurant.com; Carrer de la Infanta Isabel 4; mains €21-28; ☺1.30-3.30pm & 8.30-11pm Tue-Sat, 1.30-3.30pm Sun; ☺; ℝFGC Avinguda Tibidabo) With its grand ceiling and the scented gardens that surround the main terrace dining area, La Balsa is one of the city's premier dining addresses. The seasonally changing menu is a mix of traditional Catalan and creative expression (suckling pig with apple and cardamom, scallops with cabbage and Iberian pork loin). Lounge over a cocktail at the bar before dinner.

Via Veneto　　　　Gastronomy €€€

(☑93 200 72 44; www.viavenetobarcelona.com; Carrer de Ganduxer 10; mains €29-48; ☺1-4pm & 8-11.45pm Mon-Fri, 8-11.45pm Sat, closed Aug– mid-Sep; ℝFGC La Bonanova) Dalí was a regular in this high-society restaurant after it opened in 1967, and you can still dine at his favourite table today. The oval mirrors, orange-rose tablecloths, leather chairs and fine cutlery set the stage for intricate dishes such as prawn tartare with minced black bread and the signature roast duck. The cellar has over 1800 Spanish wines.

TREASURE HUNT

Begin your shopping adventure

Treasure Hunt

If your doctor has prescribed an intense round of retail therapy to deal with the blues, then Barcelona is the place for you. Across Ciutat Vella (Barri Gòtic, El Raval and La Ribera), L'Eixample and Gràcia is spread with a thick mantle of boutiques, historic shops, original one-off stores, gourmet corners, wine dens and designer labels. You name it, you'll find it here.

For high fashion, design, jewellery and department stores, the principal shopping axis starts on Plaça de Catalunya, proceeds up Passeig de Gràcia and turns left into Avinguda Diagonal, along which it extends as far as Plaça de la Reina Maria Cristina. The densely packed section between Plaça de Francesc Macià and Plaça de la Reina Maria Cristina is an especially good hunting ground.

In This Section

Useful Phrases

I'd like to buy ...	*Quería comprar ...*	ke·ria kom·prar ...
I'm just looking	*Sólo estoy mirando*	so·lo es·toy mee·ran·do
Can I look at it?	*¿Puedo verlo?*	pwe·do ver·lo
Do you have other sizes?	*¿Tienes más tallas?*	tee·en·es mas·tie·yas
How much is it?	*¿Cuánto cuesta?*	kwan·to kwes·ta

Previous page: Sombrerería Obach (p158)

Gràcia & Park Güell
A bit of everything in this intriguing, locally focused district
(p164)

Camp Nou, Pedralbes & La Zona Alta
Large-scale shops and the FC Barcelona stadium store
(p168)

L'Eixample
Big-name designers and upmarket boutiques
(p161)

La Ribera
Great market and numerous gourmet food outlets
(p159)

Port Olímpic

El Raval
Alternative, bohemian design, clothing and vintage stores
(p158)

La Rambla & Barri Gòtic
Intriguing quirky shops on narrow lanes among tourist traps
(p156)

Barceloneta, the Waterfront & El Poblenou
Great flea market and craft market choices
(p160)

Montjuïc, Poble Sec & Sant Antoni
Small, quirky boutiques, pop-ups and cutting-edge streetwear
(p164)

Port Vell

Mediterranean Sea

Opening Hours

In general, shops are open between 9am or 10am and 1.30pm or 2pm, and then again from around 4pm or 4.30pm to 8pm or 8.30pm Monday to Friday. Many shops keep the same hours on Saturday, although some don't bother with the evening session.

Large supermarkets, malls and department stores stay open all day Monday to Saturday, from about 10am to 10pm.

Many fashion boutiques and design stores open from about 10am to 8pm Monday to Saturday.

A few shops open on Sundays and holidays – this number increases in the run-up to key consumer holiday periods.

Sales Seasons

Winter sales start after Reis (6 January) and, depending on the shop, can go on well into February. Summer sales start in July, with shops trying to entice locals to part with one last wad of euros before summer holidays. Some shops prolong sales to the end of August. Barcelona has also succumbed to the Black Friday sales craze around the last Friday in November.

The Best...

Experience Barcelona's
best shopping

Fashion

Holala! Plaza (p158) Nowhere has a better vintage selection than Holala!

Bagués-Masriera (p163) Exquisite jewellery from a company with a long tradition.

Custo Barcelona (p160; picutred) Quirky, colourful clothes that are not for the shy.

Loisaida (p159) Cute, smart and somewhat retro clothing for men and women.

Markets

Mercat de la Boqueria (p50) The quintessential Barcelona food market.

Mercat de Santa Caterina (p110) A colourful alternative to La Boqueria, with fewer crowds and lower prices.

Mercat dels Encants (p160) A sprawling flea market in a modern building.

El Bulevard dels Antiquaris (p163) A labyrinth of tiny antique shops that merits a morning's browsing.

Mercat de Sant Antoni (p164) A neighbourhood market that's back in business after a beautiful restoration.

Design & Craft

Drap-Art (p157) Weird and wonderful recycled art and accessories.

Arlequí Màscares (p159) Handmade masks to rival any in Venice – the perfect souvenir.

Fantastik (p158) A temple to kitsch, with kooky wonders from all around the world.

Teranyina (p159) The 'Spider's Web', so called for its intricate textile designs.

Vintage

L'Arca (p156) Ethereal gowns, often used for film sets, in the heart of the Barri Gòtic.

El Bulevard dels Antiquaris (p163) A quirky hotchpotch of antique shops.

Mercat dels Encants (p160) Flea market where you can unearth retro homeware and kitschy bric-a-brac.

Port Antic (p160) A quirky street market with finds from vintage toys to tiny oil paintings.

Souvenirs & Gifts

El Born Centre de Cultura i Memòria (p84; pictured) The gift shop at this exhibition space stocks tasteful, well-made souvenirs and books about the city.

Les Topettes (p158) Creams, oils, perfumes and soaps that look every bit as tantalising as they smell.

Sabater Hermanos (p156) Divinely fragranced shop selling handmade soaps in pretty gift boxes.

MACBA (p94) The modern art museum's gift shop has some colourful and covetable books and gifts.

Food & Wine

Casa Gispert (p111) The speciality is roast nuts of every type, but you'll also find chocolate, conserves and olive oils.

Vila Viniteca (p111; pictured) A jaw- dropping cathedral of wines from Catalonia and elsewhere in Spain, tucked away in a Born side street.

Formatgeria La Seu (p156) Superb cheeses from small producers.

Caelum (p134) Delicious sweet treats made by nuns, has a tea room downstairs.

Lonely Planet's Top Choices

Vila Viniteca (p111) Oenophiles unite at this wonderful wine shop.

Coquette (p159) Simple and beautiful designer clothes for women.

Loisaida (p159) Men's and women's fashion, antiques and retro vinyl.

Mercat de Santa Caterina (p110) Stock up on delicacies at this vibrant food market.

⊕ La Rambla & Barri Gòtic

Torrons Vicens — Food

(Map p250; ☑93 252 80 00; www.vicens.com; Carrer del Petritxol 15; ☺10am-8.30pm Mon-Sat, 11am-8pm Sun; Ⓜ Liceu) You can find a *turrón* (nougat) treat year-round at Torrons Vicens, which has been selling its signature sweets since 1775. As well as classic almond flavours, there are also unusual kinds such as mojito and curry. There are several branches located around the city.

Sabater Hermanos — Cosmetics

(Map p250; ☑93 301 98 32; www.sabaterhermanos. es; Plaça de Sant Felip Neri 1; ☺10.30am-9pm; Ⓜ Jaume I) This fragrant little shop sells handcrafted soaps of all sizes. Varieties such as fig, cinnamon, grapefruit and chocolate smell good enough to eat, while sandalwood, magnolia, mint, cedar and jasmine add spice to any sink or bathtub.

Escribà — Food & Drinks

(Map p250; ☑93 301 60 27; www.escriba.es; La Rambla 83; ☺9am-9.30pm; 🛜; Ⓜ Liceu) Chocolates, dainty pastries and mouth-watering cakes can be nibbled behind the Modernista mosaic facade here or taken away for private, guilt-ridden consumption. This Barcelona favourite is owned by the Escribà family, a name synonymous with sinfully good sweet things. More than that, it adds a touch of authenticity to La Rambla.

Formatgeria La Seu — Food

(Map p250; ☑93 412 65 48; www.formatgeria laseu.com; Carrer de la Dagueria 16; ☺10am-2pm & 5-8pm Tue-Sat; Ⓜ Jaume I) Dedicated to artisan cheeses from across Spain, this small shop is run by the oh-so-knowledgeable Katherine McLaughlin. The antithesis of mass production, it sells only the best from small-scale farmers and the stock changes regularly. Wine and cheese tastings in the cosy room at the back are fun.

El Corte Inglés — Department Store

(Map p250; ☑93 306 38 00; www.elcorteingles. es; Av del Portal de l'Àngel 19-21; ☺9.30am-9pm Mon-Sat Oct-May, 9.30am-10.15pm Jun-Sep; Ⓜ Catalunya) A second branch of Spain's only remaining department store, selling electronics, fashion, stationery and sports gear.

L'Arca — Vintage, Clothing

(Map p250; ☑93 302 15 98; www.larca.es; Carrer dels Banys Nous 20; ☺11am-2pm & 4.30-8.30pm Mon-Sat; Ⓜ Liceu) Step inside this enchanting shop for a glimpse of beautifully crafted apparel from the past, including 18th-century embroidered silk vests, elaborate silk kimonos, and wedding dresses and shawls from the 1920s. Thanks to its incredible collection, it has provided clothing for films, including *Titanic* and *Perfume: The Story of a Murderer*.

Herboristeria del Rei — Cosmetics

(Map p250; ☑93 318 05 12; www.herboristeria delrei.com; Carrer del Vidre 1; ☺2.30-8.30pm Tue-Thu, 10.30am-8.30pm Fri & Sat; Ⓜ Liceu) Once patronised by Queen Isabel II, this timeless corner store flogs all sorts of weird and wonderful herbs, spices and medicinal plants. It's been doing so since 1823 and the decor has barely changed since the 1860s – some of the products have, however, and nowadays you'll find anything from fragrant soaps to massage oil.

Scenes from *Perfume: The Story of a Murderer* were shot here.

Cereria Subirà — Homewares

(Map p250; ☑93 315 26 06; https://cereriasubira. cat; Calle de la Llibreteria 7; ☺9.30am-1.30pm & 4-8pm Mon-Thu, 9.30am-8pm Fri, 10am-8pm Sat; Ⓜ Jaume I) Even if you're not interested in myriad mounds of colourful wax, pop in just so you've been to the oldest shop in Barcelona. Cereria Subirà has been churning out candles since 1761 and at this address since the 19th century; the interior has a beautifully baroque quality, with a picturesque *Gone With the Wind*–style staircase.

Artesania Catalunya — Arts & Crafts

(Map p250; ☑93 467 46 60; www.bcncrafts. com; Carrer dels Banys Nous 11; ☺10am-8pm Mon-Sat, to 2pm Sun; Ⓜ Liceu) A celebration of Catalan products, this nicely designed store is a great place to browse for unique gifts. You'll find jewellery with designs inspired by Roman iconography (as well as works that reference Gaudí and Barcelona's Gothic era), plus pottery, wooden toys, silk scarves, notebooks, housewares and more.

Drap-Art
Arts & Crafts

(Map p250; ☏93 268 48 89; www.drapart.org; Carrer Groc 1; ☺11am-2pm & 5-8pm Tue-Fri, 6-9pm Sat; Ⓜ Jaume I) A non-profit arts organisation runs this small store and gallery space, which exhibits wild designs made from recycled products. Works change regularly, but you might find sculptures, jewellery, handbags and other accessories from artists near and far, as well as mixed-media installations.

La Colmena
Food

(Map p250; ☏93 315 13 56; www.pastisseria lacolmena.com; Plaça de l'Angel 12; ☺9am-9pm; Ⓜ Jaume I) One of Barcelona's oldest pastry shops, La Colmena first opened in 1868. Today it's still run by the same family who acquired it in 1927, and produces its treats according to the original recipes. They sell many delicacies, but are best known for their boiled sweets, pine-nut-encrusted *panellets* (almond cakes), meringues and *bolados* (18th-century powered-sugar candy, flavoured with juice).

Taller de Marionetas Travi
Toys

(Map p250; ☏93 412 66 92; www.marionetas travi.com; Carrer de n'Amargós 4; ☺12.30-9pm Mon-Sat; Ⓜ Urquinaona) Opened in the 1970s, this atmospheric shop sells beautifully handcrafted marionettes, many of them made by the owner herself. Don Quixote, Sancho Panza and other iconic Spanish figures are on hand, as well as unusual works from other parts of the world – including rare Sicilian puppets and pieces from Myanmar (Burma), Indonesia and elsewhere.

Cómplices
Books

(Map p250; ☏93 412 72 83; www.libreriacomplices. com; Carrer de Cervantes 4; ☺10.30am-8pm Mon-Fri, from noon Sat; Ⓜ Jaume I) One of the most extensive gay-and-lesbian bookstores in the city has a mix of erotica in the form of DVDs and comics as well as books. It's a welcoming place for all ages and orientations.

La Manual Alpargatera
Shoes

(Map p250; ☏93 301 01 72; www.lamanual alpargatera.es; Carrer d'Avinyó 7; ☺9.30am-8pm Mon-Fri, from 10am Sat; Ⓜ Liceu) Clients from Salvador Dalí to Jean Paul Gaultier have ordered a pair of *espadrilles* (rope-soled canvas shoes) from this famous store. The shop was founded just after the Spanish Civil War, though the roots of the simple shoe design date back hundreds of years and originated in the Catalan Pyrenees.

Sala Parés
Arts & Crafts

(Map p250; ☏93 318 70 20; www.salapares.com; Carrer del Petritxol 5; ☺4-8pm Mon, 10.30am-2pm & 4-8pm Tue-Sat, plus 11.30am-2pm Sun Oct-May; Ⓜ Liceu) In business since 1877, this gallery has maintained its position as one of the city's leading purveyors of Catalan art, with works from the 19th century to the present. Increasingly it stocks more work from elsewhere in Spain and Europe.

FC Botiga
Gifts & Souvenirs

(Map p250; ☏93 269 15 32; Carrer de Jaume I 18; ☺10am-9pm; Ⓜ Jaume I) Need a Lionel Messi football jersey, a blue and burgundy ball, or any other football paraphernalia pertaining to what many locals consider the greatest team in the world? This is a convenient spot to load up without traipsing to the stadium.

Papabubble
Food

(Map p250; ☏93 268 86 25; www.papabubble. com; Carrer Ample 28; ☺10am-2pm & 4-8.30pm Mon-Fri, 10am-8.30pm Sat; Ⓜ Jaume I) It feels like a step into another era in this sweet shop, which makes up pots of rainbow-coloured boiled lollies, just like some of us remember from corner-store days as kids. Watch the sticky sweets being made before your eyes.

Petritxol Xocoa
Food

(Map p250; ☏93 301 82 91; www.petritxol.com; Carrer del Petritxol 11-13; ☺9.30am-9pm; Ⓜ Liceu) Tucked along 'chocolate street' Carrer del Petritxol, this den of dental devilry displays ranks and ranks of original bars in stunning designs, chocolates stuffed with sweet stuff, gooey pastries and more. It has various other branches scattered about town.

Vintage Fashion

El Raval is best for vintage fashion. You'll discover old-time stores that are irresistible to browsers, and a colourful array of affordable, mostly secondhand clothes boutiques. The central axis here is Carrer de la Riera Baixa, which plays host to '70s threads and military cast-offs. Carrer dels Tallers is also attracting a growing number of clothing and shoe shops (although music remains its core business). Small galleries, designer shops and arty bookshops huddle together along the streets running east of the MACBA towards La Rambla.

Holala! Plaza
PAUL QUAYLE/ALAMY STOCK PHOTO ©

Sombrerería Obach   Hats

(Map p250; ☑93 318 40 94; www.sombrereria obach.es; Carrer del Call 2; ⊙10am-2pm & 4-8pm Mon-Fri, 10am-2pm & 4.30-8pm Sat Oct-Jul, 10am-2pm & 4-8pm Mon-Fri, 10am-2pm Sat Aug-Sep; Ⓜ Jaume I) Since 1924 this store has been purveying all manner of head-gear. You'll find Kangol mohair berets, hipsterish short-brimmed hats, fedoras, elegant straw sun hats and a full-colour spectrum of *barrets* (berets).

🔒 El Raval

Les Topettes   Cosmetics

(Map p249; ☑93 500 55 64; www.lestopettes. com; Carrer de Joaquín Costa 33; ⊙11am-2pm & 4-9pm Tue-Sat, 4-9pm Mon; Ⓜ Universitat) The items in this chic little temple to soap and perfume have been picked for their designs as much as for the prod-

ucts themselves. You'll find gorgeously packaged scents, candles and unguents from Diptyque, Cowshed and L'Artisan Parfumeur, among others.

Chök   Food

(Map p250; ☑93 304 23 60; www.chokbarcelona. com; Carrer del Carme 3; ⊙9am-9pm; Ⓜ Liceu) Set inside an old chocolate-maker's, with original wooden shelving and stained glass, Chök now specialises in all things sweet, but especially doughnuts. These come in a huge array of colours and flavours, but there are also cookies, macarons, marsh-mallows and, of course, the ubiquitous cronut. There's a tiny space where you can order and drink coffee.

Joan La Llar del Pernil   Food

(Map p250; ☑93 317 95 29; www.joanllardel pernil.com; Stalls 667-671, Mercat de la Boqueria; ⊙8am-3pm Mon-Thu, to 8pm Fri & Sat; Ⓜ Liceu) This stall in the Mercat de la Boqueria sells some of the best ham and charcuterie in the city, much of which is sliced and pre-sented in little cones as a snack.

Fantastik   Arts & Crafts

(Map p249; ☑93 301 30 68; www.fantastik. es; Carrer de Joaquín Costa 62; ⊙11am-2pm & 4-8.30pm Mon-Fri, 11am-3pm & 4-9pm Sat; Ⓜ Universitat) Over 500 products, such as woodland dolls, tin robots and Mexican rubber tablecloths, are to be found in this colourful shop, which sources its items from countries including India, China, Morocco, Germany, Russia and Japan. It's a perfect place to buy all the things you don't need but can't live without.

Holala! Plaza   Fashion & Accessories

(Map p249; ☑93 302 05 93; www.holala-ibiza. com; Plaça de Castella 2; ⊙11am-9pm Mon-Sat; Ⓜ Universitat) Backing on to Carrer de Valldonzella, where it boasts an exhibition space (Gallery) for temporary art dis-plays, this Ibiza import is inspired by that island's long-established (and somewhat commercialised) hippie tradition. Vintage clothes are the name of the game, along with an eclectic program of exhibitions and activities.

Teranyina
Arts & Crafts

(Map p249; ☎93 317 94 36; www.textilteranyina. com; Carrer del Notariat 10; ⏱11am-2pm & 5-8pm Mon-Fri; ⓂCatalunya) Artist Teresa Rosa Aguayo runs this textile workshop in the heart of the artsy bit of El Raval. You can join courses at the loom, admire some of the rugs and other works that Teresa has created and, of course, buy them.

La Portorriqueña
Coffee

(Map p249; ☎93 317 34 38; Carrer d'en Xuclà 25; ⏱9am-2pm & 5-8pm Mon-Fri, 9am-2pm Sat; ⓂCatalunya) Coffee beans from around the world, freshly ground before your eyes, have been the winning formula in this store since 1902. It also offers all sorts of choc- olate goodies. The street it's on is good for little old-fashioned food boutiques.

🔒 La Ribera

See p108 for fabulous food shopping choic- es in La Ribera.

El Rei de la Màgia
Magic

(Map p250; ☎93 319 39 20; www.elreydelamagia. com; Carrer de la Princesa 11; ⏱10.30am-7.30pm Mon-Fri, 10.30am-2pm & 4-7.30pm Sat; ⓂJaume I) For more than 100 years, the owners have been keeping locals both astounded and amused. Should you decide to stay in Barcelona and make a living as a magician, this is the place to buy levitation brooms, glasses of disappearing milk and decks of magic cards.

MI.vintage
Vintage

(Map p250; www.mivintagelabel.com; Carrer dels Consellers 2; ⏱10am-8pm Mon-Sat; ⓂBarcelon- eta) Opened in 2017, this hip vintage store stocks a mix of secondhand and revamped clothes – treated, repaired, improved or, as the owner says, made 'street-ready'. Expect silk bomber jackets aplenty, colourful leather blazers, Hawaiian shirts and Emian sunglasses, along with Taschen books, Ca- sio digital watches and funky PVC jewellery.

Marsalada
Gifts & Souvenirs

(Map p250; ☎93 116 20 76; www.marsalada design.com; Carrer de Sant Jacint 6; ⏱10am- 2pm & 4-8pm Mon-Sat; ⓂJaume I) For souvenirs with a difference, Marsalada has hand-printed tote bags in unbleached cot- ton, engravings and T-shirts. Each of these is emblazoned with a well-known Barcelona attraction, sketched in pen and ink and adorned with abstract colour mosaics.

Coquette
Fashion & Accessories

(Map p250; ☎93 310 35 35; www.coquettebcn. com; Carrer de Bonaire 5; ⏱11am-3pm & 5-9pm Mon-Fri, 11.30am-9pm Sat; ⓂBarceloneta) With its spare, cut-back and designer look, this friendly fashion store is attractive in its own right. Women can browse through casual, feminine wear by such designers as Human- oid, Vanessa Bruno, UKE and Hoss Intropia.

Loisaida
Clothing, Antiques

(Map p250; ☎93 295 54 92; www.loisaidabcn. com; Carrer dels Flassaders 42; ⏱11am-9pm Mon-Sat, 11am-2pm & 4-8pm Sun; ⓂJaume I) A sight in its own right, housed in the former coach house and stables for the Royal Mint, Loisaida (from the Spanglish for 'Lower East Side') is a deceptively large emporium of colourful, retro and somewhat preppy clothing for men and women, costume jewellery, music from the 1940s and '50s and some covetable antiques. One space is devoted entirely to denim.

Arlequí Màscares
Arts & Crafts

(☎93 268 27 52; www.arlequimask.com; Carrer de la Princesa 7; ⏱11am-8.30pm Mon-Sat, to 7pm Sun; ⓂJaume I) A wonderful little oasis of originality, this shop specialises in masks for costume and decoration – some of the pieces are superb. Stock also includes a beautiful range of decorative boxes in Catalan themes and some old- style marionettes.

Nu Sabates
Shoes

(Map p250; ☎93 268 03 83; www.nusabates.com; Carrer dels Cotoners 14; ⏱11am-8pm Mon-Sat; ⓂJaume I) A modern-day Catalan cobbler has put together some original handmade leather shoes for men and women (and a hand-ful of bags and other leather items) in this friendly and stylish locale, which is enliv- ened by some inspired musical selections.

Custo Barcelona
Fashion & Accessories

(Map p250; ☑93 268 78 93; www.custo.com; Plaça de les Olles 7; ☺10am-8pm Mon-Sat; ⓂBarceloneta) The psychedelic decor and casual atmosphere lend this avant-garde Barcelona fashion store a youthful edge. Custo presents daring new women's and men's collections each year on the New York catwalks. The dazzling colours and cut of everything from dinner jackets to hot pants are for the uninhibited. It has three other stores around town.

⊙ Barceloneta, the Waterfront & El Poblenou

Vernita
Children's Clothing

(☑625 092341; www.facebook.com/vernitastudio shop; Carrer del Joncar 27; ☺10am-1.30pm & 5.30-8pm Tue, 10am-1.30pm & 5-8pm Wed-Fri, 10am-2pm & 5-8pm Sat; ⓂPoblenou) Three mothers, Neli, Laura and Nacha, design and hand-stitch children's clothing and accessories such as animal-print cushions, bags, kids' jewellery, bow ties, towels (including adorable dinosaur designs) and washable nappies as well as soft cuddly toys at this light, bright studio-boutique. During the evenings, they also offer sewing lessons and origami workshops for kids (English available).

System Action
Clothing

(☑93 463 85 82; www.systemaction.es; Carrer de Pere IV 122; ☺10am-7pm Thu-Sat; ⓂLlacuna) If you like discovering local producers, track down this outlet store. Though System Action has shops across northeast Spain, its design headquarters are a few blocks south in a former Poblenou ice factory. Fashions are feminine but rugged, and you'll find good basics here including very wearable sweaters, skirts, scarves and shoes. Prices are reasonable – especially when sales are on.

Ultra-Local Records
Music

(☑661 017638; Carrer de Pujades 113; ☺4-8.30pm Mon-Fri, 11am-8.30pm Sat; ⓂLlacuna) Along a fairly empty stretch of El Poblenou, this small, well-curated shop sells mostly used records from local and international artists, plus some re-releases and albums by current indie rock darlings. Vinyl aside, you'll find a smaller CD selection, zines and a few other curiosities. There's a €1 bargain bin in front of the store.

Mercat de la Barceloneta
Market

(☑93 221 64 71; www.mercatdelabarceloneta. com; Plaça del Poeta Boscà 1-2; ☺7am-2pm Mon-Thu, to 8pm Fri, to 3pm Sat; ⓂBarceloneta) Set in a modern glass-and-steel building fronting a long plaza in the heart of Barceloneta, this airy market has seasonal produce and seafood stalls, as well as several places where you can enjoy a sit-down meal. **El Guindilla** (☑93 221 54 58; tapas €5-11, mains €10-16; ☺9.30am-1am Sun-Thu, to 2am Fri & Sat) deserves special mention for its good-value lunch specials and outdoor seating on the plaza.

Mercat dels Encants
Market

(Fira de Bellcaire; ☑93 246 30 30; www. encantsbcn.com; Plaça de les Glòries Catalanes; ☺9am-8pm Mon, Wed, Fri & Sat; ⓂGlòries) In a gleaming open-sided complex near Plaça de les Glòries Catalanes, the 'Market of Charms' is the biggest flea market in Barcelona. More than 500 vendors ply their wares beneath massive mirror-like panels. It's all here, from antique furniture through to secondhand clothes. There's a lot of junk, but you'll occasionally stumble across a *ganga* (bargain). Catch some behind-the-scenes action from 7am to 9am on Monday, Wednesday and Friday, when the *subastas* (auctions) take place.

Port Antic
Market

(www.portvellbcn.com; Plaça del Portal de la Pau; ☺10am-8pm Sat & Sun; ⓂDrassanes) At the base of La Rambla under the Mirador de Colom, this small market is a requisite stop for antique hunters. Here you'll find old photographs, frames, oil paintings, records, shawls, cameras, vintage toys and other odds and ends. Arrive early to beat the crowds.

🔒 L'Eixample

Joan Múrria
Food & Drinks

(Map p254; 📞93 215 57 89; www.murria.cat; Carrer de Roger de Llúria 85; ⊘10am-8.30pm Tue-Fri, 10am-2pm & 5-8.30pm Sat; Ⓜ Girona) Ramon Casas designed the 1898 Modernista shopfront advertisements featured at this culinary temple of speciality food goods from around Catalonia and beyond. Artisan cheeses, Iberian hams, caviar, canned delicacies, smoked fish, *cavas* and wines, coffee and loose-leaf teas are among the treats in store.

Flores Navarro
Flowers

(Map p254; 📞93 457 40 99; www.floristerias navarro.com; Carrer de València 320; ⊘24hr; Ⓜ Girona) You never know when you might need flowers, and this florist never closes. Established in 1960, it's a vast space (or couple of spaces, in fact), and worth a visit for the bank of colour and wonderful fragrance.

Cacao Sampaka
Food

(Map p254; 📞93 272 08 33; www.cacaosampaka. com; Carrer del Consell de Cent 292; ⊘9am-9pm Mon-Sat; Ⓜ Passeig de Gràcia) Chocoholics will be convinced they have died and passed on to a better place. Load up in the shop or head for the bar out the back where you can have a classic *xocolata* (hot chocolate) and munch on exquisite chocolate cakes, tarts, ice cream, sweets and sandwiches. The bonbons make particularly good presents.

Altaïr
Books

(Map p254; 📞93 342 71 71; www.altair.es; Gran Via de les Corts Catalanes 616; ⊘10am-8.30pm Mon-Sat; 📶; Ⓜ Catalunya) Enter a wonderland of travel in this extensive bookshop, which has enough guidebooks, maps, travel literature and other books to induce a severe case of itchy feet. It has a travellers noticeboard and, downstairs, a cafe.

Dr Bloom
Fashion & Accessories

(Map p254; 📞93 315 41 89; www.drbloom.es; Rambla de Catalunya 30; ⊘10am-9pm Mon-Sat; Ⓜ Passeig de Gràcia) A new collection comes out every month at Dr Bloom, so the stock is

Designers

The heart of L'Eixample, bisected by Passeig de Gràcia, is known as the Quadrat d'Or (Golden Square) and is jammed with all sorts of glittering shops. Passeig de Gràcia is a bit of a who's who of international shopping – you'll find Spain's own high-end designers like Loewe, along with Armani, Chanel, Gucci, Stella McCartney and the rest.

El Born, particularly Carrer del Rec, is big on cool designers in small, cleanline boutiques. Some Barcelona-based designs are also sold here. This is a great area if you have money to spend and hours to browse.

Passeig de Gràcia
ANTON_IVANOV/SHUTTERSTOCK ©

constantly rotating. Designed and made in Barcelona, the label's dresses, tops, shawls and more have an emphasis on bright colours and bold prints no matter the season.

Lurdes Bergada
Fashion & Accessories

(Map p254; 📞93 218 48 51; www.lurdesbergada. es; Rambla de Catalunya 112; ⊘10.30am-8.30pm Mon-Sat; Ⓜ Diagonal) Mother-and-son design team Lurdes Bergada and Syngman Cucala's classy men's and women's fashions are made from natural fibres and have attracted a cult following.

El Corte Inglés
Department Store

(Map p254; 📞93 493 48 00; www.elcorteingles.es; Avinguda Diagonal 471; ⊘9.30am-9pm Mon-Sat; Ⓜ Hospital Clínic) A large department store selling clothing, electronics, books and more.

Top Five Barcelona Souvenirs

Cured Meats

Instead of *jamón*, go for local sausage such as *fuet* or *botifarra*. It's best bought in one of the market halls. They'll vacuum-pack it for you.

FC Barcelona Gear

Sure, you can buy a rip-off Messi shirt in any market in the world, but the real deal (plus harder-to-come-by Barça mementoes) are in their official shops.

Wine

Look for something you can't get back home – some unusual Catalan red, or a small-producer *cava* (sparkling wine). Shops in La Ribera have ample supplies.

Unusual Festive Decorations

The curious defecating figure of the *caganer* is part of Barcelona Christmas lore. Pick up your own version and make your mantelpiece edgier.

Fashion

Quality threads can be had all over town, but small local design boutiques ensure you go home wearing something unique.

El Corte Inglés
Department Store

(Map p254; ☑93 306 38 00; www.elcorteingles. es; Plaça de Catalunya 14; ⏾9.30am-9pm Mon-Sat; ⓜCatalunya) Spain's only remaining department-store chain stocks everything you'd expect, from computers to cosmetics and high fashion to homewares. Fabulous city views extend from the top-floor restaurant. Near- by branches include one on Avinguda Diagonal (p161).

Purificación García
Fashion & Accessories

(Map p254; ☑93 496 13 36; www.purificacion garcia.com; Carrer de Provença 292; ⏾10am-8.30pm Mon-Sat; ⓜDiagonal) Spanish designer Purificación García's collections are breathtaking as much for their breadth as anything else. You'll find all kinds of clothing over this shop's two floors, from women's cardigans to men's ties, as well as light summer dresses and jeans.

Regia
Cosmetics

(Map p254; ☑93 216 01 21; www.regia.es; Passeig de Gràcia 39; ⏾9.30am-8.30pm Mon-Fri, 10.30am-8.30pm Sat; ⓜPasseig de Gràcia) In business since 1928, Regia stocks all the name brands and also has a private **perfume museum** (www.museudelperfum. com; adult/child €5/free; ⏾10.30am-8pm Mon-Fri, 11am-2pm Sat) out the back. Fragrances aside, it carries a range of cosmetics and has its own line of bath products.

Mercat del Ninot
Market

(☑93 323 49 09; www.mercatdelninot.com; Carrer de Mallorca 133-157; ⏾9am-8pm Mon-Fri, to 2pm Sat; ☏; ⓜHospital Clínic) A gleaming, modern neighbourhood food market, Mercat del Ninot sells mostly meat and fish and also has a couple of stalls where you can grab a bite to eat.

Mercat de la Concepció
Market

(Map p254; ☑93 476 48 70; www.laconcepcio. cat; Carrer d'Aragó 313-317; ⏾8am-8pm Tue-Fri, to 3pm Mon & Sat early Sep–mid-Jul, 8am-3pm Mon-Sat mid-Jul–early Sep; ⓜGirona) Mercat de la Concepció has around 50 stalls selling food, flowers, wine and more, including three on-site bars.

Cubiña
Homewares

(Map p254; ☑93 476 57 21; www.cubinya.es; Casa Thomas, Carrer de Mallorca 291; ⏾10am-2pm & 4.30-8.30pm Mon-Sat; ⓜVerdaguer) Even if interior design doesn't ring your bell, it's worth a visit to this extensive temple to furniture, lamps and just about any home accessory imaginable, just to see this Domènech i Montaner building. Admire the enormous and whimsical wrought-iron decoration at street level before heading inside to marvel at the brick columns and intricate timber work.

El Bulevard dels Antiquaris
Antiques

(Map p254; ☑93 215 44 99; www.bulevarddels antiquaris.com; Passeig de Gràcia 55-57; ⏾10.30am-8.30pm Mon-Sat; ⓜPasseig de Gràcia) More than 70 stores are gathered under one roof to offer the most varied selection of collector's pieces. These range from old porcelain dolls through to fine crystal, from Asian antique furniture to old French goods, and from African and other ethnic art to jewellery. Be warned, most stores close for lunch.

Loewe
Fashion & Accessories

(Map p254; ☑93 216 04 00; www.loewe.com; Passeig de Gràcia 35; ⏾10am-8.30pm Mon-Sat; ⓜPasseig de Gràcia) Loewe is one of Spain's leading and oldest fashion stores, founded in 1846. It specialises in luxury leather (shoes, accessories and travel bags), and also has lines in perfume, sunglasses, cuff links, silk scarves and jewellery. This branch opened in 1943 in the Modernista **Casa Lleó Morera**.

Bagués-Masriera
Jewellery

(Map p254; ☑93 216 01 74; www.bagues-masriera.com; Passeig de Gràcia 41; ⏾10am-8.30pm Mon-Fri, 11am-8pm Sat; ⓜPasseig de Gràcia) This jewellery store, in business since the 19th century, is in thematic harmony with its location in the Modernista **Casa Amatller** (☑93 216 01 75; www. amatller.org; adult/child 1hr guided tour €24/12, 40min multimedia tour €19/9.50; ⏾10am-6pm). Some of the classic pieces to come out of the Bagués clan's workshops have an equally playful, Modernista bent.

Laie
Books

(Map p254; ☏93 318 17 39; www.laie.es; Carrer de Pau Claris 85; ⏰9am-9pm Mon-Fri, 10am-9pm Sat; Ⓜ Urquinaona) Laie has novels and books on architecture, art and film in English, French, Spanish and Catalan. It also has a great upstairs cafe where you can examine your latest purchases or browse through the newspapers provided for customers.

ⓞ Montjuïc, Poble Sec & Sant Antoni

Mercat de Sant Antoni
Market

(Map p249; ☏93 426 35 21; www.mercatdesant antoni.com; Carrer de Comte d'Urgell 1; ⏰8am-8pm Mon-Sat; Ⓜ Sant Antoni) Just beyond the western edge of El Raval is Mercat de Sant Antoni, a glorious old iron-and-brick building constructed between 1872 and 1882. The market recently underwent a nine-year renovation, reopening in 2018 with 250 stalls. It's a great place to stock up on seasonal produce or grab a bite in between browsing. The secondhand book market takes place alongside it on Sunday mornings.

Arenas de Barcelona
Mall

(Map p256; ☏93 289 02 44; www.arenasde barcelona.com; Gran Via de les Corts Catalanes 373-385; ⏰10am-10pm Mon-Sat Jun-Sep, 9am-9pm Mon-Sat Oct-May; Ⓜ Plaça d'Espanya) Housed inside the city's old bull ring, Las Arenas is one of the city's best shopping malls. From the outside, it still features the old arched windows and Moorish designs, while inside it's sleek and modern, filled with high street stores. On the middle level there's a cinema and the open-air roof top offers spectacular city views and several international restaurants.

Mercat de la Terra
Market

(Map p256; Jardins de les Tres Xemeneies, Avinguda del Paral·lel; ⏰10am-4pm Sat May-Sep; Ⓜ Paral·lel) On a summer Saturday, this market is the ultimate place to pick up pro-visions for a picnic in the neighbourhood's parks and gardens It is laden with artisan cheeses and breads, preserves, wine, cava and home- made vermouth, and bushels of fresh produce. There are also stalls with ready-to-eat snacks and drinks.

Popcorn Store
Fashion & Accessories

(Map p256; www.facebook.com/popcornstorebcn; Carrer Viladomat 30-32; ⏰11am-3pm & 4.30-8.30pm Mon-Sat) Cutting-edge Barcelona labels for women at this boutique include Sister Dew, with asymmetrical tops, jack-ets, dresses and more, and Ester Gueroa, with bold prints and lace. Men will find styl-ish shirts, trousers and belts from Italian and other European designers.

10000 Records
Music

(Map p249; ☏93 292 77 76; www.10000records. es; Carrer de Floridablanca 70-72; ⏰5-8pm Mon, 10.30am-2pm & 5-8pm Tue-Fri, 10am-2pm Sat; Ⓜ Rocafort) As its name suggests, this record shop overflows with vintage and new vinyl in all genres but especially rock, pop, metal and jazz. You'll also unearth retro radios, cassettes and music books.

GI Joe
Fashion & Accessories

(Map p249; ☏93 329 96 52; www.gijoebcn.com; Ronda de Sant Antoni 49; ⏰10am-2pm & 4.30-8.30pm Mon-Sat; Ⓜ Universitat) This is the best central army-surplus warehouse. Get your khakis here, along with urban army fashion T-shirts, boots and more. You can also find vintage WWII items.

ⓞ Gràcia & Park Güell

Family Beer
Drinks

(Map p254; ☏93 219 29 88; www.family-beer.com; Carrer de Joan Blanques 55; ⏰5-8.30pm Mon, 10am-2pm & 5-8.30pm Tue-Sat; Ⓜ Joanic) More than 130 varieties of local and international craft beers and ciders are stocked in the fridges here, so you can pick up a cold brew to go. It also has brewing kits and books, and runs regular brewing workshops (three hours €45) and hosts free demonstrations of cheese making and cookery using beer, as well as 'meet the brewer' tastings.

Colmillo
de Morsa
Fashion & Accessories

(Map p254; ☑645 206365; www.colmillode
morsa.com; Carrer de Vic 15; ☺11am-2.30pm
& 4.30-7pm Mon-Fri, 11am-2.30pm Sat; ☒FGC
Gràcia) Design team Javier Blanco and
Elisabet Vallecillo, who have made waves at
Madrid's Cibeles Fashion Week and Paris'
fashion fair Who's Next, showcase their
Barcelona-made women's fashion here
at their flagship boutique. They've also
opened the floor to promote other up-and-
coming local labels. Fabrics used by Colmil-
lo de Morsa are all sustainably produced in
Europe using non-toxic dyes.

Can Luc
Cheese

(☑93 007 47 83; www.canluc.es; Carrer de Berga
4; ☺10am-2.30pm & 5-8.30pm Mon-Sat; ☒FGC
Gràcia) At any given time this brightly lit shop
has 150 different varieties of cheese. Catalan
cheeses are the speciality, but you'll also find
a selection from France, Italy, the Nether-
lands, Switzerland and Britain. Expert staff
provide guidance. Wines, condiments, crack-
ers and cheese knives are also available.
For a gourmet picnic, pre-order a brimming
hamper (€25 to €100).

Vinil Vintage
Music

(Map p254; ☑93 192 39 99; Carrer de Ramón y
Cajal 45-47; ☺10.45am-1.30pm & 5-8.30pm Tue-
Thu, 11.15am-2pm & 5.45-9pm Fri & Sat; ☒Joanic)
Crate diggers will love rummaging through
this vinyl collection. There's a huge range
of rock, pop and jazz, and plenty of Spanish
music. It also sells turntables and speakers.

Amalia Vermell
Jewellery

(Map p254; ☑655 754008; www.amaliavermell.
com; Carrer de Francisco Giner 49; ☺11am-2pm &
5-9pm Mon-Sat; ☒Diagonal) Striking geometric
jewellery made from high-quality materials
such as sterling silver is handcrafted by
Amalia Vermell here in her atelier. Browse for
pendants, necklaces, bracelets and rings.

Rekup & Co
Homewares

(Map p254; ☑694 472297; www.rekupandco.
com; Carrer de Verdi 63; ☺11am-2.30pm & 5-9pm;
☒Fontana) Recycled timbers and metals are
used by French native Emmanuel Wagnon to
create individual works of art that are func-
tional too: chairs, tables, shelves, mirrors,
lamps and quirkier items like shutters made
from wooden pallets. International shipping
can be arranged.

Mercat de Sant Antoni

Lady Loquita
Clothing

(Map p254; ☑93 217 82 92; www.ladyloquita. com; Travessera de Gràcia 126; ☺11am-2pm & 5-8.30pm Mon-Sat; MFontana) At this hip little shop you can browse through light, locally made summer dresses by Tiralahilacha, evening wear by Japamala and handmade jewellery by local design label Klimbim. There are also whimsical odds and ends: dinner plates with dog-people portraits and digital prints on wood by About Paola.

Amapola Vegan Shop
Clothing

(Map p254; ☑93 010 62 73; www.amapolavegan shop.com; Travessera de Gràcia 129; ☺5-8.30pm Mon, 11am-2pm & 5-8.30pm Tue-Sat; MFontana)
🌿 A shop with a heart of gold, Amapola proves that you need not toss your ethics aside in the quest for stylish clothing and accessories. You'll find sleek leather alternatives for wallets, handbags and messenger bags by Matt & Nat, belts by Nae Vic and elegant scarves by Barts.

Other finds: socks made from bamboo, soft but wool-free gloves, and cheeky T-shirts with slogans like No como mis amigos ('I don't eat my friends'). Morrissey (a lifelong animal-rights advocate) plays overhead.

Tintin Shop
Gifts & Souvenirs

(Map p254; ☑93 289 25 24; www.tintinshopbcn. com; Travessera de Gràcia 176; ☺10.30am-2.30pm & 5-8.30pm Mon-Fri, 11am-2.30pm Sat, 5-8.30pm Mon-Fri Aug; MFontana) Fans of the Belgian boy wonder should make a beeline to this Gràcia store, where you'll find Tintin T-shirts, posters, action figures, book bags, wristwatches, pencil cases, and even a soft, irresistible Milou (Tintin's wire fox terrier, known as Snowy in English) – plus, of course, the books that made him famous (with titles in Catalan, Spanish and French).

Picnic
Clothing

(Map p254; ☑93 016 69 53; www.picnicstore. es; Carrer de Verdi 17; ☺11am-9pm Mon-Fri, 11am-2.30pm & 5-9pm Sat; MFontana) This tiny, beautifully curated boutique has many temptations: stylish sneakers by Meyba (a Barcelona brand), striped jerseys from

Basque label Loreak Mendian and boldly patterned Mödernaked backpacks. Other finds include animal-print ceramics for the home, small-scale art prints and fashion mags.

Mercat de l'Abaceria Central
Market

(Map p254; ☑93 213 62 86; www.mercatabaceria. cat; Travessera de Gràcia 186; ☺8am-2.30pm & 5-8.30pm Mon-Thu, to 8.30pm Fri, to 3pm Sat; MJoanic) Dating from 1892, this sprawling iron-and-brick market is an atmospheric place to browse for fresh produce, cheeses, bakery items and more. There are also several food stalls where you can grab a quick bite on the cheap.

Surco
Music

(Map p254; ☑93 218 34 39; www.facebook.com/ surcobcn; Travessera de Gràcia 144; ☺10.30am-2pm & 5.30-9pm Mon-Sat; MFontana) Surco is an obligatory stop for music lovers, especially fans of vinyl. You'll find loads of new and used records and CDs here, with a mix of Tom Waits, Mishima (a Catalan indie pop band), Calexico and more.

Be
Gifts & Souvenirs

(Map p254; ☑93 218 89 49; www.bethestore.com; Carrer de Bonavista 7; ☺10am-9pm Mon-Fri, from 10.30am Sat; MDiagonal) Be is a fun place to browse. You'll find rugged vintage-looking satchels, leather handbags, stylish (and reflective) Happy Socks, portable record players, sneakers (Vans, Pumas, old-school Nikes) and gadgets (including richly hued Pantone micro speakers and Polaroid digital cameras).

Cabinet BCN
Homewares

(Map p254; ☑933 68 43 82; www.cabinetbcn. com; Travessera de Gràcia 133; ☺5-8.30pm Mon, 11am-2.30pm & 5-8.30pm Tue-Sat; MFontana) Charming interiors shop Cabinet BCN stocks a tasteful selection of homewares – including throws, cushions, bowls, candles and lamps, as well as quirky little ornaments – that make excellent presents. It also has a small range of clothing, and custom-designed furniture made of iron, wood and other recycled materials. Shipping is available.

Bodega Bonavista — Wine

(Map p254; [📞]93 218 81 99; Carrer de Bonavista 10; ⊗10am-2.30pm & 5-9pm Mon-Fri, noon-3pm & 6-9pm Sat, noon-3pm Sun; [M]Fontana) An excellent little neighbourhood bodega, Bonavista endeavours to seek out great wines at reasonable prices. The stock is mostly from Catalonia and elsewhere in Spain, but there's also a well-chosen selection from France. The Bonavista also acts as a deli, and there are some especially good cheeses. You can sample wines by the glass, along with cheeses and charcuterie, at one of the in-store tables.

Mushi Mushi — Fashion & Accessories

(Map p254; [📞]93 292 29 74; www.mushimushi collection.com; Carrer de Bonavista 12; ⊗11am-3pm & 4.30-8.30pm Mon-Sat; [M]Diagonal) A gorgeous little fashion boutique in an area that's not short of them, Mushi Mushi specialises in quirky but elegant women's fashion and accessories. It stocks small labels such as Des Petits Hauts, Sessùn and Orion London, as well as jewellery by Adriana Llorens. The collection changes frequently, so a return visit can pay off.

Nostàlgic — Photography

(Map p254; [📞]93 368 57 57; www.nostalgic.es; Carrer de Goya 18; ⊗10.30am-2pm & 5-8pm Mon-Fri, 11am-2.30pm Sat; [M]Fontana) In a beautiful space with exposed brick walls and wooden furniture, Nostàlgic specialises in all kinds of modern and vintage photography equipment. You'll find camera bags and tripods for the digital snappers, rolls of film, and quirky Lomo cameras. There is also a decent collection of photography books to buy or browse.

Hibernian — Books

([📞]93 217 47 96; www.hibernianbooks.com; Carrer de Montseny 17; ⊗4-8.30pm Mon, 10.30am-8.30pm Tue-Sat; [M]Fontana) Barcelona's biggest secondhand English bookshop stocks thousands of titles covering all sorts of subjects, from cookery to children's classics. There's a smaller collection of new books in English, too.

Shopping Malls

Barcelona has no shortage of shopping malls. One of the first to arrive was L'Illa Diagonal (p169), designed by star Spanish architect Rafael Moneo. The city's other emporia include **Centre Comercial Diagonal Mar** ([📞]93 567 76 37; www.diagonalmarcentre.es; Avinguda Diagonal 3; ⊗9.30am-10pm Mon-Sat Jun-Sep, 9am-9pm Mon-Sat Oct-May; [M]El Maresme Fòrum), up by El Fòrum; the waterfront **Maremàgnum** a ([📞]93 225 81 00; www.maremagnum.es; Moll d'Espanya 5; ⊗10am-10pm; [M]Drassanes); **Centre Comercial de les Glòries** (www.glories. com; Avinguda Diagonal 208; ⊗9.30am-10pm Mon-Sat; [M]Glòries), in the former Olivetti factory; **SOM Multiespai** ([📞]93 276 50 70; www.sommultiespai.com; Avinguda de Rio de Janeiro 42; ⊗shops 9.30am-9pm Mon-Sat winter, to 10pm summer, cinema & restaurants 7am-1am Sun-Thu, to 3am Fri & Sat; [M]Fabra i Puig), just off Avinguda Meridiana, about 4km north of Plaça de les Glòries Catalanes; **Gran Via 2** ([📞]902 30 14 44; www.granvia2. com; Gran Via de les Corts Catalanes 75; ⊗stores 9.30am-9pm Mon-Sat, restaurants & cinema 10am-1am Sun-Thu, to 3am Fri & Sat; [R]FGC Ildefons Cerdà) in L'Hospitalet de Llobregat. Perhaps the best is **La Maquinista** ([📞]93 360 89 71; www. lamaquinista.com; Carrer de Potosí; ⊗9am-9pm Mon-Sat; [🚌]42, [M]Sant Andreu), a huge outdoor complex filled with covered walkways, palm trees and an array of both designer and high street stores.

Centre Comercial Diagonal Mar

Shopping Strips

Avinguda del Portal de l'Àngel This broad pedestrian avenue is lined with high-street chains, shoe shops, bookshops and more. It feeds into Carrer dels Boters and Carrer de la Portaferrissa, characterised by stores offering light-hearted costume jewellery and youth-oriented streetwear.

Avinguda Diagonal This boulevard is loaded with international fashion names and design boutiques, suitably interspersed with cafes to allow weary shoppers to take a load off.

Carrer d'Avinyó Once a fairly squalid old city street, Carrer d'Avinyó has morphed into a dynamic young fashion street.

Carrer de la Riera Baixa The place to look for a gaggle of shops flogging preloved threads.

Carrer del Consell de Cent The heart of the private art-gallery scene in Barcelona, between Passeig de Gràcia and Carrer de Muntaner.

Carrer del Petritxol Best for chocolate shops and art.

Carrer del Rec Another threads street, this one-time stream is lined with bright and cool boutiques. Check out Carrer del Bonaire and Carrer de l'Esparteria too. You'll find discount outlets and original local designers.

Carrer dels Banys Nous Along with nearby Carrer de la Palla, this is the place to look for antiques.

Passeig de Gràcia This is Barcelona's chic premier shopping boulevard, mostly given over to big-name international brands.

Érase una Vez   Fashion & Accessories
(Map p254; ☑697 805409; www.eraseunavez. info; Carrer de Bonavista 13; ☉11am-2pm & 5-8.30pm Tue-Sat; Ⓜ Diagonal) 'Once Upon a Time' is the name of this fanciful boutique,

which brings out the princess in you. It offers ethereal, delicate women's clothes as well as exquisite wedding dresses. You'll also find playful frocks for kids.

⓮ Camp Nou, Pedralbes & La Zona Alta

Catalina House   Homewares
(☑93 140 96 39; http://catalinahouse.net; Carrer d'Amigó 47; ☉10.30am-2pm & 5-8pm Mon-Fri, 10.30am-2pm Sat; ⓇFGC Muntaner) 🖋 After its decade-long success on the Balearic island of Formentera, Catalina House opened its second shop in Barcelona in 2016. Sustainable materials, such as linen, cotton, stone, glass, terracotta and oil-treated recycled timbers, are used in stylish Mediterranean designs for the home including cushions, tableware, vases, clocks and furniture.

Normandie   Children's Clothing
(☑93 209 14 11; www.normandiebaby.com; Plaça de Sant Gregori Taumaturg 6; ☉10.30am-2.30pm & 4.30-8.30pm Mon-Sat; ⓇFGC La Bonanova) Set up by Barcelona-born, Paris-trained designer Graziella Antón de Vez in 2000, this fashion label for babies and children up to six years utilises all-natural materials such as angora, cotton, cashmere and wool. Adorable outfits are inspired by France's Normandy region, with vintage- and retro-style lines.

Ukka   Fashion & Accessories
(☑661 919710; www.facebook.com/ukka bcn; Carrer de Laforja 122; ☉10.30am-2pm & 5-8.30pm Mon-Fri, 10.30am-2pm Sat; ⓇFGC Muntaner) Ukka makes its bohemian-inspired women's fashion and accessories (including scarves, hats and some eye-catching jewellery) at its Barcelona factory and sells them exclusively in this chic little terracotta-floored boutique.

Labperfum   Cosmetics
(☑93 298 95 12; www.labperfum.com; Carrer de Santaló 45; ☉10am-2.30pm & 5-8.30pm Mon-Sat; ⓇFGC Muntaner) This tiny shop looks like an old apothecary, with its shelves lined

with pretty glass bottles of extraordinary fragrances (for men and women) made in-house and beautifully packaged. Scents diverge from run-of-the-mill Obsession, with varieties like tobacco, black orchid and leather. You can also buy scented candles, soaps and creams.

Mercat de Galvany
Market

(www.mercatgalvany.es; Carrer de Santaló 65; ⊙7am-2.30pm Mon-Thu & Sat, to 8pm Fri; 回FGC Muntaner) Opened in 1927, Galvany is one of the city's most beautiful markets, with a brick facade and glass-and-cast-iron interior. More than 80 different stalls sell a variety of bakery items, fresh produce and deli goods.

Oriol Balaguer
Food

(☑93 201 18 46; www.oriolbalaguer.com; Plaça de Sant Gregori Taumaturg 2; ⊙9am-2.30pm & 4-9pm Mon-Fri, 8.30am-2.30pm & 4-9pm Sat, 8.30am-2.30pm Sun; 回FGC La Bonanova) Magnificent cakes, sweets, ice cream, chocolates and other sweet creations tantalise in this museumlike shop.

FC Botiga Megastore
Gifts & Souvenirs

(☑93 409 02 71; www.fcbarcelona.com; Gate 9, off Avinguda Joan de XXIII; ⊙10am-8pm, until kick-off match days; MPalau Reial) This sprawling three-storey shop at Camp Nou (p72) has footballs, shirts, scarves, socks, wallets, bags, footwear, phone covers – pretty much anything you can think of – all featuring the team's famous red-and-blue insignia.

L'Illa Diagonal
Mall

(☑93 444 00 00; www.lilla.com; Avinguda Diagonal 557; ⊙9.30am-9pm Mon-Sat Oct-May, to 10pm Jun-Sep; MMaria Cristina) One of Barcelona's best malls, this is a fine place to while away a few hours (or days), with high-end shops and a mesmerising spread of eateries.

◉ Outside the Centre

Mercantic
Market

(☑93 674 49 50; www.mercantic.com; Avinguda de Rius i Taulet 120; ⊙10am-8pm Tue-Sat, to 4pm Sun; 🛜; 回FGC line S2 to Volpelleres) Antique collectors could set aside a Sunday morning for a trip to Mercantic, a collection of gaily painted wooden huts occupied by antique and bric-a-brac dealers selling records, books, vintage clothes, jewellery, artwork, home furnishings and much more. Ample food and drink vendors on hand add to the good cheer, and there's even live music some days.

The first Sunday of the month is delivery day, when the stallholders take delivery of a new wave of old stuff. The permanent market, with some 80 stallholders, is open during the week too. There's also an activities and play area for children.

La Roca Village
Fashion & Accessories

(☑93 842 39 39; www.larocavillage.com; Santa Agnès de Malayanes; ⊙10am-9pm Mon-Fri, to 10pm Sat & Sun) For the ultimate discount-fashion overdose, head out of town for some outlet shopping at La Roca Village. Here a village has been given over to consumer madness. At a long line of Spanish and international fashion boutiques you'll find reduced-price clothes, shoes, accessories and designer homewares.

The Village runs a Shopping Express bus from Passeig de Gràcia – see the website for details. A few euros cheaper is the hourly Shopping Bus run by **Sagalés** (☑902 130014; www.sagales.com) from Carrer Casp. Alternatively, take a slower bus from the same company from Fabra i Puig metro station (four departures Monday to Friday, three in August).

DRY M
ORIGI
1/2 LONI
1/2 FREN
1 DASH C
SQUEEZE LEMON
BOMBAY
SAPPHIRE
GREY GOOSE
VODKA
DISTILLED AND BOTTLED
FRANCE

BAR OPEN

Cocktails, *cava* and clubs galore

Bar Open

Barcelona is a town for nightlife lovers, with an enticing spread of candlelit wine bars, old-school taverns, stylish lounges and kaleidoscopic nightclubs where the party continues until daybreak. The atmosphere varies tremendously – mural-covered chambers in the medieval quarter, antique-filled converted storefronts and buzzing Modernista spaces are all part of the scene. Of course, where to go depends as much on the crowd as it does on ambience – and whether you're in the mood for drinking with the stylishly woke (try Sant Antoni), a bohemian crowd (El Raval) or young expats (Gràcia), you'll find a scene that suits in Barcelona. Wherever you end up, keep in mind that eating and drinking go hand in hand here, and some of the liveliest bars serve food as well as alcohol.

In This Section

Opening Hours

Bars Typically open around 6pm and close at 2am (3am on weekends), though many are open all day. Bars get lively around 11pm or midnight.

Clubs Open from midnight until 6am Thursday to Saturday but don't start filling up until around 1.30am or 2am.

Beach bars 10am to around midnight (later on weekends) from April through October.

Gràcia & Park Güell
Young scenester crowd
(p189)

Camp Nou, Pedralbes & La Zona Alta
High-end clubs
(p191)

L'Eixample
Student bars, tiny
lounges, LGBT+ venues
(p182)

La Ribera
Cava and wine
bars, lounges
(p179)

Port Olímpic

El Raval
Bohemian bars,
small clubs
(p177)

La Rambla & Barri Gòtic
Atmospheric bars, cafes,
outdoor spots, clubs
(p176)

Barceloneta, the Waterfront & El Poblenou
Neighbourhood taverns,
seaside bars,
touristy clubs
(p180)

Montjuïc, Poble Sec & Sant Antoni
Art-minded bars, trendy cafes,
open-air spots
(p186)

Port Vell

Mediterranean Sea

Costs & Tipping

A coffee costs €1.30 to €2, a glass of wine will cost €2 to €4 in most places and mixed drinks and cocktails will set you back €6 to €10. Nightclubs charge anywhere from nothing to €20 for admission. Tipping in bars is not customary or necessary.

Useful Phrases

Coffee

con leche	half coffee, half milk
solo	an espresso
cortado	an espresso with a dash of milk

Beer

cerveza	beer (bottle)
caña	small draught beer
tubo	large draught beer
quinto	a 200mL bottle
tercio	a 330mL bottle
clara	a shandy; a beer with a hefty dash of lemonade

The Best...

Experience Barcelona's best drinking & nightlife spots

Cocktails

Paradiso (p139) Walk through a fridge to this glam speakeasy.

Balius (p181) Beautifully mixed elixirs in Poblenou.

Elephanta (p189) The place to linger over a creative concoction.

Dry Martini (p183) Expertly made cocktails in a classy setting.

Boadas (p177) An iconic drinking den that's been going strong since the 1930s.

Old-World Ambience

Raïm (p191) Old-fashioned tavern with more than a hint of Havana.

Cafè de l'Òpera (p134) Serving opera-goers and passers-by for decades.

Bar Marsella (p177) History lives on in this 1820 watering hole.

Bar Pastís (p177; pictured) Atmospheric little bar with the warble of French cabaret tunes playing overhead.

Casa Almirall (p177) Step back into the 1860s inside this atmospheric drinking den.

Wine Lovers

Viblioteca (p190; pictured) A small modern space famed for its wine (and cheese) selections.

Perikete (p180) A large and lively wine bar in Barceloneta.

Monvínic (p182) A staggering 3000 varieties of wine means you won't lack options.

La Vinya del Senyor (p179) Long wine list and tables in the shadow of Basílica de Santa Maria del Mar.

Beer

BlackLab (p180) Creative microbrewery near the waterfront.

La Cervecita Nuestra de Cada Día (p181) A Poblenou brew bar for beer nerds.

Napar BCN (p182) The glitzy space makes an upmarket setting for sipping beers made on-site.

Cat Bar (p139; pictured) Vegan burgers and microbrews make a winning combo in El Born.

El Drapaire (p177) Atmospheric tapas and creative microbrew joint in El Raval.

Bohemian Hang-outs

Gran Bodega Saltó (p188) Poble Sec icon with psychedelic decor and an eclectic crowd.

Madame George (p181) Tiny, dramatically designed space with soulful DJs.

El Rouge (p187) Bordello-esque lounge with great people-watching.

Bar Marsella (p177; pictured) Historic absinthe bar that's seen them all.

Dancing

Marula Cafè (p176; pictured) Barri Gòtic favourite for its lively dance floor.

Sala Apolo (p177) Gorgeous dance hall with varied programme of electro, funk and more.

Moog (p178) A small Raval club that draws a fun, dance-loving crowd.

Antilla BCN (p183) The top name in town for salsa lovers.

City Hall (p200) A legendary Eixample dance club.

Views

La Caseta del Migdia (p187) Great hillside spot for a sundowner.

Mirablau (p191) The whole city stretches out beneath you from the foot of Tibidabo.

La Terrrazza (p189) Party beneath palms in Poble Espanyol.

Martínez (p147; pictured) Drinking and dining with views on Montjuïc.

Lonely Planet's Top Choices

Paradiso (p139) Glamorous, cavernous, speakeasy-style cocktail bar.

Guzzo (p179) Relaxed bar with great DJs and live music and tables outside on a Born square.

La Caseta del Migdia (p187) An open-air charmer, hidden high among the trees on Montjuïc.

Sor Rita (p176) Join festive crowds in a whimsical Almodóvar-esque world.

El Xampanyet (p179) Sip cheap pink *cava* (sparkling wine) and munch on a bacon sandwich in this convivial classic.

Dry Martini (p183) This elegant drinking den serves perfect martinis and goldfish-bowl-sized gin and tonics.

Nightlife Guides

Clubbingspain.com (www.clubbing spain.com)
Miniguide (www.miniguide.es)
enBarcelona (www.enbarcelona.com)
Xceed (https://xceed.me)

La Rambla & Barri Gòtic

L'Ascensor   Cocktail Bar

(Map p250; ☎93 318 53 47; Carrer de la Bellafila 3; ⏱7pm-3am Mon-Sun Apr-Sep, to 2am Oct-Mar; 🛜; Ⓜ Jaume I) Named after the lift doors that serve as the front entrance, this clandestine drinking den – with its vaulted brick ceilings, vintage mirrors and marble-topped bar – gathers a faithful crowd that comes for old-fashioned cocktails and lively conversation set to a soundtrack of up-tempo jazz and funk.

Sor Rita   Bar

(Map p250; ☎93 176 62 66; www.sorritabar.es; Carrer de la Mercè 27; ⏱7pm-2.30am Sun-Thu, to 3am Fri & Sat; 🛜; Ⓜ Jaume I) A study in all things kitsch, Sor Rita is pure eye candy, from leopard-print wallpaper to a high-heel-festooned ceiling to deliciously irreverent decorations inspired by the films of Pedro Almodóvar. It's a fun and festive scene, with special-event nights including tarot readings and cocktails on Mondays (€14 includes a cocktail), all-you-can-eat snack buffets (€7) on Tuesdays and karaoke on Thursdays.

Polaroid   Bar

(Map p250; ☎93 186 66 69; www.polaroidbar.es; Carrer dels Còdols 29; ⏱7.30pm-2.30am Sun-Thu, to 3am Fri & Sat; 🛜; Ⓜ Drassanes) For a dash of 1980s nostalgia, Polaroid is a blast from the past, with its wall-mounted VHS tapes, old film posters, comic-book-covered tables, action-figure displays and other kitschy decor. Not surprisingly, it draws a fun, unpretentious crowd who come for cheap *cañas* (draught beer), mojitos and free popcorn.

Marula Café   Bar

(Map p250; ☎93 318 76 90; www.marulacafe. com; Carrer dels Escudellers 49; cover up to €10; ⏱11pm-5am Wed, Thu & Sun, to 6am Fri & Sat; Ⓜ Liceu) A fantastic find in the heart of the Barri Gòtic, Marula will transport you to the 1970s and the best in funk and soul. James Brown fans will think they've died and gone to heaven. It's not, however, a monothematic place: DJs slip in other tunes, from breakbeat to house. Samba and other Brazilian dance sounds also penetrate here.

Bosc de les Fades   Lounge

(☎93 317 26 49; Passatge de la Banca 5; ⏱10am-1.30am Mon-Thu, to 2am Fri, 11am-2am Sat, to 1.30am Sun; Ⓜ Drassanes) The 'Forest of the Fairies' is popular with tourists but offers a whimsical retreat from the busy Rambla nearby and has a wonderfully kitsch charm. Lounge chairs and lamp-lit tables are scattered within an indoor forest complete with trickling fountain and grotto. *Bocadillos* (filled baguettes) and snacks are available.

Manchester   Bar

(Map p250; ☎627 733081; Carrer de Milans 5; ⏱6.30pm-2.30am Sun-Thu, to 3am Fri & Sat; 🛜; Ⓜ Liceu) ✐ A drinking den that has undergone several transformations over the years now treats you to the sounds of great Manchester bands, from Joy Division to Oasis, but probably not the Hollies. It has a pleasing rough-and-tumble feel, with tables jammed in every which way. There are DJs on Thursdays.

Karma   Club

(Map p250; ☎93 302 56 80; www.karmadisco. com; Plaça Reial 10; ⏱noon-5am Tue-Thu, to 6am Fri & Sat; Ⓜ Liceu) During the week Karma plays good, mainstream indie music, while at weekends the DJs spin anything from rock to disco. A golden oldie in Barcelona, tunnel-shaped Karma is small and becomes quite tightly packed (claustrophobic for some) with a good-natured crowd of locals and out-of-towners. The bar and terrace on the Plaça Reial open from noon to 3am every day of the week.

La Macarena — Club

(Map p250; ☑93 301 30 64; www.macarenaclub. com; Carrer Nou de Sant Francesc 5; cover €5-10; ⊗midnight- 5am Sun-Thu, to 6am Fri & Sat; Ⓜ Drassanes) You won't believe this was once a tile-lined Andalucian flamenco musos' bar. Now it's a dark dance space, of the kind where it's possible to sit at the bar, meet people around you and then stand up for a bit of a shake to the DJ's electro and house offerings, all within about 5 sq metres.

Boadas — Cocktail Bar

(Map p250; ☑93 318 95 92; www.boadascocktails. com; Carrer dels Tallers 1; ⊗noon-2am Mon-Thu, to 3am Fri & Sat; Ⓜ Catalunya) One of the city's oldest cocktail bars, Boadas is famed for its daiquiris. Bow-tied waiters have been serving up unique, drinkable creations since Miguel Boadas opened it in 1933 – in fact Miró and Hemingway both drank here. Miguel was born in Havana, where he was the first barman at the immortal La Floridita.

⊙ El Raval

La Confitería — Bar

(Map p256; ☑93 140 54 35; http://confiteria.cat; Carrer de Sant Pau 128; ⊗7pm-2am Mon-Thu, 6pm-3am Fri & Sat, 5pm-2am Sun; 🛜; Ⓜ Paral·lel) This is a trip into the 19th century. Until the 1980s it was a confectioner's shop, and although the original cabinets are now lined with booze, the look of the place barely changed with its conversion. The back room is similarly evocative, and the vibe these days is lively cocktail bar. Later in the evening, it fills with those falling out of the nearby BARTS (p201) and Sala Apolo (p201) concert halls.

La Monroe — Bar

(Map p250; ☑93 441 94 61; www.lamonroe.es; Plaça Salvador Seguí 1-9; ⊗noon-1am Sun-Thu, to 2.30am Fri & Sat; Ⓜ Liceu) Peer through the glass walls of this gay-friendly hang-out inside the Filmoteca de Catalunya (p197) building, and you'll spot long wooden tables, industrial touches and a cobbled floor that mimics the square outside. It's all softened

with a burst of bright colours and leafy plants. Venture inside and you'll find great cocktails, delectable tapas and a lively vibe.

Bar Pastís — Bar

(Map p250; www.facebook.com/barpastisraval; Carrer de Santa Mònica 4; ⊗8pm-2am Tue-Thu & Sun, to 3am Fri & Sat; 🛜; Ⓜ Drassanes) A French cabaret theme (with lots of Piaf on the stereo) pervades this tiny, cluttered classic, which has been going, on and off, since the end of WWII. You'll need to be in before 9pm to have any hope of sitting or getting near the bar. On some nights it features live acts, usually performing *chanson* (French song).

Bar Marsella — Bar

(Map p250; ☑93 442 72 63; Carrer de Sant Pau 65; ⊗6pm-2am; Ⓜ Liceu) Bar Marsella has been in business since 1820, and has served the likes of Hemingway, who was known to slump here over an *absenta* (absinthe). The bar still specialises in absinthe, a drink to be treated with respect. Your absinthe glass comes with a lump of sugar, a fork and a little bottle of mineral water. Hold the sugar on the fork, over your glass, and drip the water onto the sugar so that it dissolves into the absinthe, which turns yellow. The result should give you a warm glow.

Casa Almirall — Bar

(Map p249; ☑93 318 99 17; www.casaalmirall.com; Carrer de Joaquín Costa 33; ⊗4.30pm-1.30am Mon, 4pm-2.30am Tue & Wed, noon-2.30am Thu, noon-3am Fri & Sat, noon-12.30am Sun; 🛜; Ⓜ Universitat) In business since the 1860s, this unchanged corner bar is dark and intriguing, with Modernista decor and a mixed clientele. There are some great original pieces in here, such as the marble counter, and the cast-iron statue of the muse of the Universal Exposition, held in Barcelona in 1888.

El Drapaire — Bar

(Map p249; ☑93 302 76 28; www.drapaire.com; Carrer de les Sitges 11; ⊗5pm-1am Sun-Thu, to 2.30am Fri & Sat; 🛜; Ⓜ Catalunya) Part of the recent explosion in the craft-beer scene, this cosy, beamed tavern has been given a new lease on life and now has 14 taps, featuring Spanish and international beers

Streets & Plazas for Bar-Hopping

Plaça Reial Barri Gòtic
Carrer dels Escudellers Barri Gòtic
Carrer de Joaquín Costa El Raval
Carrer Nou de la Rambla El Raval
Carrer del Parlament Sant Antoni
Platja de la Barceloneta La Barceloneta
Carrer d'Aribau L'Eixample
Plaça del Sol Gràcia
Passeig del Born La Ribera
Rambla del Raval El Raval
Plaça de la Vila de Gràcia Gràcia
Carrer Nou de la Rambla Poble Sec
Carrer de Blai Poble Sec

Ocaña (p136), Plaça Reial

of all styles. There are tapas and platters of cheese and charcuterie to share. Live music on Friday.

33 | 45 — Bar

(Map p249; ☎93 187 41 38; www.facebook.com/3345bar; Carrer de Joaquín Costa 4; ☺1pm-2am Tue-Thu, to 2.30am Fri & Sat, to 1.30am Sun, 5pm-2am Mon; ☎; ⓂSant Antoni) A super-trendy bar on a street that's not short of them, this place has excellent mojitos, a fashionable crowd and a frequently changing exhibition of art on the walls. There are DJs most nights, along with plenty of sofas and armchairs for a post-dancing slump.

Moog — Club

(Map p250; ☎93 319 17 89; www.masimas.com/moog; Carrer de l'Arc del Teatre 3; entry €5-10; ☺midnight-5am Sun-Thu, to 5.30am Fri & Sat; ⓂDrassanes) This fun and minuscule club is

a standing favourite with the downtown crowd. In the main dance area DJs dish out house, techno and electro, while upstairs you can groove to a nice blend of indie and occasional classic-pop throwbacks.

Marmalade — Bar

(Map p249; ☎93 442 39 66; www.marmalade barcelona.com; Carrer de la Riera Alta 4-6; ☺7pm-2am Mon-Thu, 10am-2.30am Fri & Sat, 10am-2am Sun; ☎; ⓂSant Antoni) The golden hues of this backlit bar and restaurant beckon seductively through the glass facade. There are various distinct spaces, decorated in different but equally sumptuous styles, and a pool table next to the bar. Cocktails are big business here, and a selection of them are €5 all night. It's also worth popping in for weekend brunch.

Negroni — Cocktail Bar

(Map p249; www.negronicocktailbar.com; Carrer de Joaquín Costa 46; ☺7pm-2.30am Sun-Thu, to 3am Fri & Sat; ⓂUniversitat) Good things come in small packages and this dark, teeny cocktail bar confirms the rule. The mostly black decor lures in a largely student set to try out the cocktails, among them, of course, the celebrated Negroni, a Florentine invention with one part Campari, one part gin and one part sweet vermouth.

Bar La Concha — Bar, Gay

(Map p250; ☎93 302 41 18; www.laconcha delraval.com; Carrer de la Guàrdia 14; ☺5pm-2.30am Sun-Thu, to 3.30am Fri & Sat; ☎; ⓂDrassanes) This place is dedicated to the actress Sara Montiel: the walls groan with more than 250 photos of the sultry star surrounding an incongruous large-screen TV. La Concha used to be a largely gay and trans haunt, but anyone is welcome and bound to have fun – especially when the drag queens come out to play.

Born in 1928, Sara Montiel bared all on the silver screen in an era that condemned nudity to shameful brazenness – hence 'la concha' (a word commonly used in Spanish slang) can be read as a sly salute to the female genitalia.

Betty Ford's
Bar

(Map p249; ☑93 304 13 68; Carrer de Joaquín Costa 56; ☺1pm-2.30am Tue-Fri, from 5pm Sat-Mon; ☎; Ⓜ Universitat) This enticing corner bar is one of several good stops along the student-jammed run of Carrer de Joaquín Costa. It puts together some nice cocktails and the place fills with an even mix of locals and foreigners, generally aged not much over 30. There's a decent line in burgers and soups, too.

Kentucky
Bar

(Map p250; ☑93 318 28 78; Carrer de l'Arc del Teatre 11; ☺10pm-4am Thu-Sat; Ⓜ Drassanes) Once a haunt of visiting US Navy boys, this exercise in Americana kitsch is the perfect way to finish an evening – if you can squeeze in. All sorts of odd bods from the *barri* and beyond gather here. An institution in the wee hours, Kentucky often stays open (unofficially) until dawn.

⊖ La Ribera

Guzzo
Cocktail Bar

(Map p250; ☑93 667 00 36; www.guzzoclub.es; Plaça Comercial 10; ☺6pm-3am Mon-Fri, noon-3.30am Sat & Sun; ☎; Ⓜ Jaume I) This old-school cocktail bar is run by much-loved Barcelona DJ Fred Guzzo, who is often to be found at the decks spinning his delicious selection of funk, soul and rare groove. You'll also find frequent live-music acts of consistently decent quality, and a funky atmosphere at almost any time of day.

La Vinya del Senyor
Wine Bar

(Map p250; ☑93 310 33 79; Plaça de Santa Maria del Mar 5; ☺noon-1am Mon-Thu, to 2am Fri & Sat, to midnight Sun; ☎; Ⓜ Jaume I) Relax on the *terraza*, which lies in the shadow of the Basílica de Santa Maria del Mar, or crowd inside at the tiny bar. The wine list is as long as *War and Peace* and there's a table upstairs for those who opt to sample the wine away from the madding crowd.

Rubí
Bar

(Map p250; ☑671 441888; Carrer dels Banys Vells 6; ☺7.30pm- 2.30am Sun-Thu, to 3am Fri & Sat; ☎; Ⓜ Jaume I) With its boudoir lighting and cheap mojitos, Rubí is where El Born's cognoscenti head for a nightcap – or several. Push through the narrow, cosy space to the back where you might just get one of the coveted tables. There's also superior bar food, from Vietnamese rolls to more traditional selections of cheese and ham.

El Born Bar
Bar

(Map p250; ☑93 319 53 33; www.elbornbar.com; Passeig del Born 26; ☺10am-2.30am Mon-Thu, to 3am Fri, 11am-3am Sat, noon-2.30am Sun; ☎; Ⓜ Jaume I) Moss-green paintwork, marble tables and a chequered black-and-white tiled floor create a timeless look for this popular cafe-bar. A spiral wrought-iron staircase leads to a quieter room upstairs (the twisting steps mean that there is no table service and hot drinks can't be carried upstairs). El Born is ideal for either morning coffee, an afternoon vermouth or an evening cocktail.

El Xampanyet
Wine Bar

(Map p250; ☑93 319 70 03; Carrer de Montcada 22; ☺noon-3.30pm & 7-11pm Tue-Sat, noon-3.30pm Sun; ☎; Ⓜ Jaume I) Nothing has changed for decades in this, one of the city's best-known *cava* bars. It's usually very crowded, so plant yourself at the bar or seek out a table against the decoratively tiled walls for a glass or three of the cheap house *cava* and an assortment of tapas, such as the tangy *boquerones en vinagre* (fresh anchovies in vinegar).

Miramelindo
Bar

(Map p250; ☑93 310 37 27; www.barmiramelindo bcn.com; Passeig del Born 15; ☺8pm-2am Mon-Sat, from 7pm Sun; ☎; Ⓜ Jaume I) A spacious tavern in a Gothic building, this remains a classic on Passeig del Born for mixed drinks, enjoyed to the sounds of soft jazz and soul. Try for a comfy seat at a table towards the back before the place fills to bursting. A couple of similar places sit on this side of the *passeig*.

Mudanzas
Bar

(Map p250; ☑93 319 11 37; Carrer de la Vidrieria 15; ☺9.30am-2am Mon-Fri, 10am-2.30am Sat & Sun; ☎; Ⓜ Jaume I) This was one of the first bars to get things into gear in El Born and it still attracts a faithful crowd. With its chequered floor and marble-topped tables, it's an attractive, lively place for a cocktail and perhaps a tapa. It also has a nice line in rum and malt whisky.

Magic   Club

(Map p250; ☑93 310 72 67; www.magic-club.net; Passeig de Picasso 40; ⊙11pm-6am Thu-Sat; ⓂBarceloneta) While it sometimes hosts live acts in its sweaty basement, Magic is basically a straightforward, subterranean nightclub offering rock, mainstream dance faves and Spanish pop. It's an established favourite and queues can be long.

⊖ Barceloneta, the Waterfront & El Poblenou

Perikete   Wine Bar

(Map p250; ☑93 024 22 29; www.gruporeini. net/perikete; Carrer de Llauder 6; ⊙11am-1am; ⓂBarceloneta) Since opening in 2017, this fabulous wine bar has been jam-packed with locals. Hams hang from the ceilings, barrels of vermouth sit above the bar and wine bottles cram every available shelf space – more than 200 varieties are available by the glass or bottle, accompanied by 50-plus tapas dishes. In the evening, the action spills into the street.

Bodega Vidrios y Cristales   Wine Bar

(Map p250; ☑93 250 45 01; www.gruposagardi. com/restaurante/bodega-vidrios-y-cristales; Passeig d'Isabel II 6; ⊙noon-4pm & 7pm-midnight Mon-Thu, noon-1am Fri-Sun; ⓂBarceloneta) In a history- steeped, stone-floored building dating from 1840, this atmospheric little jewel recreates a neighbourhood bodega with tins of sardines, anchovies and other delicacies lining the shelves (used in exquisite tapas dishes), house-made vermouth and a wonderful array of wines. Be prepared to stand as there are no seats (a handful of upturned wine barrels let you rest your glass).

BlackLab   Microbrewery

(Map p250; ☑93 221 83 60; www.blacklab.es; Plaça de Pau Vila 1; ⊙10.30am-1.30am Sun-Wed,

to 2am Thu, to 2.30am Fri & Sat; ⓂBarceloneta) Barcelona's first brewhouse opened back in 2014 inside historic Palau de Mar. Its taps feature 18 house brews, including saisons, double IPAs and dry stouts, and the brewmasters constantly experiment with new flavours, such as blonde ale with mandarin, or oatmeal and chocolate stout. One-hour tours (5pm Sundays; €19) offer a behind-the-scenes look at the brewers in action, plus tastings and a pint.

The kitchen sizzles up burgers, barbecued pulled-pork sandwiches and marinated ribs; other dishes include poké bowls.

Absenta   Bar

(☑93 221 36 38; www.absenta.bar; Carrer de Sant Carles 36; ⊙5pm-1am Sun, Mon & Wed, to 2am Thu, to 3am Fri & Sat; ⓂBarceloneta) Decorated with old paintings, vintage lamps and curious sculptures (including a dangling butterfly woman), this whimsical drinking den specialises in absinthe, with more than 20 varieties available. (Go easy, though: an alcohol content of 50% to 90% provides a kick!) It also has a house-made vermouth, if you're not a fan of the green fairy.

Can Paixano   Wine Bar

(Map p250; ☑93 310 08 39; www.canpaixano. com; Carrer de la Reina Cristina 7; ⊙9am-10.30pm Mon-Sat; ⓂBarceloneta) This lofty *cava* bar (also called La Xampanyeria) has long been run on a winning formula. The standard tipple is bubbly rosé in elegant little glasses, combined with bite-sized *bocadillos* and tapas. Note that this place is usually packed to the rafters, and elbowing your way to the bar can be a titanic struggle.

Woki Playa   Cocktail Bar

(www.tribuwoki.com; Passeig Marítim de la Barceloneta 1; ⊙noon-9pm Sun-Thu, to 11pm Fri & Sat; 🛜; ⓂBarceloneta) 🍸 A corrugated-iron bar, recycled timbers and repurposed industrial lights give this neo-*chiringuito* (snack bar) a sharp, contemporary edge. Ingredients from its own organic market in L'Eixample are used in cocktails such as its signature Woki Mule (jasmine-infused vodka, honey, lime, cardamom and ginger beer). Tapas, salads and burgers are all organic too.

Organic food is also served at its upstairs restaurant **Barraca** (📞93 224 12 53; mains €17-23; ⊘1-11.30pm; 🍴) 🍸.

La Deliciosa
Bar

(www.ladeliciosabeachbar.com; Passeig Marítim de la Barceloneta; ⊘9am-9pm Sun-Thu, to 10pm Fri & Sat; 🗪; MBarceloneta) Bamboo fish overhang this beach bar on the sand at Platja de la Barceloneta – an idyllic spot for fresh juices, regional wines and cocktails such as Basil Instinct (vodka, pineapple juice, lemon, ginger, raspberries and basil) or Passion Smash (Jack Daniels, passion-fruit pulp and mint). Soak them up with hot and cold sandwiches, burgers, black-bean nachos and bite-size tapas.

The Mint
Cocktail Bar

(Map p250; 📞647 737707; www.facebook.com/themintbcn; Passeig d'Isabel II 4; ⊘7.30pm-2.30am Sun-Thu, to 3am Fri & Sat; MBarceloneta) Named after the prized cocktail ingredient, this mojito-loving spot has an upstairs bar where you can peruse the first-rate house-infused gins (more than 20 on hand, including creative blends like lemon grass and Jamaican pepper). Downstairs in the brick-vaulted cellars, red lights and driving beats create a more celebratory vibe.

It's a fun setting for a night out, and well located for a bar-hop through El Born either before or after.

La Cervecita Nuestra de Cada Día
Bar

(📞93 486 92 71; www.facebook.com/lacervecitanuestradecadadia; Carrer de Llull 184; ⊘11.30am-2pm & 5.30-10.30pm Wed-Sat, 11.30am-9.30pm Sun, 5-10.30pm Mon, 5.30-10.30pm Tue; MPoblenou) Equal parts beer shop and craft brew bar, La Cervecita has a changing selection of unique beers from around Europe and the US. You might stumble across a Catalan sour fruit beer, a rare English stout, a potent Belgian triple ale or half a dozen other draughts on hand – plus many more varieties by the bottle. Low-playing music and minimal decorations keep the focus on beer chatter.

 Chiringuitos

During summer, small wooden beach bars, known as *chiringuitos*, open up along the strand from Barceloneta all the way up to Platja de la Nova Mar Bella. Here you can dip your toes in the sand and nurse a cocktail or munch a snack while watching the city at play against the backdrop of the deep-blue Mediterranean. Ambient sounds add to the laid-back environment. Some beachside bars also host big-name DJs and parties.

Chiringuito on Barcelona Beach

Madame George
Lounge

(www.madamegeorgebar.com; Carrer de Pujades 179; ⊘6pm-2am Mon-Thu, to 3am Fri & Sat, to 12.30am Sun; MPoblenou) A theatrical (veering towards campy) elegance marks the interior of this small, chandelier-lit lounge just off the Rambla del Poblenou. Deft bartenders stir well-balanced cocktails like a Lychee-tini (vanilla-infused vodka, fresh lychees, lychee liqueur and lemon juice) in vintage glassware, while a DJ spins vinyl (mainly soul and funk) in the corner.

Balius
Cocktail Bar

(📞93 315 86 50; www.baliusbar.com; Carrer de Pujades 196; ⊘6pm-2am Tue & Wed, to 2.30am Thu, to 3am Fri & Sat, 8pm-2am Sun; MPoblenou) There's an old-fashioned jauntiness to this vintage cocktail den in El Poblenou. Staff pour a mix of classic libations as well as vermouths, and there's a small tapas menu until 10.30pm. Stop by on Sunday to catch live jazz, starting around 8pm.

 Clubbing in Barcelona

Barcelona's *discotecas* (clubs) are at their best from Thursday to Saturday. Indeed, many open only on these nights. A surprising variety of spots lurk in the old-town labyrinth, ranging from plush former dance halls to grungy subterranean venues that fill to capacity.

Along the waterfront it's another story. At Port Olímpic, sun-scorched crowds of visiting yachties mix it up with tourists and a few locals at noisy, back-to-back dance bars right on the waterfront.

A handful of well-known clubs is sprinkled over the classy parts of town, in L'Eixample and La Zona Alta. They attract a beautiful crowd.

Moog (p178)

DIEGO LEZAMA/GETTY IMAGES ©

Bar Leo
Bar

(Carrer de Sant Carles 34; ⊙noon-9.30pm; MBarceloneta) An almost entirely *barcelonin* crowd spills out into the street from this hole-in-the-wall drinking spot plastered with images of late Andalucian singer and heart-throb Bambino, and a jukebox mostly dedicated to flamenco. It's at its liveliest on weekends.

Santa Marta
Bar

(Carrer de Grau i Torras 59; ⊙9.30am-midnight; MBarceloneta) Just back from the beach, this laid-back bar attracts a garrulous mix of locals and expats, who sit at the outside tables for prime people-watching. Alongside classic cocktails, craft creations include Santa Delicious (tequila, Campari, pink grapefruit and mint). More than 15 varieties of thin-crust pizzas are also available.

❷ L'Eixample

Napar BCN
Brewery

(Map p254; ☑93 408 91 62; www.naparbcn.com; Carrer de la Diputació 223; ⊙noon-midnight Tue & Wed, to 1am Thu, to 2am Fri & Sat, to 11pm Sun; ☜; MUniversitat) A standout on Barcelona's burgeoning craft-beer scene, Napar has 22 beers on tap, six of which are brewed on-site, including IPA, pale ale and stout. There's also an accomplished list of bottled beers. It's a stunning space, with a gleaming steampunk aesthetic and a great rock and indie soundtrack. Creative food changes seasonally.

Monvínic
Wine Bar

(Map p254; ☑93 272 61 87; www.monvinic.com; Carrer de la Diputació 249; ⊙1-11pm Tue-Fri, 7-11pm Mon & Sat; MPasseig de Gràcia) ✦ At this rhapsody to wine, the digital wine list details more than 3000 international varieties searchable by origin, year or grape. Some 50 selections are available by the glass; you can, of course, order by the bottle too. There is an emphasis on affordability, but if you want to splash out, there are fantastic vintage options. Feel free to talk to one of the six sommeliers who work on the list.

At the back is the **restaurant** (mains €16-36; ⊙1.30-3.30pm & 8-10.30pm Tue-Fri, 8-10.30pm Mon & Sat), which specialises in Mediterranean cuisine. Both the wine bar and restaurant are a study in locavore practices and sustainability.

Milano
Cocktail Bar

(Map p254; ☑93 112 71 50; www.camparimilano.com; Ronda de la Universitat 35; ⊙1pm-4am; MCatalunya) Completely invisible from street level, this gem of hidden Barcelona nightlife is a subterranean old-school cocktail bar with velvet banquettes and glass-fronted cabinets, presided over by white-jacketed waiters. Live music (Cuban, jazz, blues, flamenco and swing) plays nightly; a DJ takes over after 11pm. Fantastic cocktails include the Picasso (tequila, honey, absinthe and lemon) and six different Bloody Marys.

Les Gens Que J'Aime
Bar

(Map p254; ☑93 215 68 79; www.lesgensque
jaime.com; Carrer de València 286; ☺6pm-
2.30am Sun-Thu, 7pm-3am Fri & Sat; ⓂPasseig
de Gràcia) Atmospheric and intimate, this
basement relic of the 1960s follows a deceptively simple formula: chilled jazz music
in the background, minimal lighting from
an assortment of flea-market lamps and
a cosy, cramped scattering of red-velvet-
backed lounges around tiny dark tables.

BierCaB
Craft Beer

(Map p254; ☑644 689045; www.biercab.com;
Carrer de Muntaner 55; ☺bar noon-midnight Mon-
Thu, noon-2am Fri & Sat, 5pm-midnight Sun, shop
3.30-10pm Mon-Sat; �; ⓂUniversitat) Beneath
an artistic ceiling installation resembling
a forest of giant matchsticks, this brilliant
craft-beer bar has 30 brews from around
the world rotating on its taps. Burgers to ac-
company them are made from Wagyu beef
and named for Barcelona neighbourhoods.
Pop into its adjacent shop for another 500
bottled varieties kept cold in fridges.

Monkey Factory
Cocktail Bar

(☑93 681 78 93; www.facebook.com/monkey
factorybcn; Carrer de Còrsega 234; ☺6.30pm-2am
Tue & Wed, to 3am Thu-Sat; ⓇFGC Provença) DJs
spin on weekends at this high-spirited venue
but it's positively hopping from early on most
nights. 'Funky monkey' (triple sec, gin, lime
and egg white), 'chimpa sour' (cardamom-
infused pisco sour) and 'chita' (passionfruit
purée, vodka, cinnamon syrup and ginger)
are among the inventive cocktails mixed up
behind the neon-green-lit bar.

Garage Beer Co
Craft Beer

(Map p254; ☑93 528 59 89; www.facebook.com/
lesgensquejaime.pub; Carrer del Consell de Cent
261; ☺5pm-midnight Mon-Thu, to 2.30am Fri,
noon-3am Sat, 2pm-midnight Sun; ⓂUniversitat)
One of the first craft-beer bars to pop up in
Barcelona, Garage brews its own in a space
at the bar. It offers around 10 different styles
at a time: the eponymous Garage (a delicate
session IPA) and Slinger (a more robust IPA)
are always on the board. Other favourites
include Imperial Chocolate (stout) and Culture Trip (raspberry Berliner Weisse).

Dry Martini
Bar

(☑93 217 50 72; www.drymartiniorg.com; Carrer
d'Aribau 162-166; ☺1pm-2.30am Mon-Thu,
1pm-3am Fri, 6.30pm-3am Sat, 6.30pm-2.30am
Sun; ⓇFGC Provença) Waiters make expert
cocktail suggestions, but the house drink,
taken at the bar or on one of the plush
green banquettes, is always a good bet.
The gin and tonic comes in an enormous
mug-sized glass – one will take you most
of the night. Out the back hides a superb
restaurant, Speakeasy (p144).

LaBar
Bar

(www.facebook.com/labarbcn; Carrer del Consell
de Cent 442; ☺8.30am-midnight Mon-Thu, 8.30am-
1am Fri, 9am-1am Sat, 9am-11pm Sun; ⓂMonu-
mental) Desperate for a drink, but equally in
need of clean laundry? LaBar is the place for
you: a relaxed spot with low-hanging lights,
wooden tables and chairs, and exposed
stone – plus an incongruous row of washing
machines along one wall. While your clothes
get clean, enjoy coffee, juices, craft beers
and wine, and snacks like pastas, salads and
sandwiches.

El Viti
Bar

(Map p254; ☑93 633 83 36; www.elviti.com; Passeig de Sant Joan 62; ☺noon-midnight Sun-Thu,
to 1am Fri & Sat; �; ⓂGirona) Along the hip
Passeig de Sant Joan, El Viti checks all the
boxes – high ceilings, brick walls both bare
and glazed, black-clad staff and a barrel of
artisanal vermouth on the bar. It also serves
a good selection of tapas.

Antilla BCN
Club

(Map p249; ☑93 451 45 64; www.antillasalsa.
com; Carrer d'Aragó 141; cover Fri & Sat €10;
☺10pm-5am Wed, 11pm-5am Thu, 11pm-6am Fri
& Sat, 7pm-2am Sun; ⓂUrgell) *The* salsateca
in town, this is the place to come for Cuban
son, merengue, salsa and a whole lot more.

Átame
Gay

(Map p254; ☑93 421 41 33; Carrer del Consell de
Cent 257; ☺7.30pm-2.30am Tue, 8.30pm-2.30am
Wed & Thu, 8.30pm-3am Fri & Sat; ⓂUniversitat)
Cool for a coffee earlier on, Átame (Tie Me
Up) heats up later in the night when the
gay crowd comes out to play. There is a fun
drag show Thursday through Saturday.

Barcelona in a Glass

Cava consumption rockets at Christmas.

Brut Nature, Extra Brut and Brut are the driest styles.

Usually made from Macabeu, Parellada and Xarel·lo grapes.

Reserva and Gran Reserva wines have extra bottle age.

Dulce and Semi Seco are the sweet styles.

Cava also comes in rosé.

URBANBUZZ/SHUTTERSTOCK ©

CAVA
WINE OF SPAIN

Cava

¡Salud!

Produced in the vineyards of the Penedès region, *cava* is Spain's most prominent sparkling wine. It undergoes a creation process similar to that of champagne and comes in varying grades of dryness or sweetness.

Sangria, the refreshing summery blend of wine, fruit, sugar and a dash of something harder, is given a twist in Catalonia by using *cava* instead of cheap red.

Sangria
PAGE LIGHT STUDIOS/SHUTTERSTOCK ©

Top Five for Cava

El Xampanyet (p179) Nothing has changed for decades in this, one of the city's best known *cava* bars.

Can Paixano (p180) This lofty *cava* bar has long been run on a winning formula: the standard tipple is bubbly rosé in elegant little glasses.

Perikete (p180) Since opening in 2017, this fabulous wine bar has been jam-packed with locals.

Viblioteca (p190) This excellent wine bar lets you choose from numerous *cava* options.

La Vinya del Senyor (p179) Plenty of cool *cava* to try in this pretty location.

Cosmo Cafe

(Map p254; ☎93 105 79 92; www.galeriacosmo.com; Carrer d'Enric Granados 3; ⏰10am-10pm; Ⓜ Universitat) Set on a pedestrian strip behind the university, this cool cafe-gallery has a bicycle hanging from the high, white walls, bright splashy murals and painted ventilation pipes – and even makes a feature of its fire hose. Along with fresh juices, hot chocolate, teas, pastries and snacks, it serves beer and wine.

Plata Bar Gay

(Map p249; ☎93 452 46 36; www.platabar.com; Carrer del Consell de Cent 233; ⏰8pm-2am Thu & Sun, to 3am Fri & Sat; Ⓜ Universitat) Summer seats on the corner terrace of this wide-open bar attract a lot of lads hopping between the area's gay bars. Inside metallic horse-saddle stools are lined up at the bar and high tables, the music is a mix of dance and trance, and bartenders whip up eye-popping cocktails.

Cafè del Centre Cafe

(Map p254; ☎93 488 11 01; Carrer de Girona 69; ⏰10am- midnight Mon-Fri, noon-midnight Sat; 📶; Ⓜ Girona) Step back into the 19th century in this cafe that's been in business since 1873. The mahogany bar extends down the right side as you enter, fronted by marble-topped tables and wooden chairs. It exudes an almost melancholy air by day but gets busy at night, when live jazz piano plays. It stocks 50 varieties of beer and 15 loose-leaf teas.

Quilombo Bar

(☎606 144272; Carrer d'Aribau 149; ⏰9pm-2.30am Mon-Thu, 8.30pm-3am Fri & Sat; 🚆FGC Provença) Some formulas just work, and this place has been working since the 1970s. Set up some guitars in the table-packed back room, add some cheapish ready-made mojitos and plastic tubs of nuts, and let the punters do the rest. They pour in, creating plenty of *quilombo* (fuss). Live music plays most nights from 11pm and impromptu parties are common.

La Fira Bar

(Map p254; ☎682 323714; www.facebook.com/lafiraprovenza; Carrer de Provença 171; cover €14; ⏰11pm-5am Thu, to 5.30am Fri & Sat; 🚆FGC Provença) Wander in past crazy mirrors, penny slot machines and other ancient fairground attractions from Germany as well as futuristic furniture, such as glowing cuboid stools. The music swings wildly from house through '90s hits to Spanish pop classics. Admission includes at least one drink. With 150 spirits on hand, it claims to have 500 varieties of shots.

Punto BCN Gay

(Map p254; ☎93 451 91 52; www.grupoarena.com; Carrer de Muntaner 65; ⏰6pm-2.30am Sun-Thu, to 3am Fri & Sat; Ⓜ Universitat) It's an oldie but a goody. A big bar over two levels with a slightly older crowd, this place gets busy on Friday and Saturday nights with its blend of Spanish pop and dance. It's a friendly early stop on a gay night out, and you can shoot a round of pool here.

La Chapelle Gay

(Map p254; ☎93 453 30 76; Carrer de Muntaner 67; ⏰4pm- 2am Sun-Thu, to 2.30am Fri & Sat; Ⓜ Universitat) A typical long, narrow Eixample bar with white-tiled walls, La Chapelle houses a plethora of crucifixes and niches that far outdo what you'd find in any other 'chapel'. No need for six-pack abs here: this is a relaxed gay meeting place that welcomes all.

Bacon Bear Gay

(Map p249; ☎93 431 00 00; Carrer de Casanova 64; ⏰6pm-2.30am Sun-Thu, to 3am Fri & Sat; Ⓜ Urgell) Every bear needs a cave, and this is a rather friendly one. It's really just a big bar for burly gay folk. The music cranks up on weekends.

Arena Classic Gay & Lesbian

(Map p254; ☎93 487 83 42; www.grupoarena.com; Carrer de la Diputació 233; cover Fri & Sat €6-12; ⏰11pm-3am Thu, to 6am Fri & Sat; Ⓜ Passeig de Gràcia) Spinning pop hits from all decades, Arena Classic has a spacious dance floor and attracts a fun gay crowd. Entry includes a drink. Each night the 11pm to 3am slot is dedicated to popular lesbian night Aire, although in practice the crowd tends to be fairly mixed.

Catalan Wines

The bulk of DO wines (*denominación de origen*, a specific regional appellation) in Catalonia are made from grapes produced in the Penedès area, which pumps out almost two million hectolitres a year. The other DO winemaking zones (spread as far apart as the Empordà area around Figueres in the north and the Terra Alta around Gandesa in the southwest) have a combined output of about half that produced in Penedès. The wines of the El Priorat area, which tend to be dark, heavy reds, have been promoted to DOC status, an honour shared only with those of La Rioja (categorised as such since 1926). Drops from the neighbouring Montsant area are frequently as good (or close) and considerably cheaper.

Most of the grapes grown in Catalonia are native to Spain and include white macabeo, garnatxa and xarel·lo (for whites), and black garnatxa, monastrell and ull de llebre (tempranillo) red varieties. Foreign varieties (such as chardonnay, riesling, chenin blanc, cabernet sauvignon, merlot and pinot noir) are also common.

There is plenty to look out for beyond Penedès. Raïmat, in the Costers del Segre DO area of Lleida province, produces fine reds and a couple of notable whites. Good fortified wines come from around Tarragona and some nice fresh wines are also produced in the Empordà area in the north.

Organic-grape harvest
JORDI CAMÍ/ALAMY STOCK PHOTO ©

Arena Madre Gay

(Map p254; ☎93 487 83 42; www.grupoarena.com; Carrer de Balmes 32; cover Sun-Fri €10, Sat €12; ⏰12.30-5am Sun-Thu, to 6am Fri & Sat; Ⓜ Passeig de Gràcia) Popular with a hot young crowd, Arena Madre is one of the top clubs in town for boys seeking boys. Mainly pop, dance and house music, with a striptease show on Monday, reggaeton on Thursday, and live shows throughout the week. Heteros are welcome but a minority.

Michael Collins Pub Irish Pub

(Map p254; ☎93 459 19 64; www.michaelcollinspubs.com; Plaça de la Sagrada Família 4; ⏰1pm-2.30am Sun-Thu, to 3am Fri & Sat; 📶; Ⓜ Sagrada Família) To be sure of a little Catalan-Irish *craic*, this barn-sized, storming pub beloved by locals and expats is just the ticket. Traditional Irish music sessions strike up on Monday; live music also plays most weekends. It's ideal for football fans wanting big-screen action over their pints, too.

New Chaps Gay

(Map p254; ☎93 215 53 65; www.newchaps.com; Avinguda Diagonal 365; ⏰9pm-3am Mon-Wed, 7pm-3am Thu & Sun, 9pm-3.30am Fri, 6pm-3.30am Sat; Ⓜ Diagonal) Leather lovers get in some close- quarters inspection on the dance floor and especially in the dark room, downstairs past the fairly dark loos in the vaulted cellars. It's a classic handle-bar-moustache gay porn kinda place that attracts an older crowd.

Montjuïc, Poble Sec & Sant Antoni

Abirradero Brewery

(Map p256; ☎93 461 94 46; www.abirradero.com; Carrer de Vilà i Vilà 77; ⏰5pm-midnight Mon-Thu, noon-2am Fri & Sat, noon-midnight Sun; 📶; Ⓜ Paral·lel) Barcelona is spoilt for choice with craft breweries, and this bright, buzzing space has 20 of its own beers rotating on the taps, including IParal·lel (a double IPA), Imperial Choco-Icecream-Cookies Stout, and Trigotopia. Tapas, sharing boards and burgers are standouts from the kitchen. There's occasionally live jazz and blues here.

Book online for 40-minute brewery tours in English (€15), which include a tasting of three beers.

La Caseta del Migdia Bar

(☎617 956572; www.lacaseta.org; Mirador del Migdia; ⊗8pm-1am Wed-Fri, noon-1am Sat & Sun Apr-Sep, noon-sunset Sat & Sun Oct-Mar; ☐150) The effort of getting to what is, for all intents and purposes, a simple *chiringuito* is worth it. Gaze out to sea over a beer or soft drink by day. As sunset approaches the atmosphere changes, as reggae, samba and funk wafts out and over the hillside. Drinks aside, you can also order food fired on the outdoor grills.

Walk below the walls of the Castell de Montjuïc along the dirt track or follow Passeig del Migdia – look out for signs for the Mirador del Migdia.

El Rouge Bar

(Map p256; ☎666 251556; www.facebook. com/ elrougebar; Carrer del Poeta Cabanyes 21; ⊗9pm-2am Thu & Sun, 10pm-3am Fri & Sat; ☜; MParal·lel) Decadence is the word that springs to mind in this bordello-red lounge and cocktail bar, with acid jazz, drum and bass and other sounds drifting along in the background. The walls are covered in heavy-framed paintings, dim lamps and mirrors, and no two chairs are alike. You can sometimes catch DJs, risqué poetry soirées, cabaret shows or even nights of tango dancing. Jam sessions regularly take place.

Pervert Club Gay

(Map p256; ☎93 453 05 82; www.facebook. com/matineeclubgay; Avinguda Francesc Ferrer i Guàrdia 13; cover from €20; ⊗midnight-6am some Sat; ☐13, 23, 150, MEspanya) This men-only fest takes place every few Saturdays in Poble Espanyol (p59). Electronic music dominates and, in spite of the 6am finish, for many this is only the start of the night. Expect loads of tanned and buff gym hotties – and plenty of shirtless eye candy. Check the Facebook page for dates.

La Cambicha Bar

(Map p256; ☎93 187 25 13; Carrer del Poeta Cabanyes 43; ⊗6pm-2am Mon-Wed, 1pm-2am Thu-Sun; MParal·lel) This shoebox-sized bar feels a bit like a lost cabin in the woods with its newspaper-covered walls, lanterns and old sporting photos. Once you've wedged yourself alongside a tiny table, you can join the young soul- and blues-loving crowd over inexpensive empanadas and vermouth. Bands also occasionally play.

Bar Olimpia Bar

(Map p256; ☎676 828232; www.facebook.com/ bar.olimpia. 5; Carrer d'Aldana 11; ⊗5pm-1am Mon-Wed, to 2am Thu, to 3am Fri, 1pm-3am Sat, 1pm-1am Sun; MParal·lel) This great little neighbourhood bar is a small slice of Barcelona history. It was here (and on the surrounding block) that the popular Olimpia Theatre Circus performed between 1924 and 1947. Today the retro setting draws a diverse crowd, who come for house-made vermouth, snacks (like quesadillas, cheese platters and tuna tartare) and strong gin and tonics.

Redrum Bar

(Map p256; ☎670 269126; www.facebook.com/ TACOSREDRUM; Carrer de Margarit 36; ⊗6pm-1am Mon-Thu, to 2am Fri, 2pm-2am Sat, 6pm-12.30am Sun; MPoble Sec) Redrum's craft brews and cocktails are complemented by Mexican street food, including excellent tacos and ceviche. It has a brightly coloured interior and friendly service. Happy hour runs from 6pm to 8pm.

Bar Calders Bar

(Map p256; ☎93 329 93 49; Carrer del Parlament 25; ⊗5pm- 1am Mon-Thu, to 2.30am Fri, 11am-2.30am Sat, 11am-midnight Sun; MPoble Sec) It bills itself as a wine bar, but actually the wine selection at Bar Calders is its weak point. At weekends it's unbeatable as an all-day cafe and tapas bar, and its outdoor tables on a tiny pedestrian lane have become the favoured meeting point for the neighbourhood's boho set.

Gran Bodega Saltó   Bar

(Map p256; 93 441 37 09; www.bodegasalto.net; Carrer de Blesa 36; ⊙7pm-2am Mon-Thu, noon-3am Fri & Sat, noon-midnight Sun; Ⓜ Paral·lel) The barrels give away the bar's history as a traditional bodega. Now, after a little home-made psychedelic redecoration with odd lamps, figurines and old Chinese beer ads, it's a magnet for an eclectic barfly crowd. The crowd is mixed and friendly, and gets animated on nights when there's live music.

Sala Plataforma   Club

(Map p256; ☑93 329 00 29; www.salaplataforma. com; Carrer Nou de la Rambla 145; cover from €6; ⊙10pm-6am Thu-Sat, 7pm-2am Sun; Ⓜ Paral. lel) With two adjoining if smallish dance spaces, 'Platform' feels like a clandestine location in an otherwise quiet residential street. Inside this friendly, straightforward dance dive, you'll find popular '80s grooves, timeless rock and occasional live bands – plus drum and bass on Thursday.

Metro Disco   Gay

(Map p249; ☑93 323 52 27; www.metrodiscobcn. com; Carrer de Sepúlveda 185; cover before/ after 2.30am from €7/13; ⊙12.15am-5.30am Sun-Thu, to 6.30am Fri & Sat; Ⓜ Universitat) Metro attracts a fun-loving gay crowd with its two dance floors, three bars and very dark room. Keep an eye out for shows and parties, which can range from parades of dancers to bingo nights (held Wednesdays, with sometimes-interesting prizes), plus the occasional strip show.

While you'll save some cash by coming before 2.30am, you're likely to be drinking on your own, as Metro doesn't fill up till late.

Tinta Roja   Bar

(Map p256; ☑93 443 32 43; www.tintaroja.cat; Carrer de la Creu dels Molers 17; ⊙8pm-midnight Wed, 8.30pm-2am Thu, to 3am Fri & Sat, shorter hours Aug; Ⓜ Poble Sec) A succession of nooks and crannies, dotted with flea-market finds and dimly lit in violets, reds and yellows, makes Tinta Roja an intimate spot for a craft beer, cocktail or glass of Argentinean wine, as do the occasional shows in the back, featuring anything from actors to acrobats.

This was once a *vaqueria* (small dairy farm) that kept cows out the back and sold fresh milk at the front.

La Confitería (p177)

La Terrrazza   Club

(Map p256; ☑687 969825; http://laterrrazza.com/
en; Avinguda de Francesc Ferrer i Guàrdia 13; cover
from €15; ☉midnight-6.30am Thu-Sat May-Sep;
☑13, 23, 150, Ⓜ Espanya) In summer, La Terrrazza attracts squadrons of beautiful people,
locals and foreigners alike, for a full-on night
of music (house, techno and electronica)
and cocktails partly under the stars inside
the Poble Espanyol (p59) complex.

☉ Gràcia & Park Güell

Bobby Gin   Cocktail Bar

(Map p254; ☑93 368 18 92; www.bobbygin.com;
Carrer de Francisco Giner 47; ☉4pm-2am Sun-
Wed, to 2.30am Thu, to 3am Fri & Sat; Ⓜ Diagonal)
With more than 60 varieties, this whitewashed stone-walled bar is a haven for gin
lovers. Try an infusion-based concoction
(rose-tea-infused Hendrick's with strawber-
ries and lime; tangerine-infused Tanqueray
10 with agave nectar and bitter chamomile)
or a cocktail like the Santa Maria (chardonnay, milk-thistle syrup, thyme, sage
and lemon). Fusion tapas choices include
G&T-cured salmon. Shrimp coated in green
puffed rice and beef and shiitake wontons
are other great options.

Rabipelao   Cocktail Bar

(Map p254; ☑93 182 50 35; www.elrabipelao.com;
Carrer del Torrent d'En Vidalet 22; ☉7pm-1.30am
Sun-Thu, to 3am Fri & Sat, 1-4.30pm Sun; Ⓜ Joanic)
Rabipelao is a celebratory space with richly
patterned red wallpaper and DJs spinning
salsa beats. A silent film plays, walls are
decorated with vintage framed photos, and
there's a colourful mural above the bar.
Tropical cocktails such as mojitos and caipir-
inhas pair with Venezuelan snacks such as
arepas (bean, meat and cheese-filled corn-
bread patties) and Peruvian ceviche.

Tables spread across the covered patio
at the back. There's occasional live music.

El Ciclista   Cocktail Bar

(Map p254; ☑93 368 53 02; www.elciclistabar.
com; Carrer de Mozart 18; ☉7.30pm-2am Sun-
Thu, to 3am Fri & Sat; Ⓜ Diagonal) As the name
suggests, this elegant little cocktail bar has

a cycling theme - think bike-wheel chandeliers and tables, and bicycle frames stuck to
the walls. Among the list of classic cocktails
on offer is an excellent selection of gin and
tonics, as well a wide variety of flavoured
mojitos. There's live music on Friday night
and in-house DJs on Saturday.

Elephanta   Bar

(Map p254; ☑93 237 69 06; www.elephanta.cat;
Carrer del Torrent d'en Vidalet 37; ☉6pm-1.30am
Mon-Wed, to 2.30am Thu, to 3am Fri & Sat, to 10pm
Sun; ☏; Ⓜ Joanic) Tucked away off the main
drag, this petite cocktail bar has an old-
fashioned vibe, with long plush green banquettes, art-lined walls and a five-seat bar
with vintage wooden stools. Gin is the drink
of choice, with more than 40 varieties on
hand, and the cocktails are expertly mixed.

La Vermu   Bar

(Map p254; ☑93 171 80 87; Carrer de Sant
Domènec 15; ☉7pm- midnight Mon-Thu, 12.30-
4.30pm & 7.30pm-12.30am Fri-Sun; ☒FGC
Gràcia) House-made *negre* (black) and
blanc (white) vermouth, served with a slice
of orange and an olive, is the speciality
of this hip neighbourhood hang-out. The
airy space with exposed timber beams
and industrial lighting centres on a marble
bar with seating and surrounding marble-
topped tables. Vermouth aside, it also has
a small but stellar wine list and stylishly
presented tapas.

Sol de NIT   Bar

(Map p254; ☑93 237 39 37; http://sol-de-nit.
eltenedor.rest; Plaça del Sol 9; ☉1-3.30pm &
9-11pm; Ⓜ Fontana) Happening little hang-
out Sol de NIT has a small, cosy interior
decorated with mosaics, old lamps and a
soundtrack of jazz, and a large terrace on
Plaça del Sol that's heated in winter. Sangría
is a speciality; there are great cocktails, too.

El Rincón Cubano   Bar

(Map p254; ☑682 113 204; www.facebook.com/
elrinconcubanobcn; Carrer de l'Or 19; mains
€8.50-9.40; ☉7pm-2am Tue-Sun, 1pm-6.30pm
Sat & Sun; ☏; Ⓜ Fontana) Cuban cocktails
(including Cuba libres and *el presidentes*)
and beers (Mayabe, Tinima and Cacique)

are served alongside authentic snacks such as *pasteles* (puff pastry with savoury fillings), Cuban sandwiches and *ropa vieja* (shredded steak in tomato sauce) at this bar with arched brickwork and terracotta-tiled floors. It's in its element on Sunday from 4pm when live acoustic Cuban music plays.

La Vermuteria del Tano   Bar

(Map p254; ☎93 213 10 58; Carrer de Joan Blanques 17; ☺9am-9pm Tue-Fri, noon-4pm Sat & Sun; Ⓜ Joanic) Scarcely changed in decades, with barrels on the walls, old fridges with wooden doors, vintage clocks and marble-topped tables, this vermouth bar is a local gathering point. Its house-speciality Peruchi is served traditionally with a glass of carbonated water. Tapas is also traditional, with most dishes utilising ingredients from tins (anchovies, smoked clams, cockles and pickled octopus).

Chatelet   Cocktail Bar

(Map p254; ☎93 284 95 90; Carrer de Torrijos 54; ☺6pm-2.30am Mon-Thu, to 3am Fri, noon-3am Sat, to 2.30am Sun; Ⓜ Joanic) A popular meeting point, Chatelet has big windows for watching passers-by parade and a buzzing, art-filled interior that sees a wide cross-section of Gràcia society. Blues music and old-school American soul play in the background. The cocktails are excellent, and the drink prices fair (with discounts before 10pm).

Viblioteca   Wine Bar

(Map p254; ☎93 284 42 02; www.viblioteca.com; Carrer de Vallfogona 12; ☺7pm-midnight; Ⓜ Fontana) A glass cabinet piled high with ripe cheese (more than 50 varieties) entices you into this small, white, cleverly designed contemporary space. The real speciality at Viblioteca, however, is wine, and you can choose from 150 mostly local labels, many of them available by the glass.

La Cigale   Cocktail Bar

(Map p254; ☎93 457 58 23; www.facebook. com/la-cigalebarcelona; Carrer de Tordera 50; ☺7.30pm-2am Sun-Thu, to 3am Fri & Sat; Ⓜ Joanic) La Cigale is a very civilised place for a cocktail, with oil paintings on the

walls, gilded mirrors and leatherbound volumes scattered about. Prop up the zinc bar, sink into a secondhand lounge chair around a teeny table or head upstairs. Music is chilled, conversation lively, and you're likely to see Charlie Chaplin in action on the silent flat-screen TV (though FC Barcelona games are also screened). Free salsa classes take place at 10pm Sunday. American-style burgers and snacks such as cheese-smothered nachos are also served.

Bar Canigó   Bar

(Map p254; ☎93 213 30 49; www.barcanigo.com; Carrer de Verdi 2; ☺10am-2am Mon-Thu, 10am-3am Fri, 8pm-3am Sat; Ⓜ Fontana) Now run by the third generation of owners, this corner bar overlooking Plaça de la Revolució de Setembre de 1868 is an animated spot to sip on a house vermouth or an Estrella beer around rickety old marble-top tables, as people have done here since 1922.

Earlier in the day, it's a great spot for a coffee paired with a croissant or *bikini* (toasted cheese and ham sandwich).

La Fourmi   Bar

(Map p254; ☎93 213 30 52; Carrer de Milà i Fontanals 58; ☺9am-1.30am Mon-Thu, to 3am Fri, 10am-3am Sat, to 1.30am Sun; Ⓜ Joanic) La Fourmi is a small, cosy spot for a cocktail or a bite, no matter the time of day; it draws a mix of students, old-timers and hipsters. Drinks range from classic mojitos and strawberry daiquiris to international beers. There's also a weekend brunch menu (€11.90), including dishes such as eggs Benedict, French toast with bacon and traditional English breakfast.

El Sabor   Bar

(Map p254; ☎674 993075; Carrer de Francisco Giner 32; ☺10pm-3am Tue-Sun; Ⓜ Diagonal) This home of *ron y son* (rum and sound) has been ruled since 1992 by the charismatic Havana-born Angelito. A mixed crowd of Cubans and fans of the Caribbean island come to drink mojitos and shake their stuff in this diminutive, good-humoured hang-out. Stop by on on Wednesdays for a free two-hour salsa or bachata lesson (starting at 9pm).

Le Journal
Bar

(Map p254; ☑93 368 41 37; Carrer de Francisco Giner 36; ☺6pm-2am; ⓜFontana) Newspapers plaster the wood-panelled walls and ceilings of this split-level bar (hence the name). Read the headlines of yesteryear while reclining in an old lounge. For a slightly more intimate feel, head upstairs to the rear gallery overlooking the bar. Try one of the gin infusions or house-speciality Hurricane (with dark rum and passionfruit juice).

Musical Maria
Bar

(Map p254; ☑93 501 04 60; Carrer de Maria 5; ☺9.30pm-3am; ☎; ⓜDiagonal) Even the music hasn't changed since this place got going in 1980. Those longing for rock 'n' roll crowd into this animated bar, listen to old hits and knock back beers. Out the back there's a pool table and the bar serves pretty much all the variants of the local Estrella Damm brew.

Raïm
Bar

(Map p254; Carrer del Progrés 48; ☺8pm-2am Tue-Thu, to 3am Fri & Sat; ⓜDiagonal) Open for more than a century, Raïm is alive with black-and-white photos and paraphernalia of Cubans and Cuba. It's like being in a bar in Old Havana, with weathered wooden chairs around marble tables, old fashioned clocks, and wood-framed mirrors hanging on the walls. It draws a friendly, garrulous crowd that piles in for first-rate mojitos and an excellent selection of rum.

⊖ Camp Nou, Pedralbes & La Zona Alta

El Maravillas
Cocktail Bar

(☑93 360 73 78; www.elmaravillas.cat; Plaça de la Concòrdia 15; ☺noon-midnight Sun-Tue, to 1am Wed, to 2am Thu, to 3am Fri & Sat; ⓜLes Corts, ⓡT1, T2, T3 Numància) Overlooking the peaceful Plaça de la Concòrdia, El

Maravillas feels like a refuge from the crowded lanes of the Ciutat Vella (Old City). The glittering bar has just a few tables, plus outdoor seating on the square in warm weather. Creative cocktails, good Spanish red wines and easy-drinking vermouths are the drinks of choice.

Café Turó
Cafe

(☑93 200 69 53; http://romainfornell.com/restaurantes/cafe-turo; Carrer del Tenor Viñas 1; ☺8am-11.30pm Mon-Fri, 9am-11.30pm Sat & Sun; ⓡFGC Muntaner) Framed by red awnings, with vivid crimson walls brightening the low-lit interior, this cafe on the edge of Turó Parc has year-round seating on the footpath at the front – ideal for catching some sun over a morning coffee, afternoon glass of wine or evening cocktail. There's a good selection of bistro plates and tapas.

Mirablau
Bar

(☑93 418 58 79; www.mirablaubcn.com; Plaça del Doctor Andreu; ☺11am-3.30am Mon-Wed, to 4.30am Thu, 10am-5am Fri & Sat, 10am-2.30am Sun; ⓡ196, ⓡFGC Avinguda Tibidabo) Views over the entire city from this balcony restaurant at the base of the Funicular del Tibidabo make up for sometimes patchy service. The bar is renowned for its gin selection, with 30 different varieties. Wander downstairs to the tiny dance space, which opens at 11.30pm; in summer you can step out onto the even smaller terrace for a breather.

Marcel
Bar

(☑93 209 89 48; Carrer de Santaló 42; ☺7.30am-1am Mon-Thu, 7.30am-3am Fri & Sat, 9.30am-midnight Sun; ⓡFGC Muntaner) A classic meeting place, Marcel has an old-world feel, with a wood bar, black-and-white floor tiles and high windows. It offers snacks and tapas as well. Space is somewhat limited and customers inevitably spill out onto the footpath, where there are also a few tables.

SHOWTIME

Listen to live jazz, check out a gig
or dance the night away

Showtime

Barcelona teems with stages hosting all manner of entertainment from underground cabaret and comic opera to high drama. Dance companies are thick on the ground and popular local theatre companies, when not touring the rest of Spain, keep folks strapped to their seats.

Almost every big international rock and pop act has passed through Barcelona at some point, and the city is also blessed with a fine line-up of theatres for grand performances of classical music, opera and more.

In This Section

Listings & Tickets

The Palau de la Virreina (p45) cultural information office has oodles of information on theatre, opera and classical music performances.

For exhibitions and other forms of entertainment, see www.barcelona-metropolitan.com or www.timeout.cat. For free activities, check out www.forfree.cat.

The easiest way to get hold of *entradas* (tickets) for most venues throughout the city is through Ticketea (www.ticketea.com) or Ticketmaster (www.ticketmaster.es). Occasionally there are discounted tickets to be had on www.atrapalo.com.

Gran Teatre del Liceu (p196)

The Best...

For Classical Music

Good coverage of classical music listings is available at www.classictic.com.

Palau de la Música Catalana (p198) A Modernista fantasy, where the fabulous interior can distract from the finest musician.

Gran Teatre del Liceu (p196) One of Europe's most splendid opera houses, built to impress.

L'Auditori (p200) Fiercely modern concert venue, with a resident orchestra.

L'Ateneu (p196) This elegant old library is hard to enter if you're not a member – unless you catch one of its occasional concerts.

For Live Bands

City Hall (p200) The perfect midsize venue for up-and-coming local and international acts.

Sala Apolo (p201) Cosy booths and a warm red glow give this hugely popular venue something special.

BARTS (p201) A key player on the live music circuit, with superb sound and every mod con.

Bikini (p203) Hidden behind a shopping centre, Bikini still pulls in some great acts.

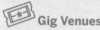

Bigger touring bands more often than not play at Razzmatazz (p199), Bikini (p203), Sala Apolo (p201) or BARTS (p201), although there are a number of other decent midsize venues. There are also abundant local gigs in institutions as diverse as **CaixaForum** (Map p256; ☑93 476 86 00; www.caixaforum.es; Avinguda de Francesc Ferrer i Guàrdia 6-8; MEspanya), La Pedrera (p76) and L'Ateneu (p196).

Audience at Bikini (p203)

✪ La Rambla & Barri Gòtic

Gran Teatre del Liceu
Theatre, Live Music

(Map p250; ☑93 485 99 00; www.liceu barcelona.cat; La Rambla 51-59; ⊗box office 11am-8pm Mon-Fri, to 6pm Sat; tours adult/ concession/under 7yr 30min €6/5/free, 45min €9/7.50/free; ⊗30min tours 1pm Mon-Sat, 45min tours hourly 2-5pm Mon-Fri, from 11am Sat MLiceu) Barcelona's grand old opera house, restored after a fire in 1994, is one of the most technologically advanced theatres in the world. To take a seat in the grand auditorium, returned to all its 19th-century glory but with the very latest in acoustics, is to be transported to another age.

Tickets can cost anything from €10 for a cheap seat behind a pillar to €200 for a well-positioned night at the opera.

L'Ateneu
Classical Music

(Map p250; ☑93 343 61 21; www.ateneubcn. org; Carrer de la Canuda 6; tickets free-€10; MCatalunya) This historic private library and cultural centre (dating back more than 150 years) hosts a range of high-brow fare, from classical recitals to film screenings and literary readings.

El Paraigua
Live Music

(Map p250; ☑93 302 11 31; www.elparaigua.com; Carrer del Pas de l'Ensenyança 2; ⊗noon-1am Sun-Wed, to 2am Thu, to 3am Fri & Sat; MLiceu) **FREE** A tiny chocolate box of dark tinted Modernisme, the 'Umbrella' has been serving up drinks since the 1960s. The turn-of-the-20th-century decor was transferred here from a shop knocked down elsewhere in the district and cobbled back together to create this cosy locale. Take a trip back in time from Modernisme to medieval by heading downstairs to the brick and stone basement bar area. Amid 11th-century walls, live bands – funk, soul, rock, blues – hold court on Friday and Saturday (from 11.30pm).

Sidecar Factory Club
Live Music

(Map p250; ☑93 933 17 76 66; http://sidecar. es; Plaça Reial 7; ⊗7pm-5am Thu & Fri, to 6am Sat, other days vary; MLiceu) Descend into the red-tinged, brick-vaulted bowels where just about any kind of live music could be on the agenda, from UK indie through to country punk, though rock and pop lead the way. DJs take over later on. Upstairs at ground level you can get food (until midnight) or a few drinks (until 3am).

Jamboree
Live Music

(Map p250; ☑93 319 17 89; www.masimas.com/ jamboree; Plaça Reial 17; tickets €5-22; ⊗8pm-6am; MLiceu) For more than half a century, Jamboree has been bringing joy to the jivers of Barcelona, with high-calibre acts featuring jazz trios, blues, Afrobeats, Latin and big-band sounds. Two concerts are held most nights (at 8pm and 10pm), after which Jamboree morphs into a DJ-spinning club at 12.30am. Jamboree Jam sessions are held on Monday (entrance a mere €5). Buy tickets online to save a few euros.

Harlem Jazz Club
Jazz

(Map p250; ☎93 310 07 55; www.harlemjazzclub. es; Carrer de la Comtessa de Sobradiel 8; tickets €7-12; ⏰8pm-3am Sun & Tue-Thu, to 5am Fri & Sat; Ⓜ Jaume I) This narrow, old-city dive is one of the best spots in town for jazz, as well as funk, Latin, blues and gypsy jazz. It attracts a mixed crowd that maintains a respectful silence during the acts. Most concerts start at 10.30pm or 11pm. Get in early if you want a seat in front of the stage.

Tarantos
Flamenco

(Map p250; ☎93 319 17 89; www.masimas. com/tarantos; Plaça Reial 17; tickets €15; ⏰shows 7.30pm, 8.30pm & 9.30pm Oct-Jun, plus 10.30pm Jul-Sep; Ⓜ Liceu) Since 1963, this basement locale has staged up-and-coming flamenco groups performing in Barcelona. Today Tarantos has become a mostly tourist-centric affair, with half-hour shows held three times a night. Still, it's a good introduction to flamenco, and not a bad setting for a drink.

✪ El Raval

Filmoteca de Catalunya
Cinema

(Map p250; ☎93 567 10 70; www.filmoteca. cat; Plaça de Salvador Seguí 1-9; adult/concession €4/3; ⏰screenings 5-10pm, ticket office 10am-3pm Tue-Fri, plus 4-9.30pm Tue-Thu & Sun, to 10pm Fri & Sat; Ⓜ Liceu) The Filmoteca de Catalunya – Catalonia's national cinema – sits in a modern 6000-sq-metre building in the midst of the most louche part of El Raval. The films shown are a superior mix of classics and more recent releases, with frequent themed cycles. A 10-session pass is an amazingly cheap €20.

In addition to two cinemas totalling 535 seats, the Filmoteca comprises a film library, a bookshop, the **La Monroe** cafe-bar (☎93 441 94 61; www.lamonroe.es; ⏰noon-1am Sun-Thu, to 2.30am Fri & Sat) offices and a dedicated space for exhibitions.

23 Robadors
Live Music

(Map p250; www.23robadors.wordpress.com; Carrer d'en Robador 23; ⏰8pm-2.30am; Ⓜ Liceu) On what remains a sleazy Raval street,

 Sardana Dancing

The Catalan dance par excellence is the *sardana*, whose roots lie in the far northern Empordà region of Catalonia. Compared with flamenco, it is sober indeed but not unlike a lot of other Mediterranean folk dances. The dancers hold hands in a circle and wait for the 10 or so musicians to begin. The performance starts with the piping of the *flabiol*, a little wooden flute. When the other musicians join in, the dancers start. Catalans of all ages come out for the dance, which takes place in a circle with dancers holding hands. Together they move right, back and then left, hopping, raising their arms and generally building momentum as the tempo picks up. All are welcome to join in, though you'll have to watch a few rounds to get the hang of it.

In Barcelona the best chance you have of seeing people dancing the *sardana* is either at 6pm Saturday or noon Sunday in front of La Catedral, or during festivals like La Mercè. It is also performed sometimes in Plaça de Sant Jaume. For more information, contact the Agrupació Cultural Folklòrica de Barcelona (https://acfbarcelona.cat).

NEIL SETCHFIELD/LONELY PLANET©

where streetwalkers and junkies hang out in spite of gentrification in the area, this narrow little bar has made a name for itself with its shows and live music. Jazz is the name of the game, but you'll also find live poetry, flamenco and plenty more.

Flamenco

Seeing good performances of this essentially Andalucian dance and music is not easy. The few *tablaos* are touristy and often tacky. You can catch flamenco on Friday and Saturday nights at the JazzSí Club; also watch out for big-name performers at the Palau de la Música Catalana.

The Festival de Flamenco de Ciutat Vella (www.ciutatflamenco.com) is held in May. A series of concerts can be seen, usually from April to July, as part of the Barcelona Guitar Festival (www.guitarbcn.com).

JazzSí Club
Live Music

(Map p249; ☎93 329 00 20; http://tallerde musics.com/jazzsi-club; Carrer de Requesens 2; entry incl drink €6-10; ☺8.30-11pm Mon & Thu, 7.45-11pm Tue & Wed, 8.45-11pm Fri & Sat, 6.30-10pm Sun; ▯Sant Antoni) A cramped little bar run by the Taller de Músics (Musicians' Workshop) serves as the stage for a varied program of jazz jams through to some good flamenco (Friday and Saturday nights). Thursday night is Cuban night, Tuesday and Sunday are rock, and the rest are devoted to jazz and/or blues sessions. Some concerts are preceded by jam sessions.

Teatre Romea
Theatre

(Map p250; ☎93 301 55 04; www.teatreromea.cat; Carrer de l'Hospital 51; ☺box office 5.30pm to start of show Tue-Fri, from 4.30pm Sat & Sun; ▯Liceu) Just off La Rambla, this 19th-century theatre was resurrected at the end of the 1990s and is one of the city's key stages for quality drama. It usually fills up for a broad range of interesting plays, often classics with a contemporary flavour, in Catalan and Spanish.

Teatre Llantiol
Theatre

(Map p249; ☎93 329 90 09; www.llantiol.com; Carrer de la Riereta 7; ▯Sant Antoni) At this small, charming cafe-theatre, which has a certain scuffed elegance, all sorts of odd stuff, from concerts and theatre to magic shows, is staged. The speciality, though, is stand-up comedy, which is occasionally in English.

El Cangrejo
Gay

(Map p250; ☎93 301 29 78; www.facebook. com/elcangrejodelraval; Carrer de Montserrat 9; ☺11pm-3am Fri & Sat; ▯Drassanes) This altar to kitsch is a dingy dance hall that has transgressed since the 1920s, and for years starred the luminous underground cabaret figure of Carmen Mairena. It exudes a gorgeously tacky feel, especially with the midnight drag shows. Due to its popularity with tourists, getting in is all but impossible unless you turn up early.

⊕ La Ribera

Palau de la Música Catalana
Classical Music

(Map p254; ☎93 295 72 00; www.palaumusica. cat; Carrer de Palau de la Música 4-6; tickets from €18; ☺box office 9.30am-9pm Mon-Sat, 10am-3pm Sun; ▯Urquinaona) A feast for the eyes, this Modernista confection is also the city's most traditional venue for classical and choral music, although it has a wide-ranging programme, including flamenco, pop and, in particular, jazz. Just being here for a performance is an experience. In the foyer, its tiled pillars all a-glitter, you can sip a pre-concert tipple. Head up the grand stairway to the main auditorium, a whirlpool of Modernista whimsy.

Tablao Nervión
Dance

(Map p250; ☎93 315 21 03; www.restaurante nervion.com; Carrer de la Princesa 2; show incl 1 drink €17, show & set dinner €30; ☺shows 8-10pm Wed-Sun; ▯Jaume I) For admittedly tourist-oriented flamenco, this unassuming bar is cheaper than most and has good offerings. Shows take place in the basement.

Palau de Dalmases   Live Performance

(Map p250; ☎93 310 06 73; www.palaudalmases. com; Carrer de Montcada 20; ⏲11.30am-1.30am; Ⓜ Jaume I) You can sip wine or cocktails (both rather expensive) inside the baroque courtyard and theatrical interior of the originally medieval Palau de Dalmases. There are flamenco shows (€25 including one drink) at 6pm, 7.30pm and 9.30pm. On Wednesday there is a free jazz concert at 11pm, and on Thursday, opera (€20), also at 11pm.

❂ Barceloneta, the Waterfront & El Poblenou

Sala Monasterio   Live Music

(☎616 287197; www.facebook.com/sala. monasterio; Moll de Mestral 30; tickets vary; ⏲10pm-5am Sun-Thu, to 6am Fri & Sat; Ⓜ Ciutadella Vila Olímpica) Overlooking the bobbing masts and slender palm trees of Port Olímpic, this pocket-sized music spot stages an eclectic line-up of live bands, including jazz, *forró* (music from northeastern Brazil), blues jams and rock.

Razzmatazz   Live Music

(☎93 320 82 00; www.salarazzmatazz.com; Carrer de Pamplona 88; tickets from €10; Ⓜ Bogatell) Bands from far and wide occasionally create scenes of near hysteria in this, one of the city's classic live-music and clubbing venues. Bands can appear throughout the week (check the website), with different start times. On weekends live music later gives way to club sounds.

Five different rooms in one huge post-industrial space attract people of all dance persuasions and ages, and the offering varies from night to night. The main space, RazzClub, is a haven for the latest international rock and indie acts. The Loft does techno, house and electro, while the Pop Bar offers anything from R&B to '80s hits. Lolita is the land of house, disco and electro, and upstairs in the Rex Room urban sounds range from hip-hop to dancehall. You can save a few euros by purchasing tickets to concerts in advance online.

Performers, Harlem Jazz Club (p197)

La Fura dels Baus

Keep your eyes peeled for any of the eccentric (if not downright crazed) performances of Barcelona's La Fura dels Baus (www.lafura.com) theatre group. It has won worldwide acclaim for its brand of startling, often acrobatic, theatre in which the audience is frequently dragged into the chaos. The company grew out of Barcelona's street-theatre culture of the late 1970s, and although it has grown in technical prowess and received great international acclaim, it has not abandoned the rough-and-ready edge of street performances.

L'Auditori Classical Music

(☑93 247 93 00; www.auditori.cat; Carrer de Lepant 150; tickets free-€60; ☺box office 5-9pm Tue-Fri, 10am-1pm & 5-9pm Sat; MMarina) Barcelona's modern home for the Orquestra Simfònica de Barcelona i Nacional de Catalunya, L'Auditori stages performances of orchestral, chamber, religious and other music. Designed by Rafael Moneo and opened in 1999, the main auditorium can accommodate more than 2000 concertgoers. The **Museu de la Música** (☑93 256 36 50; www.museu musica.bcn.cat; adult/child €6/4.50, free 3-7pm Sun; ☺10am-6pm Tue, Wed & Fri, to 9pm Thu, to 7pm Sat & Sun) is located in the same building.

Teatre Nacional de Catalunya Performing Arts

(☑93 306 57 00; www.tnc.cat; Plaça de les Arts 1; tickets free-€29; ☺box office 4-7pm Wed, 5-8pm Thu & Fri, 3-8pm Sat, 3-6pm Sun; MGlòries) The National Theatre of Catalonia hosts a wide range of performances, including dramas, comedies, musicals and dance in this ultra-neoclassical theatre designed by Barcelona architect Ricardo Bofill, which opened in 1996. Performances are in Catalan.

Sala Beckett Theatre

(☑93 284 53 12; www.salabeckett.cat; Carrer de Pere IV 228; tickets from €3; MPoblenou) One of the city's principal alternative theatres, the Sala Beckett doesn't shy away from challenging theatre, and stages an eclectic mix of productions in this lovely space in a 1920s building. Performances are primarily in Catalan.

Yelmo Cines Icària Cinema

(☑902 220922; www.yelmocines.es; Carrer de Salvador Espriu 61; adult/child €10/7.50; MCiutadella Vila Olímpica) This vast cinema complex shows films in the original language on 15 screens, making for plenty of choice. Aside from the screens, you'll find several cheerful places to eat, bars and the like to keep you occupied before and after the movies.

✪ L'Eixample

City Hall Live Music

(Map p254; ☑93 238 07 22; www.cityhallbarcelona.com; Rambla de Catalunya 2-4; MCatalunya) This former theatre is the perfect size and shape for live music, holding a crowd of around 500. The acoustics are great and the layout means everyone gets a good view of the stage. It's also home to a **nightclub** (cover from €10; ☺midnight-5am Mon-Thu, to 6am Sat).

Mediterráneo Live Music

(Map p254; www.elmedi.net; Carrer de Balmes 129; ☺10.30pm- 3am; ☒FGC Provença) Free live music plays nightly at this student favourite. Order a beer and enjoy the free nuts at one of the tiny tables while waiting for the next act to tune up at the back. The performances are usually of a high standard.

Teatre Tívoli · Theatre

(Map p254; ☑93 412 20 63; www.grupbalana.com; Carrer de Casp 8; ticket prices vary; ☺box office 5-8pm, plus 90min before shows; Ⓜ Catalunya) Dating from 1919 this grand theatre has three storeys of boxes and a generous stage hosting a fairly rapid turnover of drama, musicals and concerts; Bruce Springsteen and Radiohead have all played here.

Méliès Cinemes · Cinema

(Map p249; ☑93 451 00 51; www.meliescinemes. com; Carrer de Villarroel 102; tickets €4-7; Ⓜ Urgell) A cosy cinema with two screens, the Méliès specialises in classic films and independent releases from around the world.

❂ Montjuïc, Poble Sec & Sant Antoni

Hiroshima · Live Performance

(Map p256; ☑93 315 54 58; www.hiroshima. cat; Carrer de Vilà i Vilà 67; ☺7-11pm Wed-Sun; Ⓜ Paral·lel) Hiroshima is a creative lynchpin in Poble Sec. In a former elevator factory, it hosts emerging and avant-garde musicians, dancers and performing artists. There are two stages (for 130 and 250 people, respectively) and a lively ground-floor bar where you can grab a drink after the show. This is a good place to look for unconventional fare.

BARTS · Concert Venue

(Map p256; Barcelona Arts on Stage; ☑93 324 84 92; www.barts.cat; Avinguda del Paral·lel 62; Ⓜ Paral·lel) BARTS has a solid reputation for its innovative line-up of urban dance troupes, electro swing, psychedelic pop and other eclectic fare. Its smart design combines a comfortable midsized auditorium with excellent acoustics. Hours and ticket prices vary; check the agenda online.

Teatre Grec · Theatre

(Map p256; http://lameva.barcelona.cat/grec; Passeig de Santa Madrona; 🚍55, 150) Built in 1929 by Catalan architect Ramon Revento, this lovely stone Greek-style amphitheatre on Montjuïc stages one of the city's best summer festivals, the Festival Grec de Barcelona, with theatre, dance and music events.

 Alfresco Cinema

Outdoor screens are set up in summer in the moat of the Castell de Montjuïc (www.salamontjuic.org), on the beach and in the Fòrum. Foreign films with subtitles and original soundtracks are marked 'VO' *(versió original)* in listings.

Cinema Lliure a la Platja
IVOR M/ALAMY STOCK PHOTO ©

Fundació Mas I Mas · Chamber Music

(☑93 319 17 89; www.masimas.com/fundacio; tickets €12-15) This foundation promotes chamber and classical music, offering concerts in a couple of locations. Classical concerts, usually involving Catalan performers, are held in summer in various venues around town. For intense 30-minute sessions of chamber music, see its program of performances at **l'Ateneu** (p196), a hallowed academic institution-cum-club.

Sala Apolo · Live Music

(Map p256; ☑93 441 40 01; www.sala-apolo. com; Carrer Nou de la Rambla 113; club from €12, concerts vary; ☺concerts from 8pm, club from midnight; Ⓜ Paral·lel) This is a fine old theatre, where red velvet dominates and you feel as though you're in a movie-set dancehall scene. 'Nasty Mondays' are aimed at a die-hard, never-stop-dancing crowd. Club entry includes a drink. Earlier in the evening, concerts generally take place here and in 'La 2', a smaller auditorium downstairs.

Tastes are as eclectic as possible, from local bands and burlesque shows to big-name international acts.

Longing for Cuba

The oldest musical tradition to have survived to some degree in Catalonia is that of the *havaneres* (from Havana) – nostalgic songs and melancholy sea shanties brought back from Cuba by Catalans who lived, sailed and traded there in the 19th century. Even after Spain lost Cuba in 1898, the *havanera* tradition (a mix of European and Cuban rhythms) continued. A magical opportunity to enjoy these songs is the **Cantada d'Havaneres** (www.havanerescalella.cat), a one-day festival held on the Costa Brava in early July. Otherwise you may stumble across performances elsewhere along the coast or even in Barcelona, but there is no set program.

Palau Sant Jordi   Stadium

(Map p256; ☑93 426 20 89; www.palausantjordi. cat; Passeig Olímpic 5-7; ☐13, 55, 150) Built for the 1992 Olympics, this huge indoor arena hosts big-name concerts (Adele, Coldplay, Lady Gaga), as well as championship sports events.

Sant Jordi Club   Live Music

(Map p256; ☑93 426 20 89; www.santjordiclub. cat; Passeig Olímpic 5-7; ☐13, 55, 150) With capacity for more than 4500 people, this concert hall, annexed to the Olympic stadium Palau Sant Jordi, is used for big gigs that don't reach the epic proportions of headlining international acts.

Teatre Mercat De Les Flors   Dance

(Map p256; ☑93 256 26 00; www.mercatflors. cat; Carrer de Lleida 59; ☺box office 11am-2pm & 4-7pm Mon-Fri, plus 1hr before show; ☐55) Next door to the Teatre Lliure, and together with it known as the Ciutat de Teatre (Theatre City), this spacious modern stage is Barcelona's top venue for local and international contemporary dance acts.

Teatre Victòria   Theatre

(Map p256; ☑93 329 91 89; www.teatrevictoria. com; Avinguda del Paral·lel 67-69; ☺box office 2hr before show; MParal·lel) Rather nondescript looking from the street, this modern theatre stages musicals (usually in Catalan), flamenco and contemporary dance.

Teatre Lliure   Theatre

(Map p256; ☑93 289 27 70; www.teatrelliure.com; Plaça de Margarida Xirgu 1; ☺box office 9am-8pm, plus 2hr before performance; ☐55) Housed in the magnificent former Palau de l'Agricultura building on Montjuïc (opposite the Museu d'Arqueologia), the 'Free Theatre' consists of two modern theatre spaces, Espai Lliure and Sala Fabià Puigserver. It puts on a variety of quality drama (mostly in Catalan), contemporary dance and music.

Renoir Floridablanca   Cinema

(Map p249; ☑91 542 27 02; www.cinesrenoir.com; Carrer de Floridablanca 135; MSant Antoni) With seven screens, this cinema shows a mix of quality art-house flicks and blockbusters in their original language with Spanish subtitles. It's handily located just beyond El Raval, so you'll find no shortage of post-film entertainment options nearby.

✪ Gràcia & Park Güell

Soda Acústic   Live Music

(Map p254; ☑93 016 55 90; www.soda.cat; Carrer de les Guilleries 6; tickets free-€5; ☺8.30pm-2.30am Wed, Thu & Sun, 9pm-3am Fri & Sat; MFontana) This low-lit modern space stages an eclectic line-up of bands and performing artists. Jazz, world music, Balkan swing, Latin rhythms and plenty of experimental, not easily classifiable musicians all receive their due. The acoustics are excellent.

Verdi Park   Cinema

(Map p254; ☑93 238 79 90; www.cines-verdi. com; Carrer de Torrijos 49; MFontana) Verdi Park is a perennially popular art-house cinema with four screens. Most films are shown in their original language.

L'Auditori (p200)

Teatreneu · Theatre

(Map p254; ☎93 285 37 12; www.teatreneu.com; Carrer de Terol 26; Ⓜ Joanic) This lively theatre experiments with all sorts of material, from monologues to social comedy, and also screens films. Aside from the main theatre, two cafe-style spaces serve as more intimate stage settings for small-scale productions. Most performances are in Catalan or Spanish. The box office opens one hour before performance times.

Its bustling, rambling downstairs bar faces the street.

Cines Verdi · Cinema

(Map p254; ☎93 238 79 90; www.cines-verdi.com; Carrer de Verdi 32; tickets from €8; Ⓜ Fontana) In the heart of Gràcia, this five-screen cinema shows art-house and blockbuster films in their original language, as well as films in Catalan and Spanish. It's close to lots of local eateries and bars for pre- and post-film enjoyment.

✪ Camp Nou, Pedralbes & La Zona Alta

Luz de Gas · Live Music

(☎93 209 77 11; www.luzdegas.com; Carrer de Muntaner 246; ⊗midnight-6am Wed-Sat; ☒T1, T2, T3 Francesc Macià, ☒FGC Provença) Several nights a week this club, set in a grand former theatre, stages concerts including rock, soul, salsa, jazz and pop. From about 2am, the place turns into a club that attracts a well-dressed crowd with varying musical tastes, depending on the night.

Bikini · Club

(☎93 322 08 00; www.bikinibcn.com; Avinguda Diagonal 547; cover €8-15; ⊗midnight-6am Thu-Sat; Ⓜ Maria Cristina) This old star of the Barcelona nightlife scene has been keeping the beat since 1953. Every possible kind of music gets a run, from reggaeton to 1980s disco, depending on the night and the space you choose.

ACTIVE BARCELONA

Football, cycling and everything in between

Active Barcelona

Mediterranean oceanfront and a rambling hilly park overlooking the city make fine settings for a bit of outdoor activity beneath the (generally) sunny skies of Barcelona. For a break from museum-hopping and overindulging at tapas bars, Barcelona has plenty of options – running, swimming, cycling or simply pumping fists in the air at a never-dull FC Barcelona match. Football here has the aura of religion and for much of the city's population, support for the city's principal team is an article of faith. There's also a variety of ways to get a more active look at the city, whether on a specialised walking tour through the Old City or on a bicycle excursion around the city centre.

In This Section

Sports Seasons

Football The season runs from late August to May.

Basketball The season runs from October to June.

Asobal The handball league, runs from September to May or early June.

Tennis The professional season is in spring; the big event here is the Barcelona Open in April.

FC Barcelona fans

The Best...

Best Activities

Castell de Montjuïc (p63) Barcelona's easily accessible mountain offers a scenic setting for running and biking.

Parc de Collserola (p98) The city's best mountain biking (and home to wild boar).

Camp Nou (p209) See FC Barcelona in action at their world-famous home stadium.

Rituels d'Orient (p208) A beautiful hammam in El Born.

Piscines Bernat Picornell (p209) A truly Olympian setting for a swim.

Best Spas

Rituels d'Orient (p208) A beautiful spa in a historic setting of El Born.

Aqua Urban Spa (p208) Get the full range of relaxation treatments.

Flotarium (p208) Float weightlessly in a salt-filled chamber.

⊕ Activities

Rituels d'Orient   Spa
(📞93 419 14 72; www.rituelsdorient.com; Carrer de Loreto 50; baths per 45min €29, treatments from €21; 🕐11am-9pm Tue, Wed & Sun, to 10pm Thu-Sat; Ⓜ️Hospital Clínic) Rituels d'Orient resembles a Moroccan fantasy, with dark woods, window grills, candle lighting and ancient-looking stone walls. It's a wonderfully relaxing setting for luxuriating in a hammam and indulging in a massage, body scrub, facial or hand and foot treatments.

Molokai SUP Center   Water Sports
(📞93 221 48 68; www.molokaisupcenter. com; Carrer de Meer 39; 2hr private lesson €60, SUP rental per hour €15; Ⓜ️Barceloneta) This respected outfit will give you a crash course in stand-up paddleboarding (SUP). In addition to the two-hour beginner's class, Molokai can help you improve your technique (in intermediate and advanced lessons – all in two-hour blocks); gear and wetsuits are included. If you're experienced and would rather just hire an SUP board, staff can quickly get you out to sea.

Base Nautica
Municipal   Water Sports
(📞93 221 04 32; http://basenautica.org; Avinguda de Litoral; 2hr lessons from €40, equipment hire per hour from €20, wetsuit hire per day €10; 🕐10am-7pm; Ⓜ️Poblenou) Just back from Platja de la Mar Bella, at Base Nautica Municipal you can learn the basics of kayaking, windsurfing, catamaran sailing or stand-up paddleboarding. You can also hire equipment here. Prices for lessons are cheaper in groups of two or more. Longer courses, running from eight to 12 hours over several days, are also available.

Aire De Barcelona   Spa
(📞93 295 57 43; www.airedebarcelona.com; Passeig de Picasso 22; thermal baths Mon-Thu €38, Fri-Sun €45; 🕐9am-11pm Sun-Thu, to midnight Fri & Sat; Ⓜ️Arc de Triomf) With low lighting and relaxing aromas, this basement spa could be the perfect way to end a day. Hot, warm and cold baths, steam baths and options

for various massages, including on a slab of hot marble, make for a delicious hour or so. Book ahead and bring a swimming costume.

Boardriders
Barceloneta   Water Sports
(📞93 221 44 91; www.facebook.com/boardriders barceloneta; Plaça del Mar 1; boards per 1/2hr €15/20; 🕐10am-10pm Mon-Sat, 11am-10pm Sun Jun-Aug, shorter hours Sep-May; Ⓜ️Barceloneta) Facing the seafront, Boardriders rents out surfboards and SUPs (stand-up paddleboards). It also sells surfwear, streetwear and skateboarding equipment.

Flotarium   Flotarium
(Map p254; 📞93 217 36 37; www.flotarium.com; Plaça de Narcís Oller 3; 50min session €40; 🕐3-9pm Mon, 10am-9pm Tue-Sat, 10am-3pm Sun; Ⓜ️Diagonal) Be suspended in zero gravity and feel the stress ebb away. Each flotarium, like a little space capsule with water, is in a private room, with shower, towels and shampoo, and Epsom salts that allow you to float as if in the Dead Sea (using 300kg of salts to achieve the same density).

Claror Marítim   Swimming
(📞93 224 04 40; www.claror.cat/maritim; Passeig Marítim de la Barceloneta 33; Mon-Fri €18, Sat, Sun & holidays €21; 🕐7am-midnight Mon-Fri, 8am-9pm Sat, 9am-5pm Sun; Ⓜ️Ciutadella Vila Olímpica) Water babies will love this thalassotherapeutic (sea-water therapy) sports centre. In addition to the small pool for lap swimming, there's a labyrinth of hot, warm and freezing-cold spa pools, along with thundering massage waterfalls. Hours are shorter in August – check schedules online.

Aqua Urban Spa   Spa
(Map p254; 📞93 238 41 60; www.aquaurbanspa. es; Carrer Gran de Gràcia 7; 90min baths session from €39; 🕐9am-9pm Mon-Sat; Ⓜ️Diagonal) With treatments for everything from stress to tired legs (merciful for diehard sightseers), this spa offers smallish pool and shower areas, along with steam baths, Roman-style baths and a series of massages and beauty treatment options such as body scrubs (from €39 for 30 minutes).

Piscines Bernat Picornell   Swimming

(Map p256; 📞93 423 40 41; www.picornell. cat; Avinguda de l'Estadi 30-38; adult/child €12.15/7.45, nudist hours €6.55/4.70, outdoor pool €6.65/4.60; ⏰6.45am-midnight Mon-Fri, 7am-9pm Sat, 7.30am-4pm Sun, outdoor pool 11am-6.30pm Jul & Aug; 🚇13, 150) Admission to Barcelona's official Olympic pool on Montjuïc also includes use of the complex's fitness room, sauna, Jacuzzi, steam bath and track. On Saturday nights, between 9pm and 11pm, the pool (with access to sauna and steam bath) is open only to nudists. On Sundays between October and May the indoor pool also opens for nudists only from 4.15pm to 6pm. The outdoor pool, offering incredible panoramic city views, is open in summer only; tickets are sold separately.

⊕ Spectator Sports

Camp Nou   Football

(📞902 189900; www.fcbarcelona.com; Carrer d'Arístides Maillol; 🚇Palau Reial) The massive stadium of Camp Nou (New Field in Catalan) is home to the legendary Futbol Club Barcelona. Attending a game amid the roar of the crowds is an unforgettable experience; the season runs from August to May. Alternatively, get a taste of all the excitement at the interactive **Barça Stadium Tour & Museum** (Gate 9, Avinguda de Joan XXIII; adult/child self-guided tour €29.50/23.50, guided tour €50/35; ⏰9.30am-7.30pm mid-Apr–mid-Oct, 10am-6.30pm Mon-Sat, to 2.30pm Sun mid-Oct–mid-Apr).

Tickets to FC Barcelona matches are available at Camp Nou, online (through FC Barcelona's official website) and through various city locations. Tourist offices sell them – the **Plaça de Catalunya branch** (📞93 285 38 34; www.barcelonaturisme.com; Plaça de Catalunya 17-S, underground; ⏰8.30am-9pm; 🚇Catalunya) is a centrally located option – as do FC Botiga stores. Tickets can cost anything from €29 to upwards of €250, depending on the seat and match.

On match day the ticket windows are open at Gate 9 from 11am until kick-off and at Gate 14 from 9am to 1.30pm. Tickets are not

🏀🎾 Urban Running

The waterfront esplanade and beaches are all perfect for an early morning run, before the crowds come out. Locals wanting to log serious miles take to Parc de Collserola, which is laced with trails. Among the best is the Carretera de les Aigües, a 9km-long track from Tibidabo to the suburb of Sant Just Desvern, with superb views over the city. More convenient are the gardens and parkland of Montjuïc or the smaller park of Ciutadella. If you want to jog while you're in town, but don't want to go alone, you can join a casual group. The Hotel Brummell Running Club (www. hotelbrummell.com) has Tuesday night runs (at 8pm) around Montjuïc, departing from the hotel. Barcelona Casual Runners (www.meetup.com/barcelona-casual-runners) meet outside Parc de la Ciutadella at 8pm Tuesday and Thursday.

FERRANTRAITE/GETTY IMAGES ©

usually available for matches with Real Madrid. You will almost definitely find scalpers lurking near the ticket windows. They are often club members and can sometimes get you in at a significant reduction. Don't pay until you are safely seated.

Estadi RCD Espanyol   Football

(📞93 292 77 00; www.rcdespanyol.com; Avinguda del Baix Llobregat 100; tickets from €25; 🚇FGC Cornellà Riera) Espanyol, based at the 40,500-seat Estadi RCD Espanyol, traditionally plays second fiddle to Barça, although it does so with considerable passion.

🚲 Cycling in Barcelona

Barcelona's long enticing seafront makes a fine setting for a ride, and the bike lane separate from traffic and pedestrians ensures you can get going a good clip (though you'll have to move slowly at peak times, like summer weekends). The city itself has an extensive network of bike lanes, including along major streets like Passeig de Sant Joan, Consell de Cent, Avinguda Diagonal and Ronda de Sant Pau/Comte d'Urgell. Avid mountain bikers will want to make their way up to the vast Parc de Collserola with rambling trails on a wooded massif overlooking the city. There are also many options available for bike tours and hire.

KAPUSTIN IGOR/SHUTTERSTOCK ©

😊 Courses

Espai Boisà   Cooking

(☑93 192 60 21; www.espaiboisa.com; Passatge Lluís Pellicer 8; 2½hr course from €45; ⓂHospital Clínic) ✔ Run by a young, multilingual Venezuelan-Catalan couple, this first-rate outfit offers themed cooking courses. They emphasise organic, seasonal ingredients from local producers from outside Barcelona – put to good use in dishes including paella, a range of tapas dishes and *crema catalana* (a Catalan version of crème brûlée).

The best part is feasting on your creations, accompanied by generous glasses of organic Catalan wine or sangría.

Swing Maniacs   Dancing

(Map p254; ☑93 187 69 85; www.swingmaniacs. com; Carrer de Roger de Flor 293; group/private 55min class from €14/40; ⓒ4-11pm Mon-Fri; ⓂJoanic) Swing dancing has quite the following in Barcelona, with old-fashioned dance parties happening in far-flung corners of the city every night. To learn the moves, sign up for a class at Swing Maniacs. You can join a drop-in class, and if you don't have a partner, one can be arranged for you.

🔂 Tours

Barcelona Walking Tours   Walking

(Map p254; ☑93 285 38 32; www.barcelona turisme.com; Plaça de Catalunya 17; ⓂCatalunya) The Oficina d'Informació de Turisme de Barcelona (p239) organises several one- to two-hour guided walking tours (available in English) exploring the Barri Gòtic (adult/child €16/free), Picasso's footsteps (€22/7) and Modernisme (€16/free). A two-hour gourmet food tour (€22/7) includes tastings. Various street-art walking and cycling tours (from €21) also take place. There is a 10% discount on most tours if you book online.

Barcelona Guide Bureau   Tours

(☑93 315 22 61; www.barcelonaguidebureau. com) Barcelona Guide Bureau places professional guides at the disposal of groups for tailor-made tours of the city. Several languages are catered for. It also offers a series of daily tours, from a five-hour highlights tour (adult/child €70/35, departing at 10am and 12.30pm) to a trip to Montserrat (€52/25), leaving Barcelona at 3pm and lasting about four hours.

Devour Barcelona   Tours

(☑695 111832; www.devourbarcelonafoodtours. com; tours €70-110) Knowledgeable guides lead food tours around Gràcia, the Old City and Barceloneta mixing gastronomy with history. The various tastings and spots visited are especially focused on small, local producers and family-run joints. Most tours last three to four hours and include enough food for a full meal.

Terra BikeTours   Cycling

(Map p254; ☑93 416 08 05; www.terrabiketours.
com; Carrer de València 337; self-guided tour from
€29, 1-day guided tour from €57; ⊙10am-8pm
Mon-Sat; MVerdaguer) This outfit offers a
wide range of cycling tours from one day
to one week. Options include mountain
biking in the Parc de Collserola or outside
of Barcelona in the Pyrenees, and a
road-biking tour on Barcelona's north coast
and beyond. Self-guided trips (including
preloaded GPS routes and gear) are also
available.

If you want to just hire a bike, this is a
good place to check out; rates start at €17
per day.

Barcelona By Bike   Cycling

(☑671 307 325; www.barcelonabybike.com; Carrer de la Marina 13; tours from €24; MCiutadella
Vila Olímpica) This outfit offers various tours
by bicycle, including 'The Original', a three-
hour pedal that takes in a bit of Gothic Barcelona, L'Eixample (including La Sagrada
Família) and the Barceloneta beachfront.
Carrer de la Marina 13 is the tour meeting
point; there's no office.

Bike Tours Barcelona   Cycling

(Map p250; ☑93 268 21 05; www.biketours
barcelona.com; Carrer de l'Esparteria 3; per person
€25; ⊙10am-7pm; MJaume I) One of the oldest
bike tour operators in the city, they offer daily three-hour bicycle tours of the Barri Gòtic,
the waterfront, La Sagrada Família and other
Gaudí landmarks. Tours depart from the
tourist office on Plaça de Sant Jaume; check
the website for departure times, and for
details of vineyard tours. Bike rental (from
€5 per hour) is also available.

Runner Bean Tours   Walking

(Map p250; ☑636 108776; www.runnerbean-
tours.com; Plaça Reial; ⊙tours 11am & 4.30pm
Mar-Sep, 11am & 3pm Oct, 11am Nov-Feb; MLiceu)
Runner Bean Tours offers several daily thematic tours. It's a pay-what-you-wish tour,
with a collection taken at the end for the
guide. The Gothic Quarter tour explores the
Roman and medieval history of Barcelona,
visiting highlights in the Ciutat Vella (Old
City). The Gaudí tour takes in the great
works of Modernista Barcelona. All tours
depart from Plaça Reial.

It's wise to book ahead, as numbers are
limited. Runner Bean also offers a handful
of paid-for tours, including a Kids & Family
walking tour and the Dark Past Night tour;
check the website for departure times and
to book a spot.

Bus Turístic   Bus

(☑93 298 70 00; www.barcelonabusturistic.
cat; adult/child 1 day €30/16, 2 days €40/21;
⊙9am-7pm mid-Apr–Oct, to 8pm Nov–mid-Apr)
This hop-on, hop-off service covers three
circuits (44 stops) linking virtually all the
major tourist sights. Tourist offices, TMB
transport authority offices and many hotels
have leaflets explaining the system. Each
of the two main circuits takes approxi-
mately two hours. The third circuit, from
Port Olímpic to El Fòrum, runs from April to
October and is less interesting.

Las Golondrinas   Cruise

(☑93 442 31 06; www.lasgolondrinas.com; Moll
de les Drassanes; adult/child port tour €7.70/
2.80, catamaran tour €15.20/5.50; MDrassanes)
Las Golondrinas offers popular cruises
from its dock in front of Mirador de Colom.
The 90-minute catamaran tour takes you
out past Barceloneta and the beaches to
the Fòrum and back. For a quick overview
of the port area, take a 40-minute excursion to the breakwater and back. Both trips
depart regularly throughout the day.

BC Naval Tours   Boating

(☑93 443 60 50; www.barcelonanavaltours.com;
Moll de les Drassanes; 40/75min cruise €7.50/18;
MDrassanes) From the dock near Mirador de
Colom, BC Naval's boats run cruises including 75-minute trips out past Barceloneta
and the beaches and back. If you just want
a peek at the area around the port, opt for a
40-minute excursion to the breakwater and
back. Both run a few times a day.

REST YOUR HEAD

Top tips for the best accommodation

Rest Your Head

Barcelona has a wide range of sleeping options, from inexpensive hostels hidden in the old quarter to luxury hotels overlooking the waterfront. The small-scale B&B-style apartment rentals scattered around the city are also a good-value choice.

Wherever you stay, it's wise to book ahead. If you plan to travel during holidays such as Christmas, New Year's Eve or Easter, or in summer, reserve a room a few months before your visit. Always reconfirm if arriving late in the evening. Check-out is generally noon.

In This Section

Room Tax

Virtually all accommodation is subject to IVA, a 10% value-added tax.

There's also an additional tax of between €0.72 and €2.48 per person per night, depending on the accommodation's level of luxury.

These charges are usually included in the quoted rate.

El Avenida Palace Hotel, L'Eixample

Reservations

Booking ahead is all but essential, especially during peak periods such as Easter, Christmas and New Year, trade fairs and throughout much of summer (although August can be quite a slack month owing to the heat and lack of business visitors).

• If you arrive without a booking, the Plaça de Catalunya tourist office (p239) can help.

• Check-in is around 2pm or 3pm. If arriving earlier, you can usually leave your luggage at reception.

• Check-out is generally noon.

• Always reconfirm if arriving late in the evening.

Useful Websites

Oh-Barcelona (www.oh-barcelona.com) Good-value selection of hotels, hostels and apartment rentals.

Barcelona 30 (www.barcelona30.com) Economical options for staying on a budget.

Lonely Planet (lonelyplanet.com/spain/barcelona/hotels) Recommendations and bookings.

Accommodation Types

Hotels

There is a broad range of hotel types. At the bottom end there is often little to distinguish them from better pensiones, and from there they run up the scale to five-star luxury. Some of the better features to look out for include rooftop pools and lounges; views (either of the sea or a cityscape); and of course proximity to the important sights.

For around €100 to €160 there are extensive options for good doubles across a wide range of hotels and areas. The top-end category starts at €250 for a double, and can easily rise to €500 (and beyond for suites).

Hostales, Pensiones & Hostels

Depending on the season you can pay as little as €11 to €25 for a dorm bed in a youth hostel. If dorm living is not your thing, but you are still looking for a budget deal, check around the many *pensiones* (also known as *hostales*) – family-run, smallscale hotels, often housed in sprawling apartments. Some are fleapits, others immaculately maintained gems.

You're looking at a minimum of around €25/55 for basic *individual/doble* (single/double) rooms, mostly with shared bathrooms. It is sometimes possible to find cheaper rooms, but they may be unappealing.

Some places, especially at the lower end, offer triples and quads, which can be good value for groups. If you want a double bed (as opposed to two singles), ask for a *llit/cama matrimonial* (Catalan/Spanish). If your budget is especially tight, look at options outside the centre.

Apartment & Room Rentals

A cosier (and sometimes more cost-effective) alternative to hotels is short-term apartment rental. Many firms organise short lets across town – try Oh-Barcelona (www.oh-barcelona.com) and Barcelona 30 (www.barcelona30.com) – and, of course, Airbnb is a big player. Rentals away from the Ciutat Vella can be a good way to get to know buzzy residential areas like Poblenou or Poble Sec. Typical prices start from around €80 to €100 for two people per night, but soar for more upscale apartments.For four people you might be looking at an average of €160 a night. Bargains are sometimes available, but be aware that these are often in less salubrious areas. Many old town apartments won't have lifts or washing machines.

Airbnb and apartment rental agencies have been accused of contributing to Barcelona's overtourism problem and driving prices up for local people. Before booking your apartment, check whether it's licensed at www.fairtourism.barcelona. Apartment-rental services including the following:

Oh-Barcelona (www.oh-barcelona.com)

Aparteasy (www.aparteasy.com)

Rent the Sun (www.rentthesun.com)

Barcelona On Line (www.barcelona-on-line.es)

Friendly Rentals (www.friendlyrentals.com)

MH Apartments (www.mhapartments.com)

Accessible Travel

Many hotels claim to be equipped for guests with disabilities but the reality frequently disappoints, although the situation is improving, particularly at the midrange and high-end levels. Check out www.barcelona-access.cat for further information.

Where to Stay

Gràcia & Park Güell

Camp Nou, Pedralbes & La Zona Alta

L'Eixample

La Ribera

Port Olímpic

Barceloneta, the Waterfront & El Poblenou

El Raval

La Rambla & Barri Gòtic

Montjuïc, Poble Sec & Sant Antoni

Port Vell

Mediterranean Sea

Neighbourhood	Atmosphere
La Rambla & Barri Gòtic	Great location, close to major sights; perfect for exploring on foot; good nightlife and restaurants. Very touristy. Rooms tend to be small and noisy.
El Raval	Central, with good nightlife and access to sights; bohemian vibe with few tourists. Some parts are seedy and a bit sketchy at night.
La Ribera	Central, with a great restaurant scene and neighbourhood exploring. Can be noisy and crowded, and is quite touristy.
Barceloneta, the Waterfront & El Poblenou	Excellent seafood restaurants; handy for beaches. Not much accommodation. Barceloneta is central, the rest not very.
L'Eixample	Wide range of options for all budgets; Modernista sights; good restaurants and nightlife; prime LGBT+ scene. Can be noisy with traffic. Not as strollable as the old city.
Montjuïc, Poble Sec & Sant Antoni	Near the museums, gardens and views of Montjuïc; great local exploring in Poble Sec. Area around Sants train station isn't great.
Gràcia & Park Güell	Youthful, local scene with lively restaurants and bars. It's quite far from the old town. Lots of rental rooms.
Camp Nou, Pedralbes & La Zona Alta	Good nightlife and restaurants in parts, but very far from the action, requiring frequent metro travel. More geared for business travellers.

In Focus

STANISLAU PALAUKOU/SHUTTERSTOCK ©

Barcelona Today

No Mediterranean home is considered to be constructed properly without a balcony. However, in Barcelona, the balcony has become more than a sun trap. Today it's a barometer for current issues, a way for citizens to interact and signal their concerns, and a way to lay out their demands – you'll see independence flags, sheets scrawled with pleas for revellers to keep the noise down, yellow ribbons (symbolising the call to release Catalan political prisoners) and a fair few placards bemoaning overtourism.

The State of Catalonia?

Not so long ago, the idea that Catalonia could break away from Spain and become a sovereign republic was only held by a handful of romantics and crackpots, but over the last decade or so it has gained so much traction that it dominates the political landscape both regionally and nationally.

In September 2017, former Catalan president Carles Puigdemont pushed a referendum law through the regional parliament, and the vote (deemed illegal and unconstitutional by central government) went ahead a couple of weeks later. There was a 42% turnout (relatively few unionists – those against secession – took part in what they saw as an illegitimate referendum) and around 90% voted in favour of secession. The day was marked by the violence doled out by the Guardia Civil (the Spanish paramilitary

belief systems
(% of population)

90 Roman Catholic

10 Other

if Barcelona were 100 people

53 would have Spanish as their first language

39 would have Catalan as their first language

8 would have other first languages

population per sq km

Barcelona

Spain

✝ ≈ 90 people

police force, shipped in for the occasion) to those attempting to vote.

In the wake of the poll, independence was declared and immediately quashed by Madrid (in the shape of direct rule), with several high-profile Catalan leaders arrested and charged with crimes including 'rebellion'. Puigdemont, meanwhile, fled to Belgium (where he remained at the time of writing). Regional elections were held in December 2017 but the results simply shored up the status quo, with separatist parties losing the popular vote but maintaining a parliamentary majority. Puigdemont installed nationalist Quim Torra (widely seen as his puppet) as president. A minor thawing of relations came with a vote of no confidence in Prime Minister Mariano Rajoy, who was replaced by Socialist leader Pedro Sánchez in May 2018. Sánchez adopted a more conciliatory tone, infuriating hardliners in Madrid, but was forced to call an election for April 2019 because his minority government's budget wasn't supported by, among others, the Catalan secessionist parties. His election win played out against the backdrop of five of the imprisoned Catalan leaders, in the middle of their trial, winning parliamentary seats. How it all shakes out is anybody's guess, and no one is expecting a smooth ride.

Barcelona or Disneyland?

Ada Colau, Barcelona's progressive mayor, has drawn fire from all sides for sitting on the fence on the independence issue, but has other fish to fry in the shape of what's become known as Barcelona's *parquetematización* (the act of turning into a theme park). As ever-increasing numbers of tourists pour into the city year-round, centuries-old family businesses give way to chain cafes and souvenir shops, and pavements fill with Segways and walking tours, the city is in grave danger of losing its charm.

As part of an attempt to lure visitors out to lesser-known neighbourhoods, Colau has clamped down on new hotel openings in the centre, and has removed or restricted many central pavement terraces – a move that has been welcomed by exhausted residents but met with fury by bar-owners and restaurateurs, who see the mayor as 'anti-business'.

Her left-wing social policies have also seen a softening of the laws on the *manteros* (from *manta*, which means blanket and refers to the immigrant vendors of cheap knock-off goods spread on sheets on the pavement), which has also angered those wanting to reclaim public spaces from tourist pursuits, and will also influence the outcome of the 2019 municipal elections. To date, however, none of the mayoral hopefuls currently campaigning has come up with any real solutions.

GEORGIOS TSICHLIS/SHUTTERSTOCK ©

History

The settlement of Barcelona has seen waves of immigrants and conquerors over its 2000-plus years, including Romans, Visigoths and Franks. Barcelona's fortunes have risen and fallen: from the golden era of princely power in the 14th century to dark days of the Franco era. An independent streak has always run through Barcelona, which has often led to conflict with the Kingdom of Castille – an antagonism that continues today, with a desire for more autonomy (or, increasingly, full independence) from Spain.

15 BC
Caesar Augustus grants the town of Barcino the title of Colonia Iulia Augusta Faventia Paterna Barcino.

AD 415
Visigoths under Ataülf, with captured Roman empress Galla Placidia as his wife, make Barcino their capital.

718
Barcelona falls to Tariq's mostly Arab and Berber troops on their march north into France.

Capella Reial de Santa Agata (p67)

AGE FOTOSTOCK/ALAMY STOCK PHOTO ©

Wilfred the Hairy & the Catalan Golden Age

It was the Romans who first etched Barcino onto Europe's map in the 3rd century BC, though the nascent settlement long played second fiddle to their provincial capital in Tarragona. The Visigoths came next, followed by the Moors, whose relatively brief occupation was usurped when the Franks put the city under the control of local counts in 801 as a buffer zone against the still Muslim-dominated caliphate to the south.

Eccentrically named Wilfred the Hairy (Count Guifré el Pelós) moulded the entity we now know as Catalonia in the 9th century by wresting control over several neighbouring territories and establishing Barcelona as its key city. The hirsute one founded a dynasty that lasted nearly five centuries and developed almost independently from the Reconquista wars that were playing out in the rest of Iberia. The counts of Barcelona gradually expanded their territory south and, in 1137, Ramon Berenguer IV, the Count of Barcelona, married Petronilla, heir to the throne of neighbouring Aragón. Thus, the combined Crown of Aragón was created.

801	**1137**	**1348**
Louis the Pious, Charlemagne's son and future Frankish king, takes control and establishes the Spanish March under local counts.	Count Ramon Berenguer IV is betrothed to one-year-old Petronila, king of Aragón's daughter, creating a new state, the Corona de Aragón.	Around 25% of Barcelona's population dies during the plague. A plague of locusts in 1358 and an earthquake in 1373 deal further blows.

Museu Marítim (p90)

In the following centuries the kingdom became a flourishing merchant empire, seizing Valencia and the Balearic Islands from the Muslims and later taking territories as far flung as Sardinia, Sicily and parts of Greece. The 14th century marked the golden age of Barcelona. Its trading wealth paid for great Gothic buildings: La Catedral, the Capella Reial de Santa Àgata (inside the Museu d'Història de Barcelona) and the churches of Santa Maria del Pi and Santa Maria del Mar. King Pere III (1336–87) later created the breathtaking Reials Drassanes (Royal Shipyards) and extended the city walls yet again to include El Raval.

Marginalisation & Decline

Overstretched, racked by civil disobedience and decimated by the Black Death, Catalonia began to wobble. When the last count of Wilfred the Hairy's dynasty expired without leaving an heir, the Crown of Aragón was passed to a noble of Castile. Soon these two Spanish kingdoms merged, with Catalonia left as a very junior partner. As business shifted from the Mediterranean to the Atlantic after the 'discovery' of the Americas in 1492, Catalans were increasingly marginalised from trade. The region, which had retained some autonomy in the running of its own affairs, was dealt a crushing blow when it supported the wrong side in the War of the Spanish Succession (1702–14). Barcelona, under the auspices of British-backed archduke Charles of Austria, fell after a stubborn siege on 11 September 1714 (now celebrated as National Catalan Day) to the forces of Bourbon king Philip V, who established a unitary Castilian state. Barcelona faced a long backlash as the new king banned the writing and teaching of Catalan, swept away the remnants of local legal systems and tore down a whole district of medieval Barcelona in order to construct an immense fort (on the site of the present-day Parc de la Ciutadella), the sole purpose of which was to watch over Barcelona's troublemakers.

The Catalan Renaissance

Buoyed by the lifting of the ban on its trade with the Americas in 1778, Barcelona embarked on the road to industrial revolution, based initially on textiles but spreading to wine,

---

1469

Castilian throne heir Isabel marries Aragonese heir Fernando, uniting Spain's most powerful monarchies and subjugating Catalonia.

1640–52

Catalan peasants, after the Thirty Years War, declare their independence under French protection, but are crushed by Spain.

1888

Showcasing its grand Modernista touches, Barcelona hosts Spain's first International Exposition in the Parc de la Ciutadella.

cork and iron in the mid-19th century. It soon became Spain's leading city. As the economy prospered, Barcelona outgrew its medieval walls, which were demolished in 1854–56. Work on the grid-plan L'Eixample (the Extension) district began soon after. The so-called Renaixença (Renaissance) brought a revival of Catalan culture, as well as political activism. It sowed the seeds of growing political tension in the early 20th century, as demands for autonomy from the central state became more insistent.

Masses & Classes

Adding to the fiery mix was growing discontent among the working class. The grand Catalan merchant-bourgeois families grew richer, displaying their wealth in a slew of whimsical private mansions built with verve and flair by Modernista architects such as Antoni Gaudí. At the same time, the industrial working class, housed in cramped quarters such as Barceloneta and El Raval and oppressed by poverty and disease, became organised and, occasionally, violent. Spain's neutrality during WWI had boosted Barcelona's economy and from 1900 to 1930 the population doubled to one million, but the postwar global slump hit the city hard. Waves of strikes, organised principally by the anarchists' Confederación Nacional del Trabajo (CNT), brought tough responses. Left- and right-wing gangs took their ideological conflict to the streets. Tit-for-tat assassinations became common currency and the death toll mounted. When the Second Spanish Republic was created under a left-wing government in 1931, Catalonia declared independence. Later, under pressure, its leaders settled for devolution, which it then lost in 1934, when a right-wing government won power in Madrid. The election of a left-wing popular front in 1936 again sparked Catalan autonomy claims, but also led to the generals' rising that launched the Spanish Civil War (1936–39), from which Franco emerged the victor.

The War Years

The acting capital of Spain for much of the civil war, Barcelona was run by anarchists and the Partido Obrero de Unificación Marxista (Marxist Unification Workers' Party) Trotskyist militia until mid-1937. Unions took over factories and public services, hotels and mansions became hospitals and schools, everyone wore workers' clothes, bars and cafes were collectivised, trams and taxis were painted red and black (the colours of the anarchists) and

Jewish Barcelona

The narrow Barri Gòtic lanes of El Call were once home to a thriving Jewish population. Catalan Jews worked as merchants, scholars, cartographers and teachers. By the 11th century, as many as 4000 Jews lived in El Call. As in much of Europe, during the 13th century a wave of anti-Semitism swept through Catalonia. Pogroms followed on from repressive laws; anti-Semitism peaked in 1391 when a frenzied mob tore through El Call, looting and destroying private homes and murdering hundreds of Jews. Most of the remaining Jews fled the city.

1909	1936-1939	1992
After reserve troops are sent to fight a war in Morocco, *barcelonins* riot, and over 100 are killed in Setmana Tràgica (Tragic Week).	In the Spanish Civil War nationalist forces are defeated by left-wing militia, workers and loyalist police but Franco's troops win.	Barcelona hosts the summer Olympic Games. The city undergoes a radical renovation program, which continues today.

Anarchists & the Tragic Week

When the political philosophy of anarchism began spreading through Europe, it was embraced by many industrial workers in Barcelona, who embarked on a road to social revolution through violent means. One anarchist bomb at the Liceu opera house on La Rambla in the 1890s killed 22 people. Anarchists were also blamed for the Setmana Tràgica (Tragic Week) in July 1909 when, following a military call-up for Spanish campaigns in Morocco, rampaging mobs wrecked 70 religious buildings, and workers were shot on the street in reprisal.

one-way streets were ignored as they were seen to be part of the old system. The more radical anarchists were behind the burning of most of the city's churches and the shooting of hundreds of priests, monks and nuns. The anarchists in turn were shunted aside by the communists (directed by Stalin from Moscow) after a bloody internecine battle in Barcelona that left 1500 dead in May 1937.

Later that year the Spanish Republican government fled Valencia and made Barcelona the official capital (the government had left besieged Madrid early in the war). The Republican defeat at the hands of the Nationalists in the Battle of the Ebro in southern Catalonia in the summer of 1938 left Barcelona undefended. It fell to the Nationalists on 25 January 1939, triggering a mass exodus of refugees to France, where most were long interned in makeshift camps. Purges and executions under Franco continued until well into the 1950s. Former Catalan president Lluís Companys was arrested in France by the Gestapo in August 1940, handed over to Franco, and shot on 15 October on Montjuïc, despite international outrage. He is reputed to have died with the words '*Visca Catalunya!*' (Long live Catalonia!) on his lips.

Recent Times

When the death of Franco was announced in 1975, *barcelonins* took to the streets in celebration. The next five years saw the gradual return of democracy and in 1977 Catalonia was granted regional autonomy. Politics aside, the big event in post-Franco Barcelona was the successful 1992 Olympic Games, planned under the guidance of the popular Socialist mayor, Pasqual Maragall. The games spurred a burst of public works and brought new life to areas such as Montjuïc, where the major events were held. The once-shabby waterfront was transformed with promenades, beaches, marinas, restaurants, leisure attractions and new housing. After the turn of the millennium, Barcelona continued to invest in urban renewal. In recent years, soaring unemployment and painful austerity measures – not to mention Catalonia's heavy tax burden – have led to anger and resentment toward Madrid and fuelled the drive toward independence. Recent polls indicate about half of Catalans support the region becoming a new European state. Heavy-handed reaction to the independence movement from Madrid has increased support for it.

2015
In an election, separatists take control of Catalonia's government, with an 18-month plan for full secession.

2017
Catalonia's referendum is marked by police violence, but independence is declared. Direct Spanish rule is imposed for a period.

2026
Builders aim to finish La Sagrada Família by the centenary of Gaudí's death, over 140 years after construction began.

Mercat dels Encants (p160)

Architecture

Famed for its architectural treasures, Barcelona has striking Gothic cathedrals, fantastical Modernista creations and more-recent avant-garde works. The great building boom began in the late Middle Ages, when Barcelona was seat of the Catalan empire. In the late 19th century, the city expanded beyond its medieval confines and was transformed by bold new thinkers. The third notable era of design, from the late 1980s, continues today.

The Gothic Period

Barcelona had a major architectural flourish during the height of the Middle Ages, when its imposing Gothic churches, mansions and shipyards were raised, together creating what survives to this day as one of the most extensive Gothic quarters in Europe. Catalan Gothic did not follow the same course as the style typical of northern Europe. Decoration here tends to be more sparing and the most obvious defining characteristic is the triumph of breadth over height. While northern European cathedrals reach for the sky, Catalan Gothic has a tendency to push to the sides, stretching its vaulting design to the limit. Another notable departure from what you might have come to expect of Gothic north of the Pyrenees is the lack of spires and pinnacles.

Roof detail, Casa Amatller (p55)

★ **Best Modernista Creations**

La Pedrera (p76)

La Sagrada Família (p36)

Palau de la Música Catalana (p106)

Casa Batlló (p52)

Casa Amatller (p55)

Modernisme

The second wave of Catalan creativity, also carried on the wind of boom times, came around the turn of the 20th century. The urban expansion program known as L'Eixample (the Extension), designed to free the choking population from the city's bursting medieval confines, coincided with this blossoming of unfettered thinking in architecture that arrived in the back-draft of the 1888 International Exposition of Barcelona. A key uniting element of the Modernistas was the sensuous curve, implying movement, lightness and vitality. But as well as modernity, architects often looked to the past for inspiration. Gothic, Islamic and Renaissance design all had something to offer. At its most playful, Modernisme was able to intelligently flout the rule books of these styles and create exciting new cocktails.

Antoni Gaudí

Born in Reus to a long line of coppersmiths, Antoni Gaudí (1852–1926) was initially trained in metalwork. In childhood he suffered from poor health, including rheumatism, and became an early adopter of a vegetarian diet. He was not a promising student. In 1878, when he obtained his architecture degree, the school's headmaster is reputed to have said: 'Who knows if we have given a diploma to a nutcase or a genius. Time will tell.'

As a young man, what most delighted Gaudí was being outdoors. Throughout his work, he sought to emulate the harmony he observed in the natural world, eschewing the straight line and favouring curvaceous forms and more organic shapes.

Gaudí's masterpiece is La Sagrada Família (begun in 1882); in it you can see the culminating vision of many ideas developed over the years. Its massive scale evokes the grandeur of Catalonia's Gothic cathedrals, while organic elements emphasise its harmony with nature. The church is rife with symbols that tangibly express Gaudí's Catholic faith through architecture. As well as being a devout Catholic he was a Catalan nationalist. He lived a simple life and was not averse to knocking on doors, literally begging for money to help fund construction on the basilica.

Gaudí died in 1926, struck down by a tram while taking his daily walk to the Sant Felip Neri church. Wearing ragged clothes, Gaudí was initially taken for a beggar and driven to a nearby hospital where he was left in a pauper's ward. He died two days later. Thousands attended his funeral procession to La Sagrada Família, where he was buried in the crypt.

Lluís Domènech i Montaner

Although overshadowed by Gaudí, Lluís Domènech i Montaner (1849–1923) was one of the great masters of Modernisme. He was a widely travelled man of prodigious intellect, with knowledge in everything from mineralogy to medieval heraldry; he was also an architectural professor, a prolific writer and a nationalist politician. The question of Catalan identity and how to create a national architecture consumed Domènech i Montaner, who designed more than a dozen large-scale works in his lifetime. The exuberant, steel-framed Palau de la Música Catalana is one of his masterpieces.

Josep Puig i Cadafalch

Like Domènech i Montaner, Josep Puig i Cadafalch (1867–1956) was a polymath; he was an archaeologist, an expert in Romanesque art and one of Catalonia's most prolific architects. As a politician – and later president of the Mancomunitat de Catalunya (Commonwealth of Catalonia) – he was instrumental in shaping the Catalan nationalist movement. One of his many Modernista gems is the Casa Amatller, a rather dramatic contrast to Gaudí's Casa Batlló next door; it is a house of startling beauty and invention blended with playful Gothic-style sculpture.

Gothic Masterpieces

La Catedral (p64)

Basílica de Santa Maria del Mar (p116)

Basílica de Santa Maria del Pi (p46)

Saló del Tinell in the **Museu d'Història de Barcelona** (p112)

The Drassanes, now the site of the **Museu Marítim** (p90)

Modern Times

Barcelona's latest architectural revolution began in the 1980s when, in the run-up to the 1992 Olympics, the city set about its biggest phase of renewal since the heady days of L'Eixample.

In the new millennium, the Diagonal Mar district is characterised by striking modern architecture, including the hovering blue, triangular Edifici Fòrum by Swiss architects Herzog & de Meuron and a 24-storey, whitewashed trapezoidal prism that serves as the headquarters for the national telephone company, Telefónica.

The heart of La Ribera got a fresh look with its brand-new Mercat de Santa Caterina. The market is quite a sight, with its wavy ceramic roof and tubular skeleton, designed by Enric Miralles, one of the most promising names in Catalan architecture until his premature death. Miralles' Edifici de Gas Natural, a 100m glass tower near the waterfront in La Barceloneta, is also extraordinary.

The redevelopment of the area near Plaça de les Glòries Catalanes is another recent project. The centrepiece, completed in 2013, is the Museu del Disseny, which incorporates sustainable features in its cantilevered, metal-sheathed building. Vaguely futuristic (though some say it looks like a stapler), it has a rather imposing, anvil-shaped presence over the neighbourhood.

Nearby stands Mercat dels Encants, the 'Charms' flea market, which was given a dramatic new look by local architecture firm b720 Fermín Vázquez Arquitectos. Traders now sell their wares beneath a giant, mirrored canopy made up of geometric panels and held aloft with long, slender poles.

Roof detail, Fundació Antoni Tàpies (p55)

CAHIR DAVITT/GETTY IMAGES ©

Modern Art

Three of Spain's greatest 20th-century artists have deep connections to Barcelona. Picasso spent his formative years in the city and it was his own idea to create a museum of his works here. Joan Miró is one of Barcelona's most famous native sons, and his instantly recognisable style can be seen in public installations throughout the city. Salvador Dalí may be more commonly associated with Figueres, but Barcelona was a great source of inspiration for him, particularly the fantastical works of Antoni Gaudí.

Pablo Picasso

It wasn't until the late 19th century that truly great artists began to emerge in Barcelona and its hinterland, led by dandy portraitist Ramón Casas (1866–1932). Casas, an early Modernista, founded a Barcelona bar known as Els Quatre Gats, which became the nucleus for the city's growing art movement, holding numerous shows and expositions. An early host was a young, then unknown, *malagueño* named Pablo Picasso (1881–1973).

Picasso lived sporadically in Barcelona between the innocence-losing ages of 16 and 24, and the city heavily influenced his early painting. This was the period in which he amassed the raw materials for his Blue Period. In 1904, the then-mature Picasso moved to Paris where he found fame, fortune and cubism, and went on to become one of the greatest artists of the 20th century.

Joan Miró

At the time the 13-year-old Picasso arrived in Barcelona, his near-contemporary Joan Miró (1893–1983) was still learning to crawl in the Barri Gòtic, where he was born. Miró spent a third of his life in Barcelona but later divided his time between France, the Tarragona countryside and the island of Mallorca, where he died.

Like Picasso, Miró attended the Escola de Belles Artes de la Llotja. In Paris from 1920, he mixed with Picasso, Hemingway, Joyce and friends, and made his own mark, after several years of struggle, with an exhibition in 1925. The masterpiece from this, his so-called realist period, was *La Masia* (The Farmhouse). It was during WWII that Miró's definitive leitmotifs emerged – arrangements of lines and symbolic figures in primary colours, with shapes reduced to their essence. Declaring he was going to 'assassinate art', Miró wanted nothing to do with the constricting labels of the era, although he has often been called a pioneering surrealist, Dadaist and automatist.

Best Places for Modern Art

Museu Picasso (p80)

Fundació Joan Miró (p60)

Fundació Antoni Tàpies (p55)

MACBA (p94)

Museu Nacional d'Art de Catalunya (p56)

Salvador Dalí

The great Catalan artist Salvador Dalí i Domènech (1904–89) was born and died in Figueres, where he left his single greatest artistic legacy, the Teatre-Museu Dalí. Although few of his famed works are in Barcelona, the city provided a stimulating atmosphere, and places like Park Güell, with its surrealist-like aspects, had a powerful effect on Dalí.

Prolific painter, showman, shameless self-promoter or just plain weirdo, Dalí was nothing if not a character – probably a little too much for the conservative small-town folk of Figueres. Every now and then a key moment arrives that can change the course of one's life. Dalí's came in 1929, when the French poet Paul Éluard visited Cadaqués with his Russian wife, Gala. The rest, as they say, is histrionics. Dalí shot off to Paris to be with Gala and plunged into the world of surrealism.

In the 1930s Salvador and Gala returned to live at Port Lligat on the north Catalan coast, where they played host to a long list of fashionable and art-world guests until the war years – the parties were by all accounts memorable. They started again in Port Lligat in the 1950s. The stories of sexual romps and Gala's appetite for local young men are legendary. The 1960s saw Dalí painting pictures on a grand scale, including his 1962 reinterpretation of Marià Fortuny's Batalla de Tetuán. After his death in 1989, he was buried (according to his own wishes) in the Teatre-Museu he had created on the site of the old theatre in central Figueres, which also houses an awe-inspiring Dalí collection.

Antoni Tàpies

Picasso, Miró and Dalí were hard acts to follow. Few envied the task of Catalan Antoni Tàpies in reviving the red hot Modernista flame. An early admirer of Miró, Tàpies soon began pursuing his own esoteric path embracing 'art informal' (a Jackson Pollock–like use of spontaneity) and inventing painting that utilised clay, string and even bits of rubbish. He was arguably Spain's greatest living painter before his death in 2012.

Catalan Culture

The fortunes of Catalonia have risen and fallen over the years, as Barcelona has gone from wealthy mercantile capital to a city of repression under the Franco regime, followed by a growing push for independence in recent years. Despite today's challenges, Catalan culture continues to flourish, with a lively festival calendar and abundant civic pride manifested in aspects from the language spoken on the streets to the much-loved FC Barcelona football team.

Language

In Barcelona, born-and-bred locals proudly speak Catalan, a Romance language related to French, Spanish (Castilian) and Italian. It was only relatively recently, however, that Catalan was deemed 'legitimate'. Since Barcelona was crushed in the War of the Spanish Succession in 1714, the use of Catalan was repeatedly banned or at least frowned upon. Franco was the last of Spain's rulers to clamp down on its public use. All that changed in 1980, when the first autonomous regional parliament was assembled and adopted new laws towards *normalització lingüística* (linguistic normalisation).

Today Catalonia's state school system uses Catalan as the language of instruction, though most Catalan speakers end up bilingual, particularly in urban areas. Around town,

Catalan is the lingua franca: advertising and road signs are in Catalan, while newspapers, magazines and other publications can be found in both languages (though you'll find about twice as many options in Catalan as in Spanish). You'll also find a mix of Catalan and Spanish programming on radio and TV stations.

Festivals

Catalonia's best celebrations tend to revolve around religious holidays. *Festes* dedicated to Nostra Senyora de la Mercè (p14) and Santa Eulàlia (p7) – Barcelona's two patron saints – are the city's biggest bashes. You'll see plenty of *sardana* (Catalan folk dance) and *castell*-building (human castles) there. You'll also see *gegants* (huge papier-mâché giants: lords, princesses, sultans, fishers and historic and contemporary figures) and *capgrossos* (oversized heads worn by costumed actors).

Another feature of these Catalan fests is the *correfoc* (fire running): horned devils brandishing firework-spouting pitchforks wreak mayhem in the streets. They are sometimes accompanied by firework-spouting dragons, or even wooden carts that are set alight. Full coverings (hats, gloves, goggles) are highly recommended for anyone who wants to get near.

Best on Film

All About My Mother (1999) One of Almodóvar's best-loved films, complete with transsexual prostitutes and doe-eyed nuns.

Vicky Cristina Barcelona (2008) Woody Allen gives Barcelona the *Manhattan* treatment, showing a city of startling beauty and neuroticism.

L'Auberge Espagnole (2002) A warmly told coming-of-age story about a mishmash of foreign-exchange students thrown together in Barcelona.

Barcelona (1994) A sharp and witty romantic comedy about two Americans living in Barcelona during the end of the Cold War.

Best Barcelona Blogs

Driftwood Journals (www.driftwoodjournals.com) Beautifully photographed things to do and places to stay.

Food Barcelona (www.foodbarcelona.com) Honest and well-crafted reviews of mostly upscale restaurants.

Foodie in Barcelona (www.foodiein barcelona.com) Entertaining descriptions of cafes, restaurants and food shops.

Homage to BCN (www.homagetobcn.com) Residents explain their 'perfect day' in Barcelona.

FC Barcelona

One of the city's best-loved names is FC Barça, which is deeply associated with Catalans and even Catalan nationalism. (See p72 for more on the club.)

Music

Barcelona's vibrant music and dance scene has been shaped by artists both traditional and cutting edge. From Nova Cançó, composed during the dark years of the dictatorship, to the hybridised Catalan rumba to hands-in-the air rock ballads of the 1970s and '80s, Barcelona's music evolves constantly. Today's groups continue to push musical boundaries, blending rhythms from all corners of the globe. In the realm of dance, flamenco has a small loyal following, while the traditional folk dance *sardana* continues to attract growing numbers.

Pau Casals

Born in Catalonia, Pau Casals (1876–1973) was one of the greatest cellists of the 20th century. Living in exile in southern France, he declared he would not play in public as long as Western democracies continued to tolerate Franco's regime. In 1958 he was a candidate for the Nobel Peace Prize.

Classical, Opera & Baroque

Spain's contribution to the world of classical music has been modest, but Catalonia has produced a few exceptional composers. Best known is Camprodon-born Isaac Albéniz (1860–1909), a gifted pianist who later turned his hand to composition. Among his best-remembered works is the *Iberia* cycle.

Montserrat Caballé is Barcelona's most successful voice. Born in Gràcia in 1933, the soprano made her debut in 1956 in Basel (Switzerland). Her home-town launch came four years later in the Gran Teatre del Liceu. In 1965 she performed to wild acclaim at New York's Carnegie Hall and went on to become one of the world's finest 20th-century sopranos. Her daughter, Montserrat Martí, is also a singer and they occasionally appear together. Another fine Catalan soprano was Victoria de los Ángeles (1923–2005), while Catalonia's other world-class opera star is the renowned tenor Josep (José) Carreras.

Jordi Savall has assumed the task of rediscovering a European heritage in music that pre-dates the era of the classical greats. He and his late wife, soprano Montserrat Figueras, have, along with musicians from other countries, been largely responsible for resuscitating the beauties of medieval, Renaissance and baroque music. In 1987 Savall founded La Capella Reial de Catalunya and two years later he formed the baroque orchestra Le Concert des Nations. You can sometimes catch their recitals in locations such as the Gran Teatre del Liceu or the Basílica de Santa Maria del Mar.

Nova Cançó

Curiously, it was probably the Francoist repression that most helped foster a vigorous local music scene in Catalan. In the dark 1950s, the Nova Cançó (New Song) movement was born to resist linguistic oppression with music in Catalan (getting air time on the radio was long close to impossible), throwing up stars that in some cases won huge popularity throughout Spain, such as the Valencia-born Raimon.

More specifically loved in Catalonia as a Bob Dylan–style 1960s protest singer-songwriter was Lluís Llach, much of whose music was more or less antiregime. Joan Manuel Serrat is another legendary figure. His appeal stretches from Barcelona to Buenos Aires. Born in the Poble Sec district, this poet-singer is equally at ease in Catalan and Spanish. He has repeatedly shown that record sales are not everything to him. In 1968 he refused to represent Spain at the Eurovision song contest because he wasn't allowed to sing in Catalan. Accused of being anti-Spanish, he was long banned from performing in Spain.

Born in Mallorca, the talented singer Maria del Mar Bonet arrived in Barcelona in 1967, and embarked on a long and celebrated singing career. She sang in Catalan, and many of her searing and powerful songs were banned by the dictatorship. On concert tours abroad, she attracted worldwide attention, and she has performed with distinguished groups and soloists across the globe.

ANDREY OMELYANCHUK/500PX©

Survival Guide

Directory A–Z

Accessible Travel

Most hotels and public institutions have wheelchair access. All buses in Barcelona are wheelchair accessible and a growing number of metro stations are theoretically wheelchair accessible (generally by lift, although there have been complaints that they are only good for people with prams). Of 158 stations, all but 15 are completely adapted (you can check which ones by looking at a network map at www.tmb.cat/en/transport-accessible). Ticket vending machines in metro stations are adapted for disabled travellers, and have Braille options for those a with visual impairment.

Several taxi companies have adapted vehicles, including **Taxi Amic** (📞93 420 80 88; www.taxi-amic-adaptat.

com) and **Green Taxi** (📞900 827900; www.greentaxi.es).

Most street crossings in central Barcelona are wheelchair-friendly.

Dangers & Annoyances

o Violent crime is rare in Barcelona, but petty crime (bag-snatching, pickpocketing) is a major problem.

o You're at your most vulnerable when dragging around luggage to or from your hotel; make sure you know your route before arriving.

o Be mindful of your belongings, particularly in crowded areas.

o Try to avoid walking around El Raval and the southern end of La Rambla late at night.

o Don't wander down empty city streets at night. When in doubt, take a taxi.

o Take nothing of value to the beach and don't leave anything unattended.

Discount Cards

Articket (www.articketbcn.org) Gives admission to six sites for €30 and is valid for six months. You can pick up the ticket at the tourist offices at Plaça de Catalunya, Plaça de Sant Jaume and Estació Sants train station and at the museums themselves. The six sights are Museu Picasso, Museu Nacional d'Art de Catalunya, Museu d'Art Contemporani de Barcelona, Fundació Antoni Tàpies, Centre de Cultura Contemporània de Barcelona and Fundació Joan Miró.

Arqueoticket (www.barcelonaturisme.com) For those with an interest in archaeology and ancient history. The ticket (€14.50) is available from participating museums and tourist offices and grants free admission to the Museu d'Arqueologia de Catalunya, Museu Egipci, Museu d'Història de Barcelona and Born Centre de Cultura i Memòria.

Barcelona Card (www.barcelonacard.com) Handy if you want to see lots in a limited time. It costs €20/45/55/60 for two/three/four/five days. You get free transport, discounted admission (up to 60% off) or free entry to many museums and other sights, and minor discounts on purchases at a small number of shops, restaurants and bars. The card costs about 50% less for children aged four to 12 years. You can purchase it at tourist offices and online (the latter saves you 5%).

Practicalities

Currency Euro (€)

Smoking Banned in restaurants and bars

Major Barcelona newspapers *La Vanguardia* and *El Periódico* are available in Spanish and Catalan; *El País* publishes an online English supplement (elpais.com/elpais/inenglish.html)

Ruta del Modernisme (www.rutadelmodernisme.com) Well worth looking into for visiting Modernista sights at discounted rates. It costs €12.

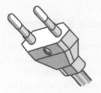

Electricity

Spain uses 230V/50Hz, like the rest of continental Europe.

Type C
220V/50Hz

Type F
230V/50Hz

Emergency & Important Numbers

Ambulance	061
EU standard emergency number	112
Country code	34
International access code	00
Tourist police	93 256 24 77

Health

● All foreigners have the same right as Spaniards to emergency medical treatment in public hospitals. EU citizens are entitled to the full range of health-care services in public hospitals, but must present a European Health Insurance Card (enquire at your national health service) and may have to pay upfront.

● Non-EU citizens have to pay for anything other than emergency treatment. Most travel-insurance policies include medical cover.

Insurance

● A travel-insurance policy to cover theft, loss, medical problems, and cancellation or delays of your travel arrangements is a good idea.

● Worldwide travel insurance is available at lonelyplanet.com/travel-insurance. You can buy, extend and claim online any time – even if you're on the road.

Internet Access

Most accommodation places offer their guests wi-fi access (usually for free). A growing array of city bars and restaurants are doing the same. The city also has dozens of free public wi-fi hotspots. The easiest way to get online is to buy a local SIM card and a data package.

LGBT+ Travellers

Barcelona has a vibrant gay and lesbian scene, with a fine array of restaurants, bars and clubs in the district known as the 'Gaixample', an area of L'Eixample about five to six blocks southwest of Passeig de Gràcia around Carrer del Consell de Cent.

Useful Websites

Patroc (www.patroc.com) A European gay guide, the Barcelona section of which has a useful selection of hotels, clubs and so on. Particularly good on upcoming events.

Tillate (www.tillate.es) Discover upcoming parties in this nightlife guide to regions around Spain, including Catalonia.

Travel Gay (www.travelgay.com) This global site has a Barcelona section with frequently updated listings.

GaySitges (www.gaysitges.com) A specific site dedicated to this LGBTI-friendly coastal town.

Money

ATMs are widely available (La Rambla has many). Credit cards are accepted in most hotels, shops and restaurants.

Tipping

Restaurants Catalans typically leave 5% or less at restaurants. Leave more for exceptionally good service.

Taxis Optional, but most locals round up to the nearest euro.

Bars It's rare to leave a tip in bars.

Opening Hours

Standard opening hours are as follows:

Restaurants 1pm to 4pm and 8.30pm to midnight

Shops 9am or 10am to 1.30pm or 2pm and 4pm or 4.30pm to 8pm or 8.30pm Monday to Saturday

Department stores 10am to 10pm Monday to Saturday

Bars 6pm to 2am (to 3am weekends)

Clubs Midnight to 6am Thursday to Saturday

Banks 8.30am to 2pm Monday to Friday; some also 4pm to 7pm Thursday or 9am to 1pm Saturday

Museums and art galleries Vary considerably; generally 10am to 8pm (though some shut for lunch around 2pm to 4pm). Many close all day Monday and from 2pm Sunday.

Public Holidays

New Year's Day (Any Nou/Año Nuevo) 1 January

Epiphany/Three Kings' Day (Epifanía or El Dia dels Reis/Día de los Reyes Magos) 6 January

Good Friday (Divendres Sant/Viernes Santo) March/April

Easter Monday (Dilluns de Pasqua Florida) March/April

Labour Day (Dia del Treball/Fiesta del Trabajo) 1 May

Day after Pentecost Sunday (Dilluns de Pasqua Granda) May/June

Feast of St John the Baptist (Dia de Sant Joan/Día de San Juan Bautista) 24 June

Feast of the Assumption (L'Assumpció/La Asunción) 15 August

Catalonia's National Day (Diada Nacional de Catalunya) 11 September

Festes de la Mercè 24 September

Spanish National Day (Festa de la Hispanitat/Día de la Hispanidad) 12 October

All Saints Day (Dia de Tots Sants/Día de Todos los Santos) 1 November

Constitution Day (Día de la Constitución) 6 December

Feast of the Immaculate Conception (La Immaculada Concepció/La Inmaculada Concepción) 8 December

Christmas Day (Nadal/Navidad) 25 December

Boxing Day/St Stephen's Day (El Dia de Sant Esteve) 26 December

Taxes & Refunds

Value-added tax (VAT, IVA in Spanish) is a 21% sales tax levied on most goods and services. For restaurants and hotels it's 10%. Most restaurants include VAT in their prices; it's usually included in hotel room prices, too, but check when booking.

Non-EU residents are entitled to a refund of the 21% IVA on purchases costing more than €90 from any shop, if the goods are taken out of the EU within three months. Ask the shop for a Cashback (or similar) refund form showing the price and IVA paid for each item and identifying the vendor and purchaser. Then present the form at the customs booth for IVA refunds when you depart from Spain (or elsewhere in the EU). You will need your passport, a boarding pass that shows you are leaving the EU, and your luggage (so do this before checking in bags).

Telephone

To call Barcelona from outside Spain, dial the international access code, followed by the code for Spain (34) and the full number (including Barcelona's area code, 93, which is an integral part of the number). To make an international call, dial the international access code (00), country code, area code and number.

Toilets

Public toilets are rare in Barcelona. Big shopping centres (or the El Corte Inglés department store) are an option, but ducking into a cafe or bar may be your best bet (it's polite to order something).

Tourist Information

Oficina d'Informació de Turisme de Barcelona (☎93 285 38 34; www.barcelona turisme.com; Plaça de Catalunya 17-S, underground; ☺8.30am-9pm; Ⓜ Catalunya) provides maps, sights information, tours, concert and events tickets, and last-minute accommodation.

Transport

Getting There & Away

Air

- After Madrid, Barcelona is Spain's busiest international transport hub. A host of airlines, including many budget carriers, fly directly to Barcelona from around Europe. Ryanair also uses Girona and Reus airports (buses link Barcelona to both).

- Most intercontinental flights require passengers to change flights in Madrid or another major European hub.

- Iberia, Air Europa, Spanair and Vueling all have dense networks across the country.

- Barcelona's main airport is El Prat (www.aena.es; ☎91 321 10 00; ☜), with the majority of international flights arriving here. In addition, there are two other airports in nearby cities, which are used by some budget airlines.

Getting To/From El Prat Airport

Bus

The **A1 Aerobús** (☎902 100104; www.aerobusbcn. com; Plaça d'Espanya; one way/return €5.90/10.20; ☺5.35am-1.05am; Ⓜ Espanya) runs from Terminal 1 to Plaça de Catalunya (30 to 40 minutes depending on traffic) via Plaça d'Espanya, Gran Via de les Corts Catalanes (corner of Carrer del Comte d'Urgell) and Plaça de la Universitat every five to 10 minutes from 5.35am to 1.05am. Departures from Plaça de Catalunya are from 5am to 12.30am

---

Climate Change & Travel

Every form of transport that relies on carbon-based fuel generates CO_2, the main cause of human-induced climate change. Modern travel is dependent on aeroplanes, which might use less fuel per kilometre per person than most cars but travel much greater distances. The altitude at which aircraft emit gases (including CO_2) and particles also contributes to their climate change impact. Many websites offer 'carbon calculators' that allow people to estimate the carbon emissions generated by their journey and, for those who wish to do so, to offset the impact of the greenhouse gases emitted with contributions to portfolios of climate-friendly initiatives throughout the world. Lonely Planet offsets the carbon footprint of all staff and author travel.

and stop at the corner of Carrer de Sepúlveda and Carrer del Comte d'Urgell, and at Plaça d'Espanya.

The **A2 Aerobús** from Terminal 2 (stops outside terminal areas A, B and C) runs from 6am to 1am with a frequency of between 10 and 20 minutes and follows the same route as the A1 Aerobús.

Buy tickets on the bus or from agents at the bus stop. Slower local buses (such as the 46 to/from Plaça d'Espanya and two night buses, the N17 and N18, to/from Plaça de Catalunya) also serve Terminals 1 and 2.

Train

Train operator Renfe runs the R2 Nord line every half-hour from the airport (from 5.42am to 11.38pm) via several stops to Barcelona's main train station, **Estació Sants** (912 432343; www.adif.es; Plaça dels Països Catalans; Sants Estació), and Passeig de Gràcia in central Barcelona, after which it heads northwest out of the city. The first service from Passeig de Gràcia leaves at 5.08am and the last at 11.07pm, and about five minutes later from Estació Sants. The trip between the airport and Passeig de Gràcia takes 27 minutes. A one-way ticket costs €4.20.

The airport train station is about a five-minute walk from Terminal 2. Regular shuttle buses run from the station and Terminal 2 to Terminal 1 – allow an extra 15 to 20 minutes.

Taxi

A taxi between either terminal and the city centre – about a half-hour ride depending on traffic – costs around €25. Fares and charges are posted inside the passenger side of the taxi; make sure the meter is used.

Train

o Train is the most convenient overland option for reaching Barcelona from major Spanish centres like Madrid and Valencia. It can be a long haul from other parts of Europe – budget flights frequently offer a saving in time and money.

o A network of *rodalies/cercanías* serves towns around Barcelona (and the airport). Contact **Renfe** (91 232 03 20; www.renfe.com).

o Frequent high-speed Tren de Alta Velocidad Española (AVE) trains between Madrid and Barcelona run daily in each direction, several of them in less than three hours.

Getting Around

Bicycle

An extensive network of bike lanes has been laid out across the city. Scenic itineraries are mapped for cyclists in the Collserola parkland, and the *ronda verda* is an incomplete 72km cycling path that extends around the city's outskirts. You can cycle a well-signed

22km loop path (part of the *ronda verda*) by following the seaside bike path northeast of Barceloneta.

You can transport your bicycle on the metro on weekdays (except between 7am and 9.30am or 5pm and 8.30pm). At weekends and during holidays and in July and August, there are no restrictions. You can use FGC trains and Renfe's *rodalies* trains to carry your bike at any time, provided there is room.

Bus

Transports Metropolitans de Barcelona (TMB; 93 298 70 00; www.tmb.cat) buses run along most city routes every few minutes from between 5am and 6.30am to around 10pm and 11pm. Many routes pass through Plaça de Catalunya and/or Plaça de la Universitat. After 11pm a reduced network of yellow *nitbusos* (night buses) runs until 3am or 5am. All *nitbus* routes pass through Plaça de Catalunya and most run every 30 to 45 minutes.

Car & Motorcycle

With the convenience of public transport and the high price of parking in the city, it's unwise to drive in Barcelona. However, if you're planning a road trip outside the city, a car is handy. Avis, Europcar, National/Atesa and Hertz have desks at El Prat airport, Estació Sants and Estació del Nord. **Cooltra** (93 221 40 70; www.cooltra.com; Via Laietana 6; scooter hire per day €29-39; 10am-8pm)

Mar-Jun, 9.30am-8.30pm Jul-Sep, shorter hours rest of year; M Barceloneta) rents scooters, as does **Mondo Rent** (📞93 295 32 68; www. mondorent.com; Passeig de Joan de Borbó 80-84; scooter rental per day from €35; ⏱10am-8pm; M Barceloneta).

Local Transport

The metro, FGC trains, *rodalies/cercanías* (Renfe-run local trains) and buses come under a combined system. Single-ride tickets on all standard transport within Zone 1 cost €2.20.

Targetes are multitrip transport tickets. They are sold at all city-centre metro stations. The prices given here are for travel in Zone 1. Children under four years of age travel free. Options include the following:

Targeta T-10 (€10.20) 10 rides (each valid for 1¼ hours) on the metro, buses, FGC trains and *rodalies*. You can change between metro, FGC, *rodalies* and buses.

Targeta T-DIA (€8.60) Unlimited travel on all transport for one day.

Two-/three-/four-/five-day tickets (€15/22/28.50/35) Unlimited travel on all transport except the Aerobús; buy them at metro stations and tourist offices.

There is support for a scheme in which visitors pay more than residents; at the time of research this was still in the works.

Train

The easy-to-use **TMB metro** (TMB; 📞93 298 70 00; www.tmb.cat) system has 11 numbered and colour-coded lines. It runs from 5am to midnight Sunday to Thursday and holidays, from 5am to 2am on Friday and days immediately preceding holidays, and 24 hours on Saturday.

Ongoing work to expand the metro continues on several lines. Línea 9 connects with the airport.

Suburban trains run by **Ferrocarrils de la Generalitat de Cata-lunya** (FGC; 📞012; www. fgc.net) include a couple of useful city lines. All lines heading north from Plaça de Catalunya stop at Carrer de Provença and Gràcia. One of these lines (L7) goes to Tibidabo and another (L6) goes to Reina Elisenda, near the Monestir de Pedralbes. Most trains from Plaça de Catalunya continue beyond Barcelona to Sant Cugat, Sabadell and Terrassa. Other FGC lines head west from Plaça d'Espanya, including one for Manresa that is handy for the trip to Montserrat.

Depending on the line, these trains run from about 5am (with only one or two services before 6am) to 11pm or midnight Sunday to Thursday, and from 5am to about 1am on Friday and Saturday.

Taxi

Taxis charge €2.20 flag fall plus meter charges of €1.17 per kilometre (€1.40 from 8pm to 8am and all day on weekends). A further €3.10 is added for all trips to/ from the airport, and €1 for luggage bigger than 55cm by 40cm by 20cm. The trip from Estació Sants to Plaça de Catalunya, about 3km, costs about €11. You can flag a taxi down in the streets or call **Fonotaxi** (📞93 300 11 00; www.fonotaxi.net) or **Radio Taxi 033** (📞93 303 30 33; www.radiotaxi033.com).

The call-out charge is €3.40 (€4.20 at night and on weekends). In all taxis it is possible to pay with a credit card, and if you have a local telephone number, you can join the T033 Ràdio taxi service for booking taxis online (www.radiotaxi033.com). You can also book online at https://catalunyataxi.com.

Taxi Amic (📞93 420 80 88; www.taxi-amic-adaptat.com) is a service for people with disabilities or in difficult situations (such as transport of big objects). Book at least 24 hours in advance.

Tram

There is a handful of **tram lines** (📞900 701181; www. tram.cat) in the city, on which all standard transport passes are valid. A scenic option is the Tramvia Blau (blue tram), which runs up to the foot of Tibidabo.

Language

Catalan and Spanish both have official-language status in Catalonia. In Barcelona, you'll hear as much Spanish as Catalan, so we've provided some Spanish to get you started. Spanish pronunciation is not difficult as most of its sounds are also found in English. You can read our pronunciation guides below as if they were English and you'll be understood just fine. And if you pronounce 'th' in our guides with a lisp and 'kh' as a throaty sound, you'll even sound like a real Spanish person.

To enhance your trip with a phrasebook, visit **lonelyplanet.com**. Lonely Planet iPhone phrasebooks are available through the Apple App store.

Basics

Hello.	*Hola.*
	o·la
How are you?	*¿Qué tal?*
	ke tal
I'm fine, thanks.	*Bien, gracias.*
	byen *gra*·thyas
Excuse me.	*Disculpe.*
(to get attention)	dees·*kool*·pe
Yes./No.	*Sí./No.*
	see/no
Thank you.	*Gracias.*
	gra·thyas
You're welcome./	*De nada.*
That's fine.	de *na*·da
Goodbye./	*Adiós./Hasta luego.*
See you later.	a·*dyos/as*·ta *lwe*·go
Do you speak	*¿Habla inglés?*
English?	*a*·bla een·*gles*
I don't understand.	*No entiendo.*
	no en·*tyen*·do
How much is this?	*¿Cuánto cuesta?*
	kwan·to *kwes*·ta
Can you reduce	*¿Podría bajar un poco el precio*
the price a little?	po·*dree*·a ba·*khar* oon *po*·ko el *pre*·thyo

Accommodation

I'd like to make	*Quisiera reservar una habitación*
a booking.	kee·*sye*·ra re·ser·*var* oo·na a·bee·ta·*thyon*
How much is it	*¿Cuánto cuesta por noche?*
per night?	*kwan*·to *kwes*·ta por *no*·che

Eating & Drinking

I'd like ..., please.	*Quisiera ..., por favor.*	
	kee·*sye*·ra ... por fa·*vor*	
That was	*¡Estaba buenísimo!*	
delicious!	es·*ta*·ba bwe·*nee*·see·mo	
Bring the bill/	*La cuenta, por favor.*	
check, please.	la *kwen*·ta por fa·*vor*	
I'm allergic to ...	*Soy alérgico/a al ... (m/f)*	
	soy a·*ler*·khee·ko/a al ...	
I don't eat ...	*No como ...*	
	no *ko*·mo ...	
chicken	*pollo*	*po*·lyo
fish	*pescado*	pes·*ka*·do
meat	*carne*	*kar*·ne

Emergencies

I'm ill.	*Estoy enfermo/a. (m/f)*
	es·*toy* en·*fer*·mo/a
Help!	*¡Socorro!*
	so·*ko*·ro
Call a doctor!	*¡Llame a un médico!*
	lya·me a oon *me*·dee·ko
Call the police!	*¡Llame a la policía!*
	lya·me a la po·lee·*thee*·a

Directions

I'm looking for a/an/the ...	
Estoy buscando ...	es·*toy* boos·*kan*·do ...
ATM	*un cajero automático*
	oon ka·*khe*·ro ow·to·*ma*·tee·ko
bank	*el banco*
	el *ban*·ko
... embassy	*la embajada de ...*
	la em·ba·*kha*·da de ...
market	*el mercado*
	el mer·*ka*·do
museum	*el museo*
	el moo·*se*·o
restaurant	*un restaurante*
	oon res·tow·*ran*·te
toilet	*los servicios*
	los ser·*vee*·thyos
tourist office	*la oficina de turismo*
	la o·fee·*thee*·na de oo·*rees*·mo

Behind the Scenes

Acknowledgements

Cover photograph:
The Museu Nacional d'Art
de Catalunya, Brian Kinney/
Shutterstock ©

This Book

This fourth edition of Lonely Planet's *Best of Barcelona* guidebook was curated by Andy Symington, and researched and written by Tom Stainer and Esme Fox. The previous edition was also curated by Andy Symington, and was written and researched by Sally Davies and Catherine Le Nevez.

This guidebook was produced by the following:

Destination Editor Tom Stainer

Senior Product Editors Genna Patterson, Jessica Ryan

Regional Senior Cartographer Anthony Phelan

Product Editor Claire Rourke

Book Designer Michael Weldon

Assisting Editors Melanie Dankel, Gabrielle Innes

Assisting Cartographers Julie Dodkins, Rachel Imeson

Cover Researcher Brendan Dempsey-Spencer

Thanks to Jessica Boland, Gwen Cotter, Mazzy Du Plessis Victoria Harrison, Kate James, Sandie Kestell

Send Us Your Feedback

We love to hear from travellers – your comments keep us on our toes and help make our books better. Our well-travelled team reads every word on what you loved or loathed about this book. Although we cannot reply individually to postal submissions, we always guarantee that your feedback goes straight to the appropriate authors, in time for the next edition. Each person who sends us information is thanked in the next edition, the most useful submissions are rewarded with a selection of digital PDF chapters.

Visit lonelyplanet.com/contact to submit your updates and suggestions or to ask for help. Our award-winning website also features inspirational travel stories, news and discussions.

Note: We may edit, reproduce and incorporate your comments in Lonely Planet products such as guidebooks, websites and digital products, so let us know if you don't want your comments reproduced or your name acknowledged. For a copy of our privacy policy visit lonelyplanet.com/privacy.

Index

A

Museu Nacional d'Art de Catalunya (p56)

VLAD GHIEA / ALAMY STOCK PHOTO ©

Barcelona Maps

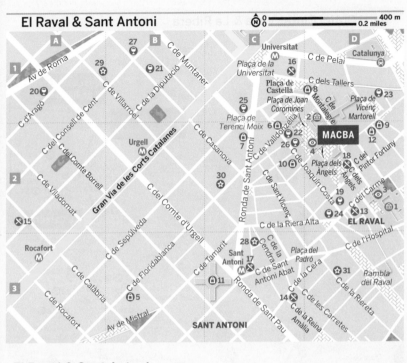

El Raval & Sant Antoni

Barri Gòtic, Ciutat Vella & La Ribera

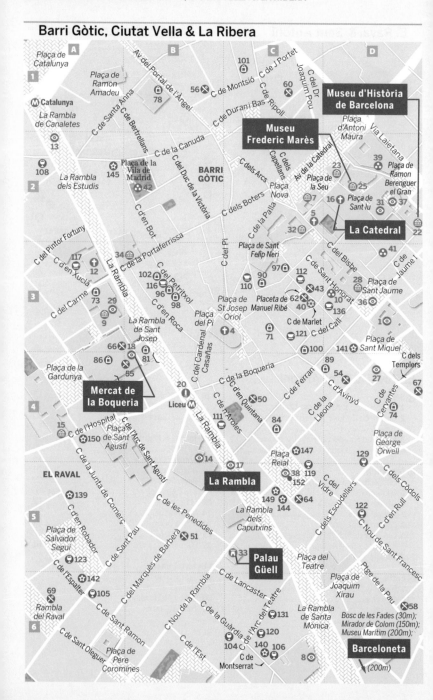

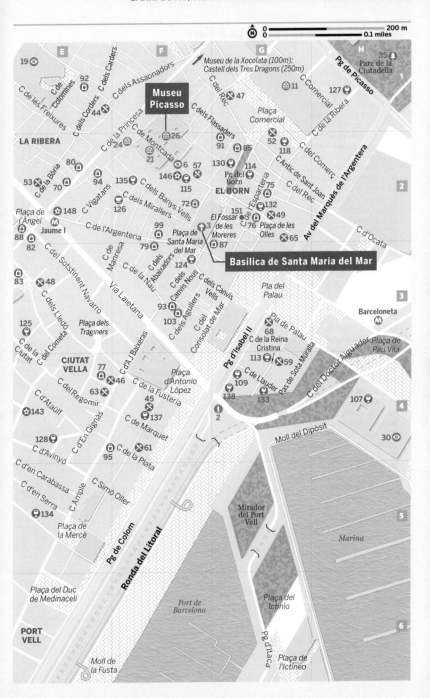

Barri Gòtic, Ciutat Vella & La Ribera

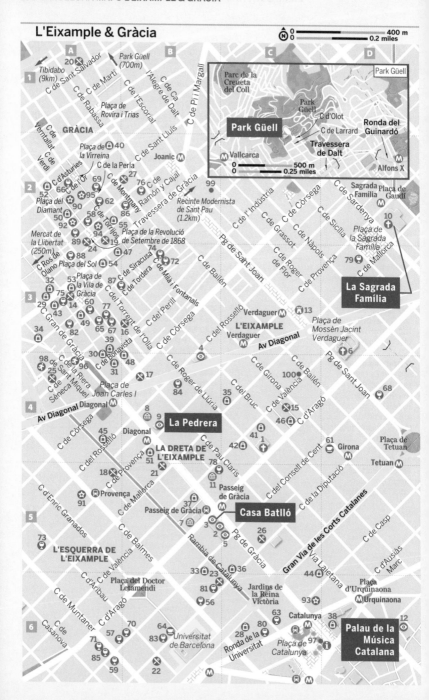

L'Eixample & Gràcia

L'Eixample & Gràcia

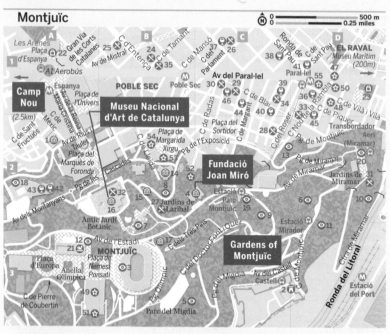

Montjuïc

Symbols & Map Key

Look for these symbols to quickly identify listings:

◎ Sights
✪ Activities
❸ Courses
❼ Tours
❽ Festivals & Events

✪ Eating
❶ Drinking
✪ Entertainment
❻ Shopping
❶ Information & Transport

These symbols and abbreviations give vital information for each listing:

🌿 Sustainable or green recommendation
FREE No payment required

☑ Telephone number
☺ Opening hours
Ⓟ Parking
❤ Nonsmoking
❄ Air-conditioning
@ Internet access
🛜 Wi-fi access
🏊 Swimming pool

🚌 Bus
⛴ Ferry
🚊 Tram
🚆 Train
🍴 English-language menu
🥗 Vegetarian selection
👪 Family-friendly

Find your best experiences with these Great For... icons.

 Art & Culture

 Beaches

 Budget

 Cafe/Coffee

 Cycling

 Detour

 Drinking

Entertainment

Events

Family Travel

Food & Drink

 History

 Local Life

 Nature & Wildlife

 Photo Op

 Scenery

 Shopping

 Short Trip

 Sport

 Walking

 Winter Travel

Sights
◎ Beach
🐦 Bird Sanctuary
☸ Buddhist
🏰 Castle/Palace
✝ Christian
☯ Confucian
🕉 Hindu
☪ Islamic
卍 Jain
✡ Jewish
◉ Monument
🏛 Museum/Gallery/ Historic Building
🏚 Ruin
⛩ Shinto
🪯 Sikh
☯ Taoist
🍷 Winery/Vineyard
🐾 Zoo/Wildlife Sanctuary
◎ Other Sight

Points of Interest
© Bodysurfing
⛺ Camping
☕ Cafe
🛶 Canoeing/Kayaking
• Course/Tour
🤿 Diving
🍸 Drinking & Nightlife
✪ Eating
🎭 Entertainment
♨ Sento Hot Baths/ Onsen
🛍 Shopping
⛷ Skiing
🛏 Sleeping
🤿 Snorkelling
🏄 Surfing
🏊 Swimming/Pool
🚶 Walking
🏄 Windsurfing
✪ Other Activity

Information
🏦 Bank
🏛 Embassy/Consulate
➕ Hospital/Medical
@ Internet
🚓 Police
✉ Post Office
☎ Telephone
🚻 Toilet
ℹ Tourist Information
? Other Information

Geographic
🏖 Beach
⤙ Gate
🛖 Hut/Shelter
🗼 Lighthouse
👁 Lookout
▲ Mountain/Volcano
🌴 Oasis
🌳 Park
)(Pass
🧺 Picnic Area
💧 Waterfall

Transport
✈ Airport
Ⓑ BART station
✕ Border crossing
Ⓣ Boston T station
🚌 Bus
+🚡+ Cable car/Funicular
—🚲— Cycling
—⛴— Ferry
Ⓜ Metro/MRT station
+🚝+ Monorail
Ⓟ Parking
⛽ Petrol station
Ⓢ Subway/S-Bahn/ Skytrain station
🚕 Taxi
+🚉+ Train station/Railway
····· Tram
Ⓤ Underground/ U-Bahn station
• Other Transport

Our Story

A beat-up old car, a few dollars in the pocket and a sense of adventure. In 1972 that's all Tony and Maureen Wheeler needed for the trip of a lifetime – across Europe and Asia overland to Australia. It took several months and at the end – broke but inspired – they sat at their kitchen table writing and stapling together their first travel guide, *Across Asia on the Cheap*. Within a week they'd sold 1500 copies. Lonely Planet was born.

Today Lonely Planet has offices in Franklin, London, Melbourne, Oakland, Dublin, Beijing, and Delhi, with more than 600 staff and writers. We share Tony's belief that 'a great guidebook should do three things: inform, educate and amuse'.

Our Writers

Andy Symington

Andy has written or worked on over a hundred books and other updates for Lonely Planet and other publishing companies, and has published articles on numerous subjects for a variety of newspapers, magazines and websites. He part-owns and operates a rock bar, has written a novel, and is currently working on several fiction and nonfiction writing projects. Andy, from Australia, moved to Northern Spain many years ago. When he's not off with a backpack in some far-flung corner of the world, he can probably be found watching the tragically poor local football side or tasting local wines after a long walk in the nearby mountains.

Contributing Writers

Tom Stainer, Esme Fox

STAY IN TOUCH LONELYPLANET.COM/CONTACT

AUSTRALIA The Malt Store, Level 3, 551 Swanston St, Carlton, Victoria 3053
📞 03 8379 8000,
fax 03 8379 8111

IRELAND Digital Depot, Roe Lane (off Thomas St), Digital Hub, Dublin 8, D08 TCV4, Ireland

USA 124 Linden Street, Oakland, CA 94607
📞 510 250 6400,
toll free 800 275 8555,
fax 510 893 8572

UK 240 Blackfriars Road, London SE1 8NW
📞 020 3771 5100,
fax 020 3771 5101

 twitter.com/
lonelyplanet

 facebook.com/
lonelyplanet

 instagram.com/
lonelyplanet

 youtube.com/
lonelyplanet

 lonelyplanet.com/
newsletter